# History.edu

# History.edu
## Essays on Teaching with Technology

Dennis A. Trinkle
Scott A. Merriman,
Editors

*M.E. Sharpe*
Armonk, New York
London, England

Copyright © 2001 by M. E. Sharpe, Inc.

**Library of Congress Cataloging-in-Publication Data**

History.edu : essays on teaching with technology / Dennis A. Trinkle and Scott A.
Merriman, editors.
   p. cm.
Includes bibliographical references and index.
ISBN 0-7656-0549-X (alk. paper) ISBN 0-7656-0550-3 (pbk : alk. paper)
   1. History—Study and teaching—United States. 2. History—Computer-assisted
instruction—United States. I. Trinkle, Dennis A., 1968– II. Merriman, Scott A.,
1968–

D16.3H53 2000
907.1'073—dc21
               00-020145
               CIP

Printed in the United States of America

The paper used in this publication meets the minimum requirements of
American National Standard for Information Sciences
Permanence of Paper for Printed Library Materials,
ANSI Z 39.48-1984.

BM (c)  10   9   8   7   6   5   4   3   2   1
BM (p)  10   9   8   7   6   5   4   3   2   1

# Contents

# Acknowledgments

Virtual communities, Web-conferencing, chat rooms, e-circles—the names for the new computer technologies of the 1990s resonate with images of collaboration. The language is indicative. The Internet and local area networks are designed to foster cooperation and collective effort. The essays in this volume reflect this synergetic emphasis. The contributors shared numerous drafts across the Internet in scholarly circles that would have been impossible to achieve before computer networks. Human beings are grounded in physical intimacy and the face-to-face exchange, however, and many of the essays reflect the role of the American Association for History and Computing (AAHC) in fostering discussions about the sensible place of technology in historical practices. Twelve of the essays contained in this volume grew out of papers initially presented at annual meetings of the AAHC. The historical profession and the contributors to this volume have profited greatly from the activities of the AAHC, and the efforts of the association are warmly appreciated.

At M.E. Sharpe, Peter Coveney has proved to be a catalyst providing motivation and guidance with good grace. Esther Clark has kept the authors and editors true to plan with helpful reminders and quick answers to unforeseen questions. One could not ask for a better team or a better publisher. Many other colleagues far too numerous to mention also helped shape the ideas and examples in this book. For their input and guidance, we are grateful. Contrary to mythology, the ultimate joys of history teachers rest not in the solitude of the ivory tower, but in the stimulation and pleasures of the historical community.

# Introduction

## Technology and the History Classroom
## Where Are We? Where Are We Headed?

### Dennis A. Trinkle

More than three decades ago, in his presidential address to the American Historical Association, Carl Bridenbaugh offered a warning to the profession about "run-away technology" that was "severing all bonds with the past" and "turning historians into the victims of a kind of collective amnesia."[1] In Bridenbaugh's eyes, nothing less than loss of "mankind's historical memory" and the decimation of the historical profession was at stake.[2] Bridenbaugh's dire warnings have proved unfounded. Radio, television, and film have not spelled the death of history. Quite the contrary—in capable and imaginative hands, these technologies have provided powerful and effective new modes for practicing the historian's craft.

What Bridenbaugh's reaction would be to the impact of computing technology upon the practices of history and memory building, one can only imagine. His concern about the effects of technology upon history and the life of the mind, however, seems characteristic of certain deeply established discourses in the Western intellectual community. Many scholars and scribes of fifteenth-century Europe greeted the printing press with analogous distrust. In late fifteenth-century Paris, the professors of the Sorbonne conjectured that the rapid production of so many books by machine must indicate "the help of the devil himself."[3] The Jeremiahs did not monopolize the rhetorical terrain, of course. The alarmed professors of the Sorbonne were well balanced by European scholars and clerics who proclaimed the hand of God, rather than the devil, in the workings of the printing press.[4]

In current critiques of the impact of computing technology upon education and the pursuit of knowledge, one finds fewer references to the supernatural, though if one reads Erik Davis's *Techgnosis: Myth, Magic, and Mysticism in the Age of Information*, one quickly discovers that they are still present.[5] More enduring are the widely divergent rhetorical statements about the promise and problems computer technologies hold for education and knowledge. Like Bridenbaugh and the troubled intellectuals of fifteenth-century Europe, the techno-gadfly Neil Postman worries loudly and publicly that the academy is embracing computer technology "hurriedly and mindlessly."[6] In a similar vein, the historian David Sicilia warns of the "risks in the purely interest-driven, student-defined investigation that information technology seems to enhance."[7]

Paralleling the optimism of those who saw the benign hand of God in the printing press, computer industry analyst and government policy adviser Esther Dyson extols the new technology: "In three school years, students benefitting from computer-assisted instruction can learn almost a full year's worth of material more than students who do not have access to the technology."[8] With similar enthusiasm, Michael McRobbie, Director of Academic Technology at Indiana University, predicts that "it is no exaggeration that those universities [that] flourish in the next millennium will be those [that] most vigorously, but thoughtfully, embrace information technology."[9] With so many variant characterizations and historical contexts, it is easy to lose one's sense of place and direction in the maze of hope, hype, and novelty that defines the Information Age.

As David Staley's imaginative and provocative article "Imagining Digital Memory Work" reveals,[10] however, historians are adept at constructing scenarios based upon historically sensitive understandings of the past and present to address the future. To help map that contextual understanding of where we stand as a profession and to foster more coherent and productive discussion about where we ought to be and where we might be headed as teachers of history, the American Association for History and Computing (AAHC) conducted a survey of current uses of technology among American college and university history professors in the fall of 1998.[11] The survey was distributed through several H-Net discussion lists and was mailed through the United States Post Office to the chairs of the approximately 660 departments listed in the American Historical Association (AHA) *Directory of History Departments and Organizations in the United States and Canada* (see Appendix). Four hundred eighty-five history instructors from 101 American colleges and universities responded.

Since the disciplinary practices of history, and education more generally, are passing through a transitional and expansive phase in which countless technology experiments are being tried, tested, adopted, and disregarded, techniques for strategic random sampling were not rigorously employed. The AAHC's modest goal was to probe the new trends and directions of historical practice, so that more informed and concrete discussions and debate about these tendencies can be encouraged.

The 485 responses represent a sample group of 3.1 percent of the 15,600 history instructors working at American colleges and universities. Because rigorous random sampling techniques were not applied, no strong statements concerning the sample's representation can be made. Several observations about the group can be offered, however. First, the replies correspond with the proportion of instructors across the various academic ranks (from adjunct to full professor). Second, one-third of the respondents sent their replies by United States Post, rather than by electronic means. The extreme ends of historical practice seem well represented. If there is a significant representative gap in the survey, it likely rests with those instructors in the middle who are not intensely opposed or favorable to technology. Given these qualifications and recognitions, the survey results offer a telling glimpse into the technological trends in historical pedagogy.

The survey clearly reveals that marriages of history and computer technologies have occurred. Those scholars who are still at the altar protesting *any* union have missed the ceremony. Every history instructor who returned the survey is using electronic mail for scholarly communication, and 93 percent of the respondents report using computers for research. The problems of access for faculty also appear to be lessening. All respondents indicated that they can now use the Internet from work. Ninety-eight percent of full-time faculty reported having a computer in their office, with 91 percent of those instructors stating that their office computer is connected to the Internet. It must be noted, however, that access for students remains problematic. A third of the respondents noted that their students have seriously insufficient access to computers.

The survey also reveals the danger in using unitary metaphors like "the marriage" or "the computer revolution" to describe the process of change occurring in American colleges and universities. Respondents' remarks clearly reveal that there is an almost overwhelming diversity of technologies being tried and tested in the teaching of history, and an equally great individual and institutional variation in how these technologies are being applied to the practices of history. The detailed comments following each of the survey questions make it clear that neither the dangers nor the promise of computer technology can be adequately addressed through broad comments about general trends affecting the profession. History is not being swept along by a single wave or carried in a single direction.

Groups like the AHA and the AAHC must organize more discussions that address the local and categorical factors in technology's impact upon the practices of history. Some possible foci for discussion suggested by the survey include distance education, technology and adjunct instruction, the role of technology in the liberal arts, the virtues of computing across the humanities programs, and the incorporation of technology into introductory survey courses, methods courses, upper division courses, undergraduate research seminars, and graduate courses, each of which is characterized by different practices and expectations.

There are, of course, some shared experiences that are reflected across the entire range of survey responses. *Experimentation* with technology in the history classroom, albeit in widely divergent forms, is a central theme. Eighty percent of those surveyed reported using computer technology in teaching, and 46 percent state that they are now requiring their students to use e-mail for course purposes. Forty-four percent also have begun requiring students to use the Internet for research exercises, papers, and seminars, though 23 percent of this latter group expressed concerns about the reliability and sheer volume of information on the Internet. Sinking into the sand while surfing the Net continues to be a concern.

Nevertheless, recognizing that Internet investigation has become an unavoidable, if limited, part of historical research, many of these instructors are addressing the problem of quality through a variety of proactive steps. Fifty-four percent of the respondents have begun devoting significant class hours to technical instruction and workshops. Many are offering students specific instruction on how to find and evaluate materials on the Internet. Respondents are also turning to printed scholarly guides to Internet resources, such as *The History Highway 2000*, and to on-line guides, such as The Argus Clearinghouse, the OCLC Internet Cataloging Project, and the *Encyclopedia Britannica*'s E-Blast to direct students to reliable materials.[12]

Many faculty are also creating their own Web sites to help guide students to dependable on-line materials and provide other useful resources. Forty-seven percent of the respondents stated that they have developed their own course sites. This measure masks great variety, however. For most of the faculty in this group, the creation of a Web site means primarily making a copy of their syllabus and schedule available on the Web and directing students to several Web sites relevant to the course. A smaller group of faculty (who report greater technical support at their university or some training in computer technology) are producing more complex Web resources for their students. The materials mentioned traverse a wide technical range from annotated course readings to interactive tutorials and sophisticated historical databases.

A significant number of faculty are also requiring students to create as well as use on-line multimedia materials. Twenty-seven percent have begun asking students to produce individual Web sites for their courses, and 21 percent require or encourage students to develop group Web projects. Many courses are now meeting at least occasionally in computer labs to work with or on multimedia materials. These projects are most frequently mentioned as part of upper-level history courses, but a number of faculty are encouraging students to create multimedia projects even at the introductory level.[13]

Anecdotal comments also reveal, however, that there are still many history instructors who are uncomfortable with the use of multimedia projects in teaching history. The rationale most often given is that requiring multimedia projects necessitates greater student preparation. The other side of this complaint is the second most repeated explanation: "teaching technical skills at the expense of historical content and methodology is a calculus of dubious value." Similarly, a number of respondents question the benefits of adopting technology relative to the high costs in purely economic terms. One representative respondent poses the question: Which leads more directly to good history teaching—"a new computer lab or a new full-time history professor"?

Importantly, a number of those already actively using multimedia projects and materials in their courses also question the benefits to learning outcomes. These complaints come primarily from faculty at community colleges and state universities, especially from those at schools moving aggressively to develop distance learning programs. These instructors echo concerns about students being poorly prepared to use computers in the classroom. They raise fundamental questions about the success of distance learning for early undergraduates in history. More than twenty instructors anecdotally claimed that participation and enthusiasm dropped in direct correlation to the amount of hours spent on-line in a course. One professor who has conducted a quantitative comparative study of his distance and traditional versions of an otherwise identical course reported that use of the Internet and multimedia projects negatively affected student interest, communication with the instructor, and performance.

Reflecting these anxieties, 73 percent of faculty worry that their present use of technology is inadequate or poorly conceived. They express concerns about outdated technology, insufficient training, lack of release time, student resistance, negative impact upon tenure and promotion decisions, and unforeseen or negative effects upon the quality of their teaching. A number of faculty also reiterate deep concerns, already being widely heard, about how technology is being implemented and used on their campuses. Thirty-five percent of the respondents claimed that they were required by their institutions to use the Internet for their courses. Some of the mandatory uses indicated include offering state-required "technology across the curriculum" courses, putting syllabi on the Internet, making course enrollment and grade records available on-line, and even using technology provided by a specific corporation as mandated by a partnership agreement. Eleven percent of the respondents specifically noted as their central concern the lack of faculty involvement in planning and policy making. More generally, 65 percent claimed to be dissatisfied with their institutions' technology policies, initiatives, and plans for the future. The most common complaint is that "the administration is imposing technology without consulting faculty" and with "little regard for its impact upon teaching or learning." Others worry that the human dimensions of the profession are being devalued and disregarded. They argue that the union of technology and history will exacerbate the job crisis, further commercialize and dehumanize the profession, and increase the use of adjuncts, part-time instructors, and graduate students. Collectively, these complaints illustrate many of the central issues that the profession must continue to address if technology is to be sensibly incorporated into the practices of history.

It would be misleading to end on a negative note. Overall, the spirit of the responses is not pessimistic. A minority of the surveys do trumpet computer technology as the late twentieth-century equivalent of either devil-work or beneficent design, but in the main, the surveys reflect a measured and pragmatic attitude. All of the responses demonstrate an acute recognition that the Internet and World Wide Web are changing, or hold the potential to change, every dimension of history—from the structures of historical knowledge to the paradigms of pedagogy. Encouragingly, the criticisms and encomiums that resonate in the responses indicate a pervasive desire by faculty to actively direct the courses these changes will follow and to shape the technologies that will be employed, and there are many indications that scholarly and professional societies have begun supporting wide discussions about the issues. The American Association for History and Computing, the American Council of Learned Societies, and the American Historical Association, for example, have all recently created committees or launched councils to determine what technology policies they ought to support and encourage.

The essays in this volume are intended to help further the discussion and formulation of successful practices. Many such volumes and explorations are needed across the full range of historical endeavors. The historian's principle occupation, however, is teaching, and the focus of the seventeen subsequent essays is, therefore, on teaching and learning. The editors and authors recognize that good history instruction occurs in many places outside the classroom, especially in this digital age. Museums, living history sites, historical societies, libraries, and archives are also the loci of vital learning activities. Nevertheless, the range and diversity of activities occurring in teaching alone are substantial enough to comprise several volumes of reflections and case studies. The essays in this collection represent only an instructive sample of history teaching as it is currently being practiced and reconfigured in settings from grade schools to retirement communities.

Collectively, the AAHC survey and the essays illustrate the varied and powerful ways that technology can enhance and expand the teaching of history if successful modes are identified and refined. They also highlight dangers and shortcomings, and they offer a common warning that technology-based instruction must be supplemented by other methods. Teaching with artifacts, visits to museums, and exploration of historic places, for example, offer distinct prisms for illuminating the past. Even the history lecture will hold a viable place in the historian's armamentarium when well-used. If the lessons of the print revolutions are indicative, the story of history's future will likely be about increased options. Despite the fears of Parisian clerics and scholars, the spoken sermon and the lecture were not replaced by the printed word; rather, in many ways, the printing press brought opportunities to refine and supplement established practices. The *histoire* of history in the electronic age will almost certainly follow this same trajectory.

## Notes

1. Carl Bridenbaugh, "The Great Mutation," *American Historical Review* 68, no. 2 (1962): 315–331.
2. Ibid.
3. As quoted in Elizabeth L. Eisenstein, *The Printing Revolution in Early Modern Europe* (Cambridge, UK: Canto, 1983), 19–20.
4. Eisenstein, *The Printing Revolution*, 12–41.
5. Erik Davis, *Techgnosis: Myth, Magic, and Mysticism in the Age of Information* (New York: Harmony, 1998).
6. Neil Postman, *Technopoly: The Surrender of Culture to Technology* (New York: Vintage, 1993), 107–122.
7. David Sicilia, "Options and Gopherholes," in *Writing, Teaching, and Researching History in the Electronic Age*, ed. Dennis A. Trinkle (Armonk, NY: M.E. Sharpe, 1998), 73–82.
8. Esther Dyson, *Release 2.1* (New York: Broadway, 1998), 97–124.
9. As quoted in Barb Albert, "Technology Upgrades Top Colleges' Wish Lists," *Indianapolis Star*, 30 December 1998, 1.
10. Daniel Staley, unpublished paper, 1999.
11. The full results of the survey and a précis of representative comments is available in Dennis A. Trinkle, "History and the Computer Revolutions: A Survey of Current Practices," *Journal of the Association for History and Computing* 2, no. 2 (1999), which can be found online at: http://mcel.pacificu.edu/JAHC/JAHCI2.HTML.
12. Dennis A. Trinkle and Scott A. Merriman, *The History Highway 2000* (Armonk, NY: M.E. Sharpe, 2000). The Argus Clearinghouse: http://www.clearinghouse.net/index.html; The OCLC Internet Cataloging Project: http://orc.rsch.oclc.org:6990; and the *Encyclopedia Britannica*'s E-Blast: http://www.ebig.com.
13. As an aside, it is worth pointing out that the most confusion, frustration, and dissatisfaction in using computers in teaching history appears to be occurring in survey courses. Here, many respondents seem to be struggling with how to balance content and skills instruction with technology-enhanced student-centered learning practices.

**Appendix: History and Computer Technology**

*A Survey for the Profession*

Professional information (optional)
Name:_____
Professional Title/Rank:_____
Institutional Affiliation:_____
E-mail address:_____
Web site(s):_____

Do you have a computer in your office? Yes ____ No ____
What operating system/s do you use?_____
Do you have Internet access from your office? Yes ____ No____
From home? Yes ____ No ____

1. Does your university *require* you to use computer technology in any way?
   Yes ____ No ____
   How? Please describe:

2. Do you currently use computer technology in your research?
   Yes ____ No ____
   How? Please describe:

3. Do you currently use computer technology for scholarly communication?
   Yes ____ No ____
   How? Please describe:

4. Do you currently use computer technology in your teaching?
   Yes____ No____
   a. Do you offer distance learning courses? Yes ____ No ____
   b. Do you require students to use e-mail in your courses?
      Yes ____ No ____
      Please describe:
   c. Do you require students to use any software packages in your courses?
      Yes ____ No ____
      Please describe:
   d. Do you require students to use discussion groups, chat rooms, or Web
      bulletin boards in your courses? Yes ____ No ____
      Please describe:
   e. Do you require students to use the Internet for research in your courses?
      Yes ____ No ____
      Please describe:

f. Do you require/encourage students to create *individual* multimedia presentations or Web sites as an assignment in your courses?
Yes ___ No ___
Please describe:

g. Do you require/encourage students to create *group* multimedia presentations or Web sites as an assignment in your courses?
Yes ___ No ___
Please describe:

h. Do you create a Web site for students in your courses? Yes ___ No ___
Please describe:

i. Do you use the Internet to offer students interactive or self-directed opportunities to learn? Yes ___ No ___
Please describe:

j. Do you use computers for assessment purposes? Yes ___ No ___

k. Please describe any additional ways in which you use computer technology in your teaching:

5. Do you provide students in your courses with any specific technological training (either personally or through computing support services)?
Yes ___ No ___
Please describe:

6. Does your institution provide technology support or training for you?
Yes ___ No ___
Please describe:

7. Do you consider your institution's support adequate? Yes ___ No ___
How could it specifically be improved?

8. Does your department have any special technological facilities?
Yes ___ No ___
Please describe:

9. Are you satisfied with your present use of technology in your teaching?
Yes ___ No ___
Please explain:

10. Are you satisfied with your present use of technology in your research?
Yes ___ No ___
Please explain:

11. Are you satisfied with your present use of technology for scholarly communication? Yes ___ No ___
Please explain:

12. Do you feel that your institution has an appropriate plan for present and future purchase and use of technology?
Please explain:

13. What would you like to be able to do with technology that you are presently unable to accomplish?

14. What problems do you presently see or foresee with your use of technology?

15. What problems do you presently see or foresee with your institution's use of technology?

# History.edu

# 1

# Academic Historians, Electronic Information Access Technologies, and the World Wide Web

## A Longitudinal Study of Factors Affecting Use and Barriers to That Use

*Deborah Lines Andersen*

## Introduction

The following paper is actually a story about research conducted from 1992 until 1998 on the four University Center campuses of the State University of New York. The research on Web sites reported in this paper is as of April 1998. Due to the rapid rate of technological innovations, some of the results presented here will not reflect the actual state of the Web sites in the future. Academic historians participated in two survey research projects and two sets of interviews that assessed their use of electronic information access technologies and the barriers to that use. A body of information and organizational theory helped to explain the empirical data that arose from these projects. In particular, theory about diffusion of innovations, technology gatekeepers, and critical success factors was important in understanding historians' use of information technologies.

In order, the sections that follow introduce the methodological issues for this project, background about the State University of New York, previous research about historians' information use, and theoretical foundations. The empirical discussion focuses on the quantitative data collected in a 1996 survey of academic historians and upon a 1998 pilot study of four departmental home pages. The final sections look at pertinent findings and critical success factors that arose from analysis of the data. By looking at technological applications that historians have successfully used and by studying the roadblocks to technological success, we should be able to derive a series of lessons that inform the introduction of current technologies into the work of academic historians and also more general lessons that will advance the adoption of future technologies.

## Methodology

This research came out of a series of studies between 1992 and 1998 that initially surveyed academics across the four University Center campuses of the State University of New York at Albany, Binghamton, Buffalo, and Stony Brook. The first research project, started in 1992, looked at all faculty members on the four University Center campuses. This study centered on the electronic information access technologies that were available to these faculty members, since the express purpose of the study was to assess the feasibility of using electronic document delivery instead of duplicating journal subscriptions across the four campuses.[1] A small number of historians (n=twenty-nine) returned questionnaires for this survey.

In 1993, a new project looked at historians on just the Albany campus, interviewing them about their use of electronic information access technologies and about the barriers they perceived to that use.[2] Their stories, taped and transcribed, formed the pilot (n=six) for a much larger research project in 1996 that both interviewed a sample of twenty-eight historians across the four University Center history departments and surveyed the entire population of ninety-four academic historians. The purpose of this study was again to look at use of electronic information access technologies and also to record stories about the use of information, including electronic information, in the historians' research and teaching. The interviewed historians were chosen in a purposive sample to take into account gender, subject specialization, administrative functions, and reported technological expertise. (In each department there was at least one individual identified as the "technology gatekeeper" of the department, the person others went to with problems and questions. These individuals were purposely selected as informants for the interview section of the research.)[3]

Finally, in 1998, an experiment was conducted to assess the Web presence of each of the four history departments. In 1996, all four chairpersons had indicated that their departments were planning a home page. The question remained as to how many of the four departments had succeeded in their plans. In mid-February and again in mid-April 1998, a Web search was conducted for each of the university home pages, looking for links to the history department at each campus center. When a link was located, the history home page was analyzed for content and currency.

## The State University of New York

Although this research focuses on history faculty on the four University Center campuses of the State University of New York, these faculty exist in a much larger organizational context of the State University of New York, the four University Center campuses, and the four departments of history in which they work. The State University system is composed of four University Centers, thirteen University Colleges, two Health Science Centers, six Colleges of Technology, four specialized colleges (environmental science and forestry, maritime, optometry, and technology), five statutory colleges (four on the campus of Cornell University and one at Alfred University), and thirty community colleges.[4] Formally designated in the 1960s, the four University Centers, which conduct research and advanced graduate and professional studies and confer baccalaureate, master's, and doctoral degrees, were selected for this study because of this student mix and their size, necessary for maintaining undergraduate as well as master's and doctoral programs. In 1996, the four history departments had between twenty-one and twenty-five tenure track faculty members each, for a total of ninety-four academic historians across the four campuses.

## Historians as Consumers of Information

The work patterns of historians, the process by which they move from topic to evidence to argument, have been studied and discussed by a variety of researchers. Peter Uva uses a five-stage process to describe this work, including (1) problem selection (including preliminary work and hypotheses), (2) detailed planning of data collection, (3) data collection, (4) analysis and interpretation of data, and (5) presentation of findings.[5] Similarly, Michael Stanford developed a five-stage logical (but not necessarily chronological) model of the historian's work that consists of (1) the choice of subject; (2) the selection and, where necessary, the preparation of the evidence; (3) an alert and thorough reading, or other study, of the sources; (4) the tentative construction of a mental picture or model to fit the subject; and (5) a firm version of this model, constructed in a way that is fit to be made public.[6] These models are designed to look primarily at the information needs of historians in the context of their research, not in that of their teaching or departmental duties and communications.

Environmental factors additionally affect the work patterns of historians. Mary-Hilda Ebert created a laundry list of such items, including denied access to collections, crowded or nonexistent work areas, closed stacks, limited hours, low availability of microform readers, and loss of materials by theft and mutilation.[7] H.J. Hanham, emphasizing the importance of hands-on access, states that "the historian is rarely happy to see a single page. . . . He clings to the notion that browsing through a book in a library may suggest just the idea he needs to solve a problem that is worrying him."[8] Both written twenty-seven years ago, these descriptions portray a historian who is closely tied to print media, not electronic sources, for research. Nonetheless, in 1991, José Igartua, in noting shifts in historians' perceptions of information technology, stated that "it seems to have become current for history departments to view their 'quantifier' or 'computer expert' much as they view feminist historians, that is, as people at the edge of the historical profession rather than insurgents aiming at its core."[9] Central to the research presented here is the shifting view of information technology among historians. How far have they come toward becoming "insurgents aiming at the core"?

Electronic information access technologies have undergone an enormous revolution during these twenty-seven years. Not only have personal computers become nearly a saturated technology in the university environment, but software programs and the graphical user interfaces designed to create access to them have eliminated the need to know the basics of computer operating systems and DOS-based commands. Since "an information system will not be used when it is more trouble than it is worth,"[10] those who create and teach technologies have decreased the "trouble," so that the benefits of new technologies will outweigh the costs, in time, effort, and money, of adopting them when they arise. Decreasing the trouble might take the form of new technologies or new techniques that make such technologies and resources available to particular populations.[11] It might also take the form of creating standards for documents that are being generated only in electronic format so that historians in the future will have access to them.[12] Standardization of electronic information access systems could go a long way toward making historians more comfortable with the materials that are available on-line.[13] Additionally, as Donald Case suggests, information system developers should take into account cognitive aspects of their user populations and "consider segmenting the audience for computer interfaces, as well as designing generic tools that apply to all users."[14]

## Theoretical Foundations

The next four sections concern the theoretical underpinnings of this project. The broad categories encompass diffusion of innovations, technological gatekeepers, critical success factors, and evaluation of Web site design. Each of these theoretical frameworks helps to explain aspects of historians' use or nonuse of electronic information access technologies.

## Diffusion of Innovations

The process of introducing a new product or function into a system has been generalized into four steps.[15] Initially, a problem or need is perceived. Next, thorough research into the problem is undertaken, and a possible solution is developed. Third, agents (individuals or groups with decision-making and implementing ability) decide that the innovation should be diffused. Finally, the actual diffusion takes place.

While the emphasis in the above four-step process is upon problems and innovations, Everett Rogers and F. Floyd Shoemaker also look at the culture in which the diffusion of innovations takes place, concentrating on the actors in the society or external to it.[16] They believe there are four types of change:

1.  Imminent change, which occurs when people internal to the society create and develop the innovation on their own.
2.  Induced imminent change, when the innovation is catalyzed by someone who is a temporary member of the society, though the primary burden of the creation rests with the members of the society.
3.  Selective contact change, when members of one system adopt an innovation as a result of their exposure to the innovation outside their own system or society.
4.  Directed contact change, caused by actors external to the system who seek to induce change in order to achieve goals defined by them.[17]

This analysis of types of change was originally constructed to deal with institution building within organizations, but can be generalized to define diffusion of innovation patterns across a wide variety of circumstances, including those within academic departments, especially when seen in light of communication channels employed by academics, including invisible colleges, conferences, and electronic information exchange.

The process of diffusion has been likened to the contagion process in epidemiological research, by which one individual passes a communicable disease on to others in a potentially geometric progression until the disease is fully diffused or saturated in the population.[18] This disease metaphor, with its possibility for resistance to a particular virus or bacteria or lack of exposure due to isolation, works equally well for diffusion of innovations, as does the potential for isolating carriers of the disease (read "innovation") so that it does not spread to others.

## Technological Gatekeepers

In one definition, gatekeepers are "individuals who either limit access to information or restrict the scope of information, thereby decreasing opportunities within the organizational structure."[19] This sense of "gatekeeper" is an inhibiting one and as such includes organizations that establish college admissions policies, closed stacks in a library, or Internet access fees that restrict economically disadvantaged portions of populations.

Second, however, there is the gatekeeper as disseminator of information and innovation. Individuals in this role positively influence the use or transfer of information in an organization. They act as "communications channel, link, intermediary, helper, adapter, opinion leader, broker, and facilitator."[20] Both of these definitions can be useful in describing members of academic departments and their informal networks for information transfer.

Finally, in discussing gatekeepers and channels of communication, Jane Klobas and Tanya McGill tested five propositions about technological gatekeepers, confirming that "self-reported information dissemination behavior can be used to identify gatekeepers among individuals with diverse information-gathering behaviors, but a common group of potential interpersonal communications channels."[21] Their propositions include

1. Experience: Few gatekeepers have been in the information technology (IT) profession less than five years.
2. Education: Gatekeepers are no more likely to hold a doctorate than others in the IT profession.
3. Number of information channels: Gatekeepers use more information channels to gather information than others.
4. Importance of information channels: Gatekeepers consider more information channels more important than nongatekeepers.
5. Information strategy: Gatekeepers use different groups of information channels to gather information.[22]

Since Klobas and McGill were working with information technology professions outside of the academic arena, their proposition concerning amount of education was a critical factor. Within academic circles, the other four propositions are perhaps more pertinent.

**Critical Success Factors**

Institution building within organizations has been studied many ways, another being the development of critical success factors that allow organizations to keep track of a small set of goals critical to their success. John Rockart,[23] building on D. Ronald Daniel's original work,[24] posits a series of critical success factors (CSF) that could support organizational goals. Attainment of these goals ensures the success of the organization. Although each organization will have a small number of critical success factors at any one time, these factors need constant and careful attention, as well as adjustment as the organization changes.

Rockart presents four sources of critical success factors for private sector organizations. "Structure of the particular industry" will define, by the nature of the organization, what factors need to be developed. "Competitive strategy, industry position, and geographic location" look at the size and location of the organization in relation to others in the same market. "Environmental factors" take into account external forces, such as economics and politics, that could change the critical success factors for an organization. Finally, "temporal factors" are those that occur for a short time due to unexpected change, such as the replacement of an executive or severe fluctuations in the market for a product.[25] Rockart is dealing with private sector, for-profit organizations, but it is not a great leap of theory to apply his analysis to public sector or not-for-profit colleges and universities that also deal with a particular market for students, faculty, and research grants. Additionally, these same academic institutions compete at some level with a wide variety of other academic institutions defined by their size, rank, and geographic location, and find themselves dealing with political and economic forces that shape their culture. Finally, all academic institutions undergo temporal change with incoming classes, changes in academic faculty, and shifts in their administrations. For the purposes of this paper, Rockart's critical success factors will be applied to the academic rather than to the for-profit arena.

**Web Sites: Their Creation, Use, and Evaluation**

The creation, use, and evaluation of Web sites is a fairly new concept in the theoretical literature, primarily because Web sites themselves, a maturing technology, are very new. Whereas focus in the past has centered on the creation of HTML documents, a growing body of literature deals with the evaluation of these sites.

This evaluation literature is in part driven by a phenomenon peculiar to Web sites as information dissemination media. Historically, the materials that were produced for public consumption arose from a carefully reviewed print publishing industry that took great care to control for the design and contents of publications. With the advent of personal computers, more individuals became desktop publishers, able to produce quality documents, but probably without the marketing force of large publishing houses. Electronic mail made possible widespread distribution of these materials from the desktops of individuals. Now there is the phenomenon of the Web page. Information is far more easily distributed internationally in this medium than in print, but the centralization and review process of a formal publishing industry have been removed.

In academic institutions, thousands of dollars are spent every year to produce brochures that will attract the best students. At the same time, individual departments are producing home pages that can be accessed by these same potential students, but the home pages potentially lack the review, administrative approval, and editing process that go into print.[26] Many of these pages are of excellent quality, but the lack of central control means that a university can find itself with a hodgepodge of Web page styles, looks, and content. It is no wonder that Web page information evaluation has become a very important topic in medicine,[27] in government,[28] in the private sector,[29] and at universities.[30] Additionally, there are quality and content issues yet to be explored in the digital scanning of primary source documents for Web page mounting.[31]

**Empirical Results**

The next sections deal first with findings from the 1996 survey of historians, augmented with materials from the 1996 interviews, and second with information gathered from the 1998 pilot review of departmental home pages.

**Findings from the 1996 Survey**

The following tables display data from the 1996 survey of academic historians' use of electronic information access technologies, including World Wide Web technologies. It is critical to realize that in 1996 these historians had created no Web pages of their own, although several of them were at the cusp of using Web pages. Throughout this discussion, a major distinction exists between using Web pages and creating Web pages. These four departments did not create Web pages at all during the course of the 1996 study.

Table 1 displays the response rate for the 1996 survey of historians. The sixty returned surveys represented a 64 percent response rate that was fairly representative of full, associate, and assistant professors across the four campuses. Full professors were overrepresented while associate and assistant professors were underrepresented. (One respondent represented approximately 1.7 percent (1/60) of the total survey sample.)

Table 2 examines the first use of a variety of electronic information access technologies by these historians. Predictably, use of telefacsimile was greatest, with a total of fifty historians reporting first use between 1986 and 1996, and with a peak in the number of users in 1990 to 1991. Electronic mail had the next highest number of first users (forty-five), but the peak in

Table 1

**1996 Survey of Ninety-four Historians on the Four University Center Campuses of the State University of New York: Distribution of Responses**

|  | Full | Associate | Assistant | Total |
|---|---|---|---|---|
| Population (P) | 42 | 36 | 16 | 94 |
| Respondents (R) | 29 | 22 | 9 | 60 |
| Percent (R/P) | 69% | 61% | 56% | 64% |

Table 2

**1996 Survey of Historians: First Use of Technologies—1986 to 1996**

| Technology or Resource | 1986–87 | 1988–89 | 1990–91 | 1992–93 | 1994–95 | 1996 |
|---|---|---|---|---|---|---|
| E-mail | 0 | 4 | 9 | 12 | 17 | 3 |
| Fax (telefacsimile) | 1 | 6 | 18 | 16 | 9 | 0 |
| CD-ROM players | 0 | 0 | 2 | 5 | 11 | 2 |
| Electronic journals | 0 | 1 | 1 | 1 | 8 | 0 |
| Listservs, newsgroups, electronic bulletin boards | 0 | 0 | 2 | 9 | 9 | 1 |
| World Wide Web resources | 0 | 0 | 0 | 1 | 14 | 6 |

these responses came in 1994 to 1995. While World Wide Web resource first use was also at its highest in 1994 to 1995, the total number of first users was twenty-one, or approximately one-third of the respondent group.

Table 3 displays a variety of methods by which historians reported obtaining publications for their research and teaching. As with the information in Table 2, the modal responses for each variable help to describe the sample. While the modal response for use of campus library was "daily," personally purchasing books or subscriptions was "monthly." The modal responses for interlibrary loan requests, use of regional libraries, and travel to regional collections (overnight stay) were "infrequently." Use of network-based sources or on-line (remote) databases was one of the three variables measured that received a modal response of "never," although there were seven historians who reported using these resources on a daily or weekly basis. In general, these historians reported most frequent acquisition of locally available, paper-based materials, while distant and electronic sources received least attention.

Tables 4 and 5 examine these historians' access to and use of equipment for information access, manipulation, and retrieval. Whereas Table 4 reports

Table 3

**1996 Survey of Historians:  Methods of Obtaining Publications**

| Method | Daily | Weekly | Monthly | Infrequently | Never |
|---|---|---|---|---|---|
| Local campus library | 11 | 36 | 12 | 1 | 0 |
| Interlibrary loan | 2 | 8 | 20 | 29 | 1 |
| Go oneself or send someone to other libraries in the region | 1 | 2 | 13 | 31 | 13 |
| Personally purchase books or subscriptions | 3 | 12 | 34 | 10 | 1 |
| Use books or subscriptions purchased by department | 0 | 3 | 0 | 15 | 42 |
| Use fee-based commercial document service | 0 | 0 | 0 | 5 | 55 |
| Travel to a library or research collection (overnight stay) | 0 | 1 | 10 | 47 | 2 |
| Borrow materials from colleagues | 0 | 1 | 3 | 40 | 16 |
| Use network-based sources or on-line (remote) databases | 3 | 4 | 7 | 17 | 29 |

Table 4

**1996 Survey of Historians:  Perceived Access to Equipment**

| Equipment | Have Access | Do Not Have Access |
|---|---|---|
| Personal computer | 59 | 1 |
| Communications modem/software | 49 | 11 |
| Connection to campus network | 52 | 8 |
| Printer | 58 | 2 |
| Fax (telefacsimile) machine or fax modem | 52 | 8 |
| CD-ROM player connected to computer | 23 | 37 |
| Microfilm reader | 51 | 9 |
| Microform camera | 6 | 54 |
| Photocopier | 53 | 7 |

historians' responses to what technologies they *believed* were available to them, Table 5 reports historians' *use* of those technologies. It is important to note that there was a gap between many historians' perceptions of what was available to them and what technologies were actually at their disposal. In particular, historians on all four campuses had access to fax machines and photocopiers, but a number of individuals believed they had no access.

Table 5

**1996 Survey of Historians: Use of Equipment**

| Equipment | Daily | Weekly | Monthly | Infrequently | Never |
|---|---|---|---|---|---|
| Personal computer for word processing | 50 | 1 | 1 | 3 | 5 |
| Personal computer for databases | 4 | 4 | 5 | 17 | 30 |
| Personal computer for spreadsheets | 0 | 0 | 3 | 6 | 51 |
| Personal computer for communications | 34 | 6 | 2 | 6 | 12 |
| Communications modem/ software | 30 | 6 | 2 | 6 | 16 |
| Connection to campus network | 33 | 8 | 1 | 6 | 12 |
| Printer | 45 | 7 | 1 | 2 | 5 |
| Fax (telefacsimile) machine or Fax modem | 8 | 18 | 7 | 17 | 10 |
| CD-ROM player connected to computer | 5 | 9 | 1 | 6 | 39 |
| Microfilm reader | 0 | 4 | 14 | 31 | 11 |
| Microform camera | 1 | 0 | 0 | 5 | 54 |
| Photocopier | 28 | 23 | 1 | 1 | 7 |

When looking at actual use of these technologies in Table 5, the numbers that stand out concern not only high daily use of computers for word processing, computers for communications, printers, and photocopiers, but also low daily or weekly use of computers for databases or spreadsheets, CD-ROM players, and microform readers. Almost none of these results were counterintuitive, simply reinforcing the types of information use that had been reported in previous studies of historians. The exception was the use of electronic communications (measured with variables for communications modem/software and connection to campus network). Although historians have been described as avoiding technological innovations, sixty-six percent (forty of the sixty respondents) were using their personal computers for communications on a daily or weekly basis. At least a partial explanation for this high percentage came from the interviews of history department chairmen on the four campuses. In one of these departments, the faculty had been told that all departmental business would be conducted electronically and that there would be no departmental funds available for postage. Having been forced to communicate electronically, all departmental members (n=twenty-five) were frequent users of e-mail.

Table 6

**1996 Survey of Historians: Information Resources Available Through Networks**

| Resource | Daily | Weekly | Monthly | Infrequently | Never |
|---|---|---|---|---|---|
| Campus on-line catalog | 14 | 28 | 11 | 3 | 4 |
| Other libraries' on-line catalog | 4 | 15 | 16 | 13 | 12 |
| Journal index/abstract databases on campus library on-line catalog | 3 | 6 | 16 | 17 | 18 |
| Journal index/abstract database via commercial vendor (i.e., CompuServe, America Online) | 1 | 0 | 0 | 7 | 52 |
| Discipline-based electronic bulletin boards, listservs, etc. | 7 | 0 | 4 | 15 | 34 |
| Electronic journals and newsletters | 5 | 2 | 3 | 5 | 45 |
| Electronic mail (e-mail) | 35 | 6 | 1 | 2 | 16 |
| Full-text electronic databases (Nexis/Lexis; ARTFL) | 0 | 1 | 2 | 8 | 49 |
| Statistical databases (e.g., U.S. census datafiles) | 0 | 1 | 2 | 5 | 52 |
| CD-ROM index/abstract databases available at workstations at the library | 0 | 3 | 7 | 14 | 36 |
| Information available on the World Wide Web | 5 | 6 | 1 | 12 | 36 |
| Newsgroups and listservs | 10 | 3 | 3 | 7 | 37 |

Historians in this research reported varying use of networks for access to information sources. Table 6 displays these historians' reported use of information resources available through networks. Several bimodal response variables stand out for the purposes of this research report. Discipline-based electronic bulletin boards and listservs, electronic journals and newsletters, e-mail, and information available on the World Wide Web all elicited split responses from the sample with peaks of responses both at the "daily/weekly" level of use and at the "never" level of use.

It appeared that while there were many historians in the sample who made little or no use of these electronic information access technologies, there was also a small group of historians on each campus who were heavy users of these technologies. The subsequent interviews of these historians uncovered groups of information gatekeepers on each campus who not only used the technologies themselves but also served as technology educators for the department. (Note the unexplained discrepancy between the number of indi-

Table 7

**1996 Survey of Historians: Obstacles**

| Obstacle | Frequency | Percent |
|---|---|---|
| Lack of time | 31 | 52 |
| Lack of necessary hardware (computer, modem, etc.) | 15 | 25 |
| Lack of necessary software (communications package, Kermit, etc.) | 12 | 20 |
| Lack of CD-ROM player | 21 | 35 |
| Lack of necessary training | 39 | 65 |
| Lack of information about available databases | 23 | 38 |
| Lack of information about accessing information | 28 | 47 |
| Lack of operating funds to pay costs of searching and/or document delivery | 9 | 15 |
| Lack of funds to acquire hardware/software | 11 | 18 |

viduals who reported no use of electronic mail [sixteen] and the number who reported no use of their personal computer for communications in Table 5 [twelve].) Additionally, in interview discussion, historians reported a high use of libraries, electronic mail, and listservs for verification of the existence and content of primary and secondary sources before travel or before interlibrary loan requests for appropriate materials.

Table 7 shifts from the access to or use of a variety of information access technologies to the obstacles to the use of these technologies that historians reported encountering. The most often reported obstacles, lack of time, lack of necessary training, and lack of information about accessing information, were noted by 47 percent or more of the sixty respondents. Although lack of hardware, software, and funding were all reported as obstacles, they were secondary to a lack of information about information. An additional obstacle that surfaced during interviews was fear of lost productivity. Several historians believed that learning and using these technologies would take away from research and teaching time as opposed to streamlining these tasks.

## Conclusions Based on the 1996 and Previous Studies

There were nine categories of findings that surfaced as a result of the analysis of the quantitative data collected in the research.

*Ownership of publications.* Approximately half of the historians in this study owned between 25 and 50 percent of the materials they considered key for their research and teaching.

*Library ownership of publications.* Approximately half of the historians in this study believed that their campus library owned between 50 and 75 percent of the materials they considered key for their research and teaching.

*Archival sources.* Essentially all (99 percent) used primary sources located in archives, museums, special collections, and private collections for their research.

*Travel.* Ninety percent of the historians traveled in order to conduct their research.

*Translation.* All but three of the forty-two historians who used non-English materials translated those materials themselves as their sole means of access. Those three made use of translators in addition to doing some of their own translation.

*Personal computers and printers.* Access to these technologies was almost universal (99 percent) although some individuals indicated that they did not presently "own" a computer, and several stated they had never used one. Eighty percent of the historians stated that they used personal computers for word processing on a daily basis.

*Communications.* Ninety percent of the historians had access to electronic communications technologies, while more than 50 percent used electronic communications (e-mail) daily.

*Instruction in electronic technologies.* Historians reported the use of manuals, self-instruction, or colleagues and friends as their primary method of learning to use their first computer. They preferred individual, hands-on instruction over classroom instruction, and in-house colleagues over outside technicians or technical manuals. They reported the desire for many transactions that could be performed from home or office computer with the aid of communications devices, but appeared not to know about services that were available to them.

*Obstacles.* The three obstacles to using electronic information access technologies that were most frequently mentioned were lack of time, lack of training, and lack of information about information. Funding was reported as an obstacle by less than 20 percent of the respondents.

## Critical Success Factors for Historians' Use of Electronic Information Access Technologies

Although not all of the findings in the previous section related directly to electronic information access, those that did inform a small list of critical matters that allow historians to use these technologies, and that need to be watched in order to ensure their continued success with these technologies.

*Equipment.* New information technologies require up-to-date hardware and software. Historians who had no personal computer could not make use of these technologies. *Periodic technology inventories and updates are critical to information access success.*

*Training.* Since technologies change at a rapid pace, training in new technologies needs to keep up with that pace. Historians preferred individual, hands-on instruction from in-house colleagues. They also reported that lack of time was one of their major obstacles to using new technologies. *Regularly scheduled, individual, in-house education in new technologies will best meet the needs of these historians.*

*Support.* Technical support follows equipment and training as a critical success factor. Historians preferred in-house colleagues, technological gatekeeper historians who were right down the hall and accessible, to computer center support staff who were hard to find and usually not immediately available. *Support mechanisms need to present short turnaround times between problems and help.*

*Information.* Historians reported lack of information about information as a major obstacle to the use of electronic information access technologies. They did not know about new databases or about how to gain access to electronic information. A fourth and final critical success factor concerns diffusion of innovations—the creation of mechanisms that will get current information about new software, hardware, programs, and information sources to historians in a timely, predictable manner. Frequent updates, arriving on the historians' desks, will supply essential knowledge about new information sources and services.

## Web Pages in 1998

Although no history department on the four University Center campuses had a departmental Web site in place in 1996, all four campuses planned to have a Web page in the near future. In February 1998, three of the four departments had accessible home pages. In April 1998, the fourth departmental page was accessible through its university's home page after being off-line for an unspecified amount of time. These Web pages varied widely in ease of access, Webmaster profile, type of information, and number of links to external sites. Using text-based presentation software (Lynx), these four sites were analyzed to look for similarities and differences in content. Text-based materials avoid the additional variables of color, placement, and graphics, thereby eliminating all but content-specific variables.

Tables 8, 9, 10, and 11 compare the links available on the home pages of the four sites that were extant in April of 1998. All four of these sites could be found through the home page of their respective universities, although

---

Table 8

**History Department A:  Home Page Information and Link Map as of April 1998**

| | |
|---|---|
| Undergraduate programs | Internal link |
| Graduate study | Internal link |
| History department faculty | Internal link |
| History department events, 1997–1998 | Internal link |
| History department courses | Internal link |
| Other history department sites | Internal link |
| Department of history links | *External link* |

---

Table 9

**History Department B:  Home Page Information and Link Map as of April 1998**

| | |
|---|---|
| Faculty of social sciences | Internal link |
| E-mail (comments) | Internal link |
| Faculty and staff | Internal link |
| Events and colloquia | Internal link |
| Program information | Internal link |
| Course offerings | Internal link |
| Undergraduate history council | *External link* |

---

Table 10

**History Department C:  Home Page Information and Link Map as of April 1998**

| | |
|---|---|
| Faculty | Internal link |
| Graduate | Internal link |
| Undergraduate | Internal link |
| Events | Internal link |
| Resources | *External link* |
| Courses | Internal link |
| Alumni newsletter | Internal link |
| University home page | Internal link |

---

sites B, C, and D required two links from the home page, through academic departments and then history, while site A required three links, through lists of colleges and schools before arriving at the history site, a much more cumbersome process. Additionally, sites C and D could also be found immediately by attaching /history/ to the URL for the university. Sites A and B generated an error message when this technique was used.

Tables 8, 9, and 10 present a fairly straightforward series of links from their respective home pages. They differed in their number of initial link categories, and each had one link to sites external to its home university. These pages were informational, taking the place of the materials one would normally find in print catalogs or brochures created specifically for the department with the external links presenting materials that would not normally be in a brochure, information about other history sites for primary or secondary source materials as well as electronic journals and listservs that one could browse. Departmental administrators and faculty used graduate students as their Webmasters. At each site there was a direct electronic contact to the Webmaster as well as an update statement at the bottom of the home page.

Table 11 displays the link categories for Department D. In stark contrast to the first three, Department D not only included most categories seen in Tables 8, 9, and 10 (no alumni newsletter), but also included seven external links to journals, course materials at other universities, newspapers, magazines, and search engines. Additionally, the second to last link cautioned students about the pitfalls of electronic plagiarism. The Webmaster for Department D, a faculty technology gatekeeper, chose to insert update information at the *beginning* of the home page, a critical feature since the Webmaster was committed to a "Feature of the Month" for the departmental home page.

The categories of information found on Department D's home page included materials that would typically be seen in print advertising and admissions brochures but then expanded to include materials that would be useful to students and faculty within the department (as well as to other individuals outside of the department who wished to do historical research). The inclusion of several search engines also allowed faculty and students to move from the home page directly to additional Web-based research.

## Critical Success Factors for History Department Web Pages

The examples of Web page materials in Tables 8, 9, 10, and 11 present a variety of issues that influence the development and design of home pages for history departments. From these it is possible to derive a small set of factors that need attention and success if Web pages are to further the strategic goals of the department.

*Ease of access.* In a situation that is not internal to individual history departments, university home pages in this pilot study were designed in such a way as to make access to the history department home page more or less difficult. In the one case where the user had to make three decisions before finding the history department home page, the department runs the risk of never being found because accessing it is too much trouble. Inactive links from the university home page (the case of Department B in February of

Table 11

**History Department D: Home Page Information and Link Map as of April 1998**

| | |
|---|---|
| Feature of the month | Internal link |
| Faculty web pages | Internal link |
| Graduate program and faculty research | Internal link |
| Faculty and undergraduate program | Internal link |
| The Public History Program | Internal link |
| Upcoming history events and speakers | Internal link |
| Course descriptions | Internal link |
| History department course materials on the Web | Internal link |
| Other history courses on the Web | *External link* |
| History and media initiative | *External link* |
| Grants, fellowships, meetings, and other announcements | Internal link |
| Historical resource sites | *External link* |
| History journals edited by history department faculty | *External link* |
| History related journals on-line | *External link* |
| Newspapers and magazines on-line | *External link* |
| Electronic plagiarism: We know about it, so why try it? | Internal link |
| Search engines | *External link* |

1998) also make departments inaccessible. *Webmasters need to check periodically to make sure that the university home page makes finding the department page nearly transparent.*

*Ease of navigation.* Web pages should be designed for ease of navigation, ensuring the success of any user in finding information. Clarity of link labels, pages that have appropriate amounts of information and explanation on each page, and clear methods of getting back to the home page all make navigation easier. *Paying attention to the organization of information at a Web site, perhaps hiring an outside designer to create the site as one would a glossy brochure, is a critical success factor, especially if prospective students who are becoming more and more technologically sophisticated might shop for a college or university over the World Wide Web.*

*Currency of materials.* Universities usually run on quarter, trimester, or semester systems. Information about course offerings changes at the beginning of each of these academic periods. Unless the departmental Webmasters have committed themselves to more frequent updates (the "Feature of the Month"), *updates must correspond to, and anticipate, these academic periods.* (All four of the sites in this study were updated in April 1998 to reflect summer and fall 1998 course schedules.)

*Continuity of Webmasters.* At one of the four history department sites, the Webmaster was a graduate student—the second graduate student the department had used as Webmaster in two years. In on-line interviews with this

Webmaster, it became apparent that some information about the site had been lost. *A critical success factor for Web sites is the organization's ability to "remember" the decisions that have been made about the site and maintain continuity through various Webmasters.*

*Targeting informational content.* The four Web sites used for this pilot study appeared to target at least five customer bases: prospective students, present students, alumni, faculty, and individuals not directly related to the university who could be interested in historical research. *Strategic planning would dictate that not just the Webmaster, but stakeholders in the success of the department, need to decide who might access, read, and make use of materials on the department's Web site.* Alumni giving, student applications, faculty research and teaching, and administrative agendas all might be critical targets for a department's Web site.

## Critical Success Factors for Web Pages Housing Primary Source Documents

The final section of this paper deals with areas for future research. The issue of primary source documents is also an area for future research. At the time of the 1996 survey and interviews, several historians were considering putting primary source materials on Web sites for their classes. Several historians were using primary source documents that were "out there" on Web sites not attached to the university's home page. Research is definitely needed in order to assess the electronic information needs of historians in their research and teaching, and to decide what the critical success factors are for making primary source documents available in electronic formats. Central to these critical success factors appear to be electronic surrogates for print sources and verification of their authenticity, as well as the archiving of and access to materials that have only appeared in digital formats.

## Conclusions

There were four theoretical issues that drove the analysis of the data in this study: diffusion of innovations, technological gatekeepers, critical success factors, and Web site evaluation. The research has highlighted the areas in which historians have seen measurable diffusion of a series of technologies into their work environments, personal computers, electronic communications, and World Wide Web access among them. Similarly highlighted were those factors that have created barriers to the diffusion of innovation—insufficient time and information about information arising as the most critical issues. Central to the diffusion of innovation among historians is the technology gatekeeper of each department. These individuals can keep others in the department technologically "up to speed," but only if they have enough time and energy (and perhaps enough compensatory time from the department) to help when help is needed. These technology gatekeepers can potentially take on the task of Webmaster in the department, another role that requires large numbers of information channels and strategic planning in gathering and disseminating information.

Critical success factors for historians' use of electronic information access technologies center upon historians' need for individual attention in a timely manner, and upon their learning about new technologies that would assist them in their research and teaching. Additionally, as computing moves from a centralized function of the university to a distributed function that has become the responsibility of various departments, there is a critical need to think strategically about how these resources can be used to benefit the department, its students and faculty, and additional stakeholders beyond the walls of the university. Finally, World Wide Web dissemination of departmental information, as well as primary source documents, has the potential to change the way historians do their work. Since Web technologies are still developing, maturing, and changing, all user populations, historians included, will need to find efficient ways of learning about and using these technologies without wasting valuable time and energy. Although it appears that the technology expert in these history departments has moved at least somewhat from the edge of the profession, it remains to be seen whether we will enter an age where it is possible to speak of these individuals as "insurgents aiming at its core."

**Future Research**

The 1996 survey of historians across the four University Center campuses of the State University of New York was a picture of academics in flux. This is equally apparent from the recent creation of home pages in the departments as well as from the emerging listing of course materials that were on the Web. A profusion of research topics could follow from this study. In particular, a repeat of the 1996 survey would create a second picture of academic historians, allowing for longitudinal analysis of their use of electronic information access technologies and of the process of diffusion of these technologies. Additionally, the same questionnaire could be administered to historians at other academic institutions, or to a group of high-tech historians, in order to look for the sources of varying electronic information access use within the community of academic historians. Finally, the pilot study of the four departmental home pages is not generalizable to any larger population as a result of its small sample size. Future research needs to involve the creation and dissemination of materials for the World Wide Web, concentrating not only on the evaluation of Web materials and presentation, but also upon the use of Web pages as strategic tools for attracting students and faculty as well as for providing critical information sources for these individuals in their research, teaching, and studies.

## Notes

1. Judith A. Adams and Sharon C. Bonk, "Electronic Information Technologies and Resources: Use by University Faculty and Faculty Preferences for Related Library Services," *College & Research Libraries* 56, no. 2 (1995): 199–231.

2. Deborah Lines Andersen, "Can Electronic Libraries Work for History Faculty at the University at Albany: An Ethnographic Investigation of Barriers to Information Access" (The University at Albany, 1993).

3. Deborah Lines Andersen, "User-driven Technologies: Assessing the Information Needs of History Faculty as a Special User Population" (Ph.D. diss., State University of New York, The University at Albany, 1996).

4. State University of New York, "Fact Sheet," 1–2.

5. Peter A. Uva, "Information Gathering Habits of Academic Historians: Report of the Pilot Study" (Syracuse: State University of New York, Upstate Medical Center, 1977), 16, ERIC, ED 142483.

6. Michael Stanford, *A Companion to the Study of History* (Oxford: Blackwell, 1994), 148.

7. Mary-Hilda Ebert, "Contrasting Patterns of Specialized Library Use," *Drexel Library Quarterly* 7, no. 1 (1971): 22–23.

8. H.J. Hanham, "Clio's Weapons," *Daedalus* 100, no. 2 (1971): 512–513.

9. José E. Igartua, "The Computer and the Historian's Work," *History and Computing* 3, no. 2 (1991): 73.

10. Calvin N. Mooers, "Mooers' Law, or Why Some Retrieval Systems Are Used and Others Are Not," *American Documentation* 11, no. 3 (1960): ii.

11. Marcia Pankake, "Humanities Research in the 90s: What Scholars Need, What Librarians Can Do," *Library Hi Tech* 9, no. 1 (1991): 9–15.

12. Ronald Zweig, "Historians as Users of Electronic Records" (paper presented to the Archives & Museum Informatics Professional Seminar, Pittsburgh, PA, April 1994).

13. Edward Shreeves, "Between the Visionaries and the Luddites: Collection Development and Electronic Resources in the Humanities," *Library Trends* 49, no. 4 (1992): 579–595.

14. Donald O. Case, "Conceptual Organization and Retrieval of Text by Historians: The Role of Memory and Metaphor," *Journal of the American Society for Information Science* 42, no. 9 (1991): 657.

15. Everett M. Rogers, *Diffusion of Innovations*, 3rd ed. (New York: Free Press, 1983).

16. Everett M. Rogers and F. Floyd Shoemaker, *Communication of Innovations: A Cross Cultural Approach* (New York: Free Press, 1971).

17. Ibid., 219–220.

18. Diana Crane, *Visible Colleges: Diffusion of Knowledge in Scientific Communities* (Chicago: University of Chicago Press, 1972).

19. Cheryl Metoyer-Duran, "Information Gatekeepers," *Annual Review of Information Science and Technology* 28 (1993): 118.

20. Ibid.

21. Jane E. Klobas and Tanya McGill, "Identification of Technological Gatekeepers in the Information Technology Profession," *Journal of the American Society for Information Science* 46, no. 8 (1995): 581.

22. Ibid., 583–584.

23. John F. Rockart, "Chief Executives Define Their Own Data Needs," *Harvard Business Review* 57, no. 2 (1979): 81–92.

24. D. Ronald Daniel, "Management Information Crisis," *Harvard Business Review* 39 (1961).

25. Rockart, "Chief Executives," 86–87.

26. Christine A. Quinn, "From Grass Roots to Corporate Image—The Maturation of the Web," (1994); available from http://www.ncsa.uiuc.edu/SDG/IT94/Proceedings/Campus.Infosys/quinn/quinn.html

27. Alejandro R. Jadad and Anna Gagliardi, "Rating Health Information on the Internet: Navigating to Knowledge or to Babel?" *Journal of the American Medical Association* 279, no. 8 (1998): 611–614.

28. Sharon S. Dawes et al., *Developing and Delivering Government Services on the World Wide Web: Recommended Practices for New York State* (Albany: Center for Technology in Government, 1996); available from http://www.ctg.albany.edu

29. Sun Microsystems, "Guide to Web Style" (1996); available from http://www.sun.com/styleguide/

30. Sarah Hinman, "Best Practice Web Page Design: An Evaluation of Five ALA-Accredited Schools' Home Pages," seminar paper, State University of New York, The University at Albany, 1998.

31. Jessica Lacher-Feldman, "Evaluating Primary Source Documents on the World Wide Web," seminar paper proposal, State University of New York, 1998.

# 2

# History Instruction and the Internet

## A Literature Review

*Ann Wynne*

### Old Wine—New Bottles

The Internet is a worldwide computer network. It decentralizes and democratizes access to knowledge bases in ways that used to be impossible. Likewise, the new social history democratizes pedagogy because it deals with evidence from a variety of sources to give voice to a range of human endeavors.[1] The advent of powerful computer-controlled, interactive, multimedia databases moves sources of material culture such as photos, images, sound, and motion pictures into the foreground in the analysis of this social history orientation.[2]

The technology of educational delivery has evolved from the oral lecture, an artifact from the Middle Ages. To "lecture" derives from the Latin verb "to read," reflecting the reading of a text by the professor when books were one-copy handwritten manuscripts. The advent of the Industrial Revolution required the mass education of workers via the group lecture model in large bureaucratic schools, intended to mirror the economies of scale of the factory system.[3] In the early twentieth century, the teaching-learning function became organized around behavioral psychology strategies of measurable objectives. This method came to dominate computer-aided instruction (CAI) such as programmed learning. As Timothy Koschmann notes in "Paradigm Shifts and Instructional Technology," "CAI applications utilize a strategy of identifying a specific set of learning goals, decomposing these goals into a set of simpler component tasks, and, finally, developing a sequence of activities designed to eventually lead to the achievement of the original learning objectives."[4] Such drill and practice computer programs emphasize instructional efficiency.

In the early 1970s, the direction of instructional design was influenced by the cognitive science of artificial intelligence (AI). In this research, the computer program simulates the role of an intelligent tutor in a complex knowledge domain. The critical issue for these types of studies is instructional competence, because AI attempts to properly represent expert knowledge.[5]

A newer concept in cognitive learning is labeled constructivism. Both the historian and the learner construct their own mental models of the past based on the interaction of new information with their prior knowledge. Learning is a reflective, generative process best facilitated by active, collaborative forms of pedagogy.[6] Challenging, participatory assignments using a variety of print and graphical nonprint sources accommodate a portfolio of methods to assess the ways students acquire and demonstrate historical understanding by making personal connections to subject matter.[7]

While constructivist theory stresses the individual's cognitive self-regulation, the theory of situated cognition posits that the mind forms a reciprocal loop from the individual to the wider social community. Knowledge is situated in a particular learning community and its culture. Teachers must mimic professional historians and develop activities akin to historical apprenticeships to induct students into the historian's distinct academic culture, patterns of discourse, and ways of conceptualizing the world.[8] In a teacher-centered class, the source of authority is the instructor and the text. In a learner-centered environment, the instructor is turned into a facilitator, guiding collaborative learning groups. This idea represents "instruction as enacted practice."[9]

To some educational researchers, the move toward an apprenticeship model of history education revealed a naive assumption about a student's readiness to learn because of a lack of prerequisite content knowledge and literacy skills.[10] In this light, the most recent national assessment of the historical abilities of American high school students indicated that students experienced great difficulties interpreting primary source documents beyond merely superficial levels.[11]

Similar to history curriculum culture wars of the 1980s, the current discussion of traditional versus digital history instruction suffers from useless polarization.[12] Instead of incrementally matching a student's learning style to appropriate delivery systems, debate participants have divided the discourse into the forces of the past against those of the future.[13] Detractors of Web-based pedagogy fear a worst-case scenario. They predict a marriage between higher education and technology that permits the deskilling of professors and the commodification of education at the cost of its core humanistic values.[14] Others compare faculty members who resist technology-based pedagogy to a modern form of academic priesthood fearful of losing its authority to the new networked knowledge revolution.[15] Such a two-valued approach to the problem has proved counterproductive. A networked history class constitutes a kind of historical learning community and culture. The question is how does historical understanding manifest itself in such a community and how can we come to know its properties?

## The Research Agenda

In "The Future of the University in an Age of Knowledge," James Duderstadt states that the modern university is experiencing pressures from an accelerating and shifting set of conditions. These include the primacy of intellectual capital in the new economic order; globalization; the connection between multimedia technology and the instantaneous exchange of information; and the replacement of hierarchical institutions such as corporations, universities, and governments with democratic networked groups. Today knowledge resides as digitally encoded forms and is universally accessible. It no longer is "the prerogative of the privileged few in academe."[16]

As experts with core competencies, history educators have reason to resist change. Academic professions enjoy market niches and partial knowledge monopolies. Disciplinary specialization reduces the ability to sense important changes in the wider environment. Although resistance to change may be in part motivated by self-interest, this resistance may prove beneficial because it forces people to distinguish between lasting versus transitory knowledge. Studies find that self-appointed famous experts predict future events with the same poor track record as average people.[17] Yet the educational horizon appears crowded at this juncture with all sorts of pundits predicting this and that about the demise of the physical institutions of higher learning in favor of virtual ones.[18]

Effective history educators need not fear change. They own a repertoire of skills developed from years of practice that is now referred to as the tacit dimension of a new knowledge base for teaching.[19] In a case study of expert high school history teachers I discovered these theories-in-action are influenced by the teacher's entrepreneurial drive, flair for performance art, personally mediated curricular ideas, and intuitive sensitivity to students in personal contexts.[20] These are hardly a set of procedural routines easily captured by a computer program. As Rushworth Kidder suggests, in the rush to get on the technology bandwagon, institutions may favor hiring techno-wizards and not instructors who understand students. He notes the old adage that if you want to teach history, geography, or math to Mary, it is as important to know Mary as it is to know the subject.[21]

The competition to bring courses on-line may be based on exaggerated and unproven claims of improved learning outcomes. Most educational software developed in the last thirty years lacks an empirical research base of longitudinal studies involving large numbers of students.[22] Ian Forsyth has noted that the first generation of Internet courseware was largely hype, consisting of electronic page turning overlaid with some random access search and indexing features.[23] In a survey of current distance learning programs, Donna Pogroszewski discovered that relatively few institutions were successfully adopting interactive technology tools such as chat rooms, groupware conferencing programs, or threaded discussion lists to deliver electronic courses.[24] This fact is especially disturbing because cooperative student learning is the stated preferred pedagogical strength of Web-based instruction.[25] As with the dearth of published findings on the nature of exemplary collegiate history instruction, more research is needed comparing face-to-face with virtual forms of classroom communications.[26] The same instructor would have to use the same readings and assessments, teach the same material, and use similar pedagogical methods for both the on-campus and on-line class history course. Students of fairly similar abilities would have to be randomly assigned to each course treatment.

It logically follows that this much-needed research would aid in a theory-building process to identify how exemplary history educators at all levels of schooling successfully adapt both content and pedagogical knowledge to computer-mediated learning worlds.[27] What subject-specific practices work best in tapping the democratic educational potential of the World Wide Web? Ethnographic studies should document how teams of history instructors, instructional designers, and programmers structure highly complex and critically demanding interactive virtual courseware. This courseware needs to be beta-tested in on-campus networked computer labs, with students of varying ability levels, to diagnose students' difficulties interpreting the program's navigational structure and in mastering course materials.[28] In the formative and summative evaluation of these learning objects, the educational community must also be sensitive to the aforementioned skills in the affective domain. For a student of history, such affective skills include the development of historical empathy for the problems and solutions of past generations and a passionate excitement and enjoyment of history as a grand narrative story.[29] Although research indicates there is no significant difference in learning outcomes when comparing traditional classroom instruction to alternative delivery systems, including new media, educators should not assume that computer-mediated teaching is neutral.[30] As Perry Robinson warns in *Technology and Higher Education*, "we need to think about the substitution of cyberspace for shared human space, the difference between interaction with the computer and interaction with other humans" and how [cyberspace] will affect academic life and all our communities."[31]

## History Instructors On-Line

Far from eliminating the primacy of the instructor, the art of authoring, teaching, and maintaining a Web-based history course may be more time intensive than teaching lecture courses. Similar feedback has been anecdotally reported by college history instructors who have pioneered in teaching distance education Western Civilization courses.[32] This finding is not surprising because the shift toward constructivist interactive pedagogy demands a steep learning curve involving not only mastery of Internet-based history resources, but cross-disciplinary forays into computer graphics, course design, cognitive psychology, human-computer interface issues, and so forth.[33] But at the core of the enterprise are the domain-specific skills of the history educator. Margaret Honey and Jan Hawkins find that teacher ownership—"the process of generating ideas and strategies that make sense within the particular circumstances of one's own classroom and curriculum—is a key to successful use of digital archives."[34] Teachers and students must be provided with analytic tools to enable them to access digital source materials in ways that make sense to them. These tools might include storyboards, spreadsheets, image analysis tools, databases, time lines, and templates, but the relevant content links should be assembled by the instructor. It is common sense to state that "indexing schemes that work well for a classroom teacher are likely to be very different from those that function effectively for a scientist or scholar."[35]

The history teacher who chooses to experiment with virtual teaching will be challenged to spend time filtering and evaluating historical Web sites. In a recent review of such sites, Michael O'Malley and Ray Rosenzweig discovered that commercial search engines did not expend as much rigor in ranking history sites as they expended energy pursuing advertising dollars.[36] On the *Yahoo!* annotated history list, a site promoting racist and anti-Semitic historical views was listed side by side with a national women's history program.[37] These reviewers conclude that commercial history Web sites push glitzy, canned treatments of subject matter rather than serious historical productions. They lament that politically controversial and independent history sites will not be able to compete financially with the commercial ones.[38] Web site reviews should focus on pedagogical rather than commercial uses; one such pedagogical site was constructed by Dr. Skip Knox of Boise State University.

The metaphor of a community of scholars is used by Knox to describe his on-line asynchronous freshman Western Civilization course.[39] When Knox first offered a virtual course, he tried to act as a "guide on the side," rather than a "sage on the stage." He translated this to mean he was to provide objectives, course requirements, and weekly discussion questions and then wait for a spontaneous student reaction. Nothing happened. He realized that without his leadership students were merely "separate individuals who would separately earn three credits of history and who might by accident have something to say to one another."[40] The sense of a common educational community with a common purpose is essential to either a virtual or a real class. For Dr. Knox, his course's discussion group is the lifeline for his community of scholars.

He has retooled his Web pedagogy with a writing style he referred to as Web rhetoric—writing both formal and conversational in the tradition of dramatic storytelling.

> Each Web page serves to present a thought, a concept, a scene in a narrative. The link between one page and the next is a caesura, and the end of a page is a dramatic moment, rather like a dramatic pause in public speaking. The reader has to click on the mouse button and wait a moment (but not too long!) for the next screen to appear. Just as the end of a chapter in a book should propel the reader forward to the next chapter, so the words at the end of one Web page should create a little tension and lead the reader forward.[41]

Knox believes that external hyperlinks should be sparsely used. To him, solid Web pedagogy involves designing the material in such a manner that the learner is able to create a quick mental model of the boundaries of the work expected. There are internal links of sound files to help a student with pronunciation of difficult terms. Graphics are not embedded in Web lectures because of long download times. External links are provided under supplemental activities, but Internet exploration is subordinated to formal study requirements.

Several points of interest can be made. First, the dramatic flair for storytelling in Knox's Web lectures has been identified in one case study as a pedagogical characteristic of the teaching style of exemplary history lecturers.[42] Experienced history teachers are not content-managers of some bureaucratic, teacher-proof, canned curriculum. They are managers of meaning and content transformers through their own agencies. Secondly, Knox's students were socialized by years of teacher-led schooling and were naturally confused by an open-ended environment. Students, as well as teachers, will require retooling of old habits to adapt to a learner-centered model of instruction. And, finally, Knox came to discover what the research seems to indicate. The most powerful factor of the instructional event is the elegance of the curricular-instructional design and not the properties of the particular delivery system.[43]

In a more radical departure from current practice, other practitioners have begun to experiment with knowledge-building communities. Marlene

Scardamalia and Carl Bereiter explain this process by distinguishing between first and second order environments. In the former, learning is asymptotic, evidencing little progressive complex problem solving in a given domain. In the latter, intentional progress made by one member advances the knowledge of the collective environment.[44] This was the original idea behind the invention of hypertext, whereby the ability to think in a nonlinear fashion would enfranchise people's creativity in learning communities. Instructors may someday assess an individual's or group's progressive learning by studying the complexity of their hyperlinked-knowledge maps' structure for a given historical topic. Such complex structures seem to indicate deeper understanding.[45] Detractors of hypertext have suggested it degrades the reader's search for deep meaning and internal complexity as in a study of linear text because hypertext reading rewards superficial thinking in which "the linkages between texts now matter rather than the internal coherence of the texts themselves."[46]

Konnilyn Feig has described a distance learning course in Western Civilization as a developing knowledge-building community. Students worked for extra credit in multimedia computer labs researching topical history links. This project became the basis of two fifty-page Internet books on the ancient and modern worlds that form the core of Feig's on-line courses at Foothill Community College in California. New groups of virtual and campus-bound students continue to add to the project. She encourages her students to chart changes in their perceptions of organizing and understanding historical subjects. The instructor builds Web research exercises around the Internet books into the course requirements and moderates this discussion by posting weekly conceptual, collaborative position papers to guide her novice Internet historians. These on-line conferences are held synchronously and students respond in real-time e-mail. Feig stated in a telephone interview with this researcher that her own thinking about history has been transformed by involvement in the project.[47] We are no longer bound to a particular time or place for historical sources. For example, this is a statement from her on-line syllabus: "Each week, students peruse the Internet through the *Ancient World* with the wonderful range of things to think about. Archeology, art, music, theater, books and writing, language, philosophy, politics, war and peace, life and living, psychology, sociology, history, geometry, and astronomy and biology, building and architecture and engineering. Economics and geography, women and men and children, farming and town planning, rivers and deserts and mountains, gods and goddesses. Birth and death, magic and mystery, aspiration and despair, palaces and mud huts, the freedom to rule empires, and the chains of everlasting slavery. Poetry, logic, weaponry, sports, courage and cowardice, love and hate, and genius.[48]

These topics most likely serve as a mirror into ways students identify with aspects of subject matter as well as the signature of the instructor's philosophical curricular framework. Dr. Feig is a Holocaust history scholar and has worked with others on worldwide human rights issues. This passionate commitment to a curricular vision and to dramatization of the curriculum to teach historical empathy may also be a key to good teaching practices.[49] Talking head researchers, either in a telecourse, CD-ROM, or a multimedia Internet history course, do not necessarily understand how to successfully get material across to undergraduates. Reputational and evaluative criteria should be established to identify and reward exemplary history instructors whose wisdom from years of practice proves they do. For any on-line project to succeed, history educators with core competencies essential to the production process must be accorded partnership in the enterprise in terms of intellectual property rights.[50] As Knox puts it, "The information is free, but the teaching costs."[51]

Another example of a knowledge-building community is the American Studies Web program at the University of Virginia. This project started in 1996 as part of a new master's degree program in American Studies designed to emphasize the use of new technologies. Alan Howard reports that it is far more expensive and time intensive than university administrators, state legislators, and members of the public had envisioned.[52] This electronic village features samples of graduate and undergraduate work in American Studies; a digital library of public domain books; and a continuously growing virtual museum exhibit of the nation's capital. Students believe that their projects are bound together in the progression of building the entire site. The site has become a joint stock company, with student pride of ownership continuing after graduation. Intellectual property is now defined as communal property.

> The value of the by-product can be realized only when someone else expropriates the material, changes it, adds to it. It can't be sold, only given away. Title, it seems, is vested more in the user than in the producer. It also yields old-style, low-tech rewards: "The ability to think, to write, and to work intensely on matters of genuine concern, things that have always seemed to me the central goals of a liberal education."[52]

## In Search of the Learning Community

It seems that this essay has only briefly illustrated both the potentialities and problems of distance education Web-based history instruction. Education jargon has picked up the phrase the "learning community" from business organization literature, but what is needed are real blueprints on how to achieve this goal within academic domains.[54] Research funds need to be carefully targeted to publish a body of educational case literature illustrating the teacher lore developed by pioneer on-line history educators across levels of schooling. Or else, to paraphrase a line from *Alice in Wonderland*, if we don't know where we are going, then any road will do. History educators need not buy into the overly optimistic rhetoric of technological determinism, but neither should they be blinded to the historic learning and research opportunities that are unfolding in their midst in other university disciplines. Technology may contribute to our understanding of the processes that transform novice history students into outstanding ones. History pedagogues could participate in triangulated research teams of content-area specialists, cognitive scientists, natural language acquisition experts, and computer scientists to develop new curricular-instructional models emphasizing apprentice historical internships along four dimensions: knowledge integration, authentic real-world problems, product-oriented course outcomes, and collaborative teamwork.[55] Because student-teacher and student-student academic conversations can be electronically archived, researchers from these fields will begin to build theories of how a student vicariously learns from peers and how an individual's domain-specific mental schema develops by recognizing connections made through reusable historical dialogues.[56] The model-building process could include inventing expert software to tutor students in historical essay writing, using primary source documents, or creating reliable objective tests based on cognitive mapping of historical concepts.

James O'Donnell has lamented the absence of a critical climate of discourse beyond the university walls in the present-day worlds of politics, radio, and television.[57] Just as no one confuses Oprah Winfrey with Plato, Dan Rather cannot substitute for Herodotus. This is one reason there may be a cultural divide between academics and industry representatives who arrive on campus hawking the latest million-dollar technology system. It is the job of teachers to teach students how to become aware of "massive manipulation by the media and the information industry."[58] Teaching has a long history as a service profession. According to Walker,

> This observation reveals a new appreciation for the complexity of human understanding. Expertise means far more than having the right answers or formulating rules and principles to govern professional behavior. It refers to that sense of familiarity, grounded in experience and practice, that appeals primarily to intuition and "feel." Knowledge, some theorists are given to say, is inextricably bound up in what it means to be human—in culture,

in moral vision, and in the particular relationships that frame the learning event. This insight is again substantiated by a wealth of new literature in which teachers describe their work as less hierarchical and less dependent on a detached and calculating rationality. Rather, knowledge is bound up in teachers' sense of pedagogical mission, in their own biographies, and in the special conditions under which they work.[59]

What appears at first view as faculty resistance to technology and change may be in reality a resistance to any Faustian bargain that might violate concern for students. If the old myths and stories about education are not working, we may need new ones. The new ones should focus less on the technical language of reengineering and more on new metaphors of what it means to be an educated, historically aware citizen of the new millennium.[60]

## Notes

1. P. Burke, "Overture: The New History: Its Past and Its Future," in *New Perspectives on Historical Writing*, ed. P. Burke (University Park: The Pennsylvania State University Press, 1992), 1.

2. Ann M. Wynne, "Using Non-Print Instructional Materials," in *Instructor's Guide to The Enduring Vision: A History of the American People*, ed. Robert B. Grant and James L. Lorence (Lexington, MA: Heath, 1996), 30.

3. A.W. Bates, *Technology, Open Learning and Distance Learning* (London and New York: Routledge, 1995), 1.

4. Timothy Koschmann, "Paradigm Shifts and Instructional Technology: An Introduction," in *CSCL: Theory and Practice of an Emerging Paradigm*, ed. T. Koschmann (Mahwah, NJ: Lawrence Erlbaum, 1996), 5–6.

5. Ibid., 12.

6. J. L. Herman, P.R. Aschbacher, and L. Winter, *A Practical Guide to Alternative Assessment* (Alexandria, VA: Association for Supervision and Curriculum Development, 1992).

7. Howard Gardiner, *Art, Mind, and Brain* (New York: Basic Books, 1982).

8. J. Brown, A. Collins, and P. Duguid, "Situated Cognition and the Culture of Learning," *Educational Researcher* 18, no. 1 (1989): 32.

9. Koschmann, "Paradigm Shifts," 14.

10. S. Wineberg, "Remembrance of Theories Past," *Educational Researcher* 18, no. 4 (1989): 7.

11. E. Hawkins et al., *Learning About Our World and Our Past: Using the Tools and Resources of Geography and U.S. History–A Report of the 1994 NAEP Assessment* (Washington, DC: National Center for Education Statistics, 1998), 189.

12. G. Nash, C. Crabtree, and R. Dunn, *History Wars on Trial: Culture Wars and the Teaching of the Past* (New York: Knopf, 1997).

13. Judith V. Boettcher, "The Journey to the Web: Simple Adaptations or New Curricula?" *Syllabus* (January 1998): 48; Lawrence A. Tomei, "Instructional Technology: Pedagogy for the Future," *T.H.E. Journal* 25 (December 1997): 56.

14. David Noble, "Digital Diploma Mills: The Automation of Higher Education," *First Monday* (1998), 2. Available from http://www.firstmonday.dk/issues/issue3_1/noble/index.html; Kenneth R. Weiss, "Wary Academia Eyes Cyberspace," *Los Angeles Times*, 31 March 1998, 1.

15. Carl Raschke, "Digital Culture, The Third Knowledge Revolution, and the Coming of the Hyperuniversity," *Syllabus* (March 1998): 16.

16. James J. Duderstadt, "The Future of the University in an Age of Knowledge," *Journal of Asynchronous Learning Networks* (1997), 3; available from http://www.aln.org/alnweb/journal/issue2/duderstadt.htm

17. William Starbuck, "Learning by Knowledge–Intensive Firms," in *Knowledge in Organizations*, ed. L. Prusak (Boston and Oxford: Butterworth-Heinemann, 1997).

18. Eli Noam, "Eli Noam on the Future of the University," *Educom Review* (July–August 1996): 4; available from http://www.educom.edu/web/pubs/review/Articles/31438.htm

19. L. Shulman, "Knowledge and Teaching: Foundations of the New Reform," *Harvard Educational Review* 57 (1987): 100.

20. Ann M. Wynne, "Keepers of the Gates: An Inquiry into the Curricular-Instructional Gatekeeping Practices of Exemplary High School History Teachers" (Ph.D. diss., University of California at Los Angeles, 1994), 308–309.

21. Rushworth M. Kidder, "The Ethics of Teaching and the Teaching of Ethics," in *The Electronic Classroom: A Handbook for Education in the Electronic Environment*, ed. Erwin Boschmann (Medford, NJ: Learned Information, 1995), 223.

22. Alfred Bork, "The Future of Computers and Learning," *T.H.E. Journal* (1997): 3; available from http://www.thejournal.com/SPECIAL/25thani/0697feat03.html

23. Ian Forsyth, *Teaching and Learning Materials and the Internet* (London: Kogan Page, 1996), 13.

24. Donna Pogroszewski, "Survey of Current Distance Learning Programs" (cited 25 February 1998); available from http://www.rit.edu/~djp6549/research.html

25. Badrul Kahn, ed., *Web-Based Instruction* (Englewood Cliffs, NJ: Educational Technologies Publications, 1997).

26. David W. Brooks, *Web-Teaching: A Guide to Designing Interactive Teaching for the World Wide Web* (New York and London: Plenum Press, 1997), 88–91.

27. M.S. McIssaac and C.N. Gunawardena, "Distance Education, in *Handbook of Research for Educational Communications and Technology*, ed. D.H. Jonassen (New York: Simon and Schuster), 403–437.

28. Bork, "The Future of Computers and Learning," 5; Steve Draper, "Constructivism and Instructional Design" (cited 7 December 1997); available from http://www.psy.gla.ac.uk/~steve/constr.htm

29. Wynne, "Keepers," 166–172.

30. Stephen C. Ehrmann, "Asking the Right Question: What Does Research Tell Us About Technology and Higher Learning?" (cited August 1997); available from http://www.georgetown.edu/crossroads/guide/ehrmann.html

31. Perry M. Robinson, *Technology and Higher Education* (Washington, DC: American Federation of Teachers, 1997), 23.

32. Konnilyn Feig, "History 4A—History of Western Civilization: The Ancient World," (1998), 1; available from http://www.omnibusol.com/ancientcourse.html; Skip Knox, "The Pedagogy of Web Site Design," *ALN Magazine*, August 1997; available from http://www.idbsu.edu/people/skip; James O'Donnell, "Humanities in the 21st Century," *Humanities* (September–October

1995); available from http://ccat.sas.upenn.edu/jod/hackney.html; Norman G. Raiford, "Why Would a History Teacher Venture into Teaching On-Line or, Yes, Old Doggies Can Learn New Tricks but Should They Have To?" conference presentation to the League for Innovation in the Community College, Atlanta, GA, 12 October 1997.

33. C. McCormack and D. Jones, *Building a Web-Based Education System* (New York: John Wiley, 1998); Dennis A. Trinkle and D. Auchter, eds., *The History Highway: A Guide to Internet Resources* (Armonk, NY: M.E. Sharpe, 1997).

34. Margaret Honey and Jan Hawkins, "Digital Archives: Creating Effective Designs for Elementary and Secondary Educators" (Center for Children and Technology, Educational Development Center, Inc., May 1996), 30; available from http://www.ed.gov/Technology/Futures/honey.html

35. Ibid., 5.

36. Michael O'Malley and Ray Rosenzweig, "Brave New World or Blind Alley? American History on the World Wide Web," *Journal of American History* (June 1997); available from http://chnm.gmu.edu/chnm/jah.html

37. Ibid.

38. Ibid., 13.

39. Knox, "The Pedagogy of Web Site Design," 2.

40. Ibid.

41. Ibid., 4.

42. S. Wineberg and S.M. Wilson, "Models of Wisdom in the Teaching of History," *Phi Delta Kappa* (September 1988): 50–58.

43. Ehrmann, "Asking the Right Question," 5.

44. M. Scardamalia and C. Bereiter, "Computer Support for Knowledge Building Communities," in *CSCL: Theory and Practice of an Emerging Paradigm*, ed. T. Koschmann (Mahwah, NJ: Lawrence Erlbaum, 1996), 249.

45. Linda Harasim et al., *Learning Networks: A Field Guide to Teaching and Learning On-Line* (Cambridge and London: MIT Press, 1997), 253.

46. Graeme Davison, "History and Hypertext," *The Electronic Journal of Australian and New Zealand History* (August 1997), 4; available from http://www.jcu.edu.au/aff/history/elehist/davison.htm n, 51.

47. Personal telephone interview with K. Feig, September 1997.

48. Feig, "History 4A."

49. Wynne, "Keepers," 168.

50. Robinson, "Technology and Higher Education," 51.

51. Knox, "The Pedagogy of Web Site Design," 10.

52. Alan B. Howard, "AS@UVA: Virtual Space—Actual Learning" (1997), 1; available from http://xroads.virginia.edu/%7EAS@UVA/vistreal.html

53. Ibid., 7.

54. L. Prusak, *Knowledge in Organizations* (Boston and Oxford: Butterworth-Heinemann, 1997).

55. Mark Guzdial, "Generalized Technological Support for Project-Based Learning in Undergraduate Engineering Education" (cited 5 May 1997), 3; available from http://guzdial.cc.gatech.edu/rcpp/final.html

56. Human Communication Research Center of Edinburgh University, "The Vicarious Learner," (1998), 1; available from http://www.hcrc.ed.ac.uk/site/VICARIOU.html

57. O'Donnell, "Humanities in the 21st Century," 6.

58. Robert N. Nigohosian, "Scholarly Internet Research: Is It Real?" (July 1977) 7; available from http://net.slcc.edu/bio/ecn274/ethictxt.html

59. R. Welker, *The Teacher as Expert: A Theoretical and Historical Explanation* (New York: State University of New York Press, 1992), 131–132.

60. A. Carvin, "The Future of Networking Technologies for Learning: Workshop Report," Office of New Media, Corporation for Public Broadcasting (cited 1 May 1996), available from http://www.ed.gov/Technology/Futures/carvin.html

# 3

# Hypertext "Papers" on the Web
## Students Confront the Linear Tradition

*Arne Solli*

## Introduction

A decade ago, the World Wide Web (WWW) did not exist. Only five years ago, the WWW was unknown to most history students. Today, the Internet and the World Wide Web are increasingly becoming a part of history courses and the students are finding their way around the Web themselves. There are certainly many uses of the Internet, perhaps the most "natural" link between history and the WWW coming from viewing the latter as a library and an archive containing electronic texts. However, the WWW can also be seen as a hypertext or hypermedia system, which opens other possibilities.[1]

In the History Department at the University of Bergen, Norway, one class of undergraduate students is now being trained to explore these aspects of the WWW. Bergen has introduced the Internet as a tool for historical research and for dissemination of knowledge. As a part of this project, students must publish their papers (assignments) or projects as Web pages. The content of these Web pages must be historical, following the paradigms for standard written assignments and theses in a history program.

Although the WWW is new, the underlying concept, hypertext, has been known for nearly six decades among a relatively small group of enthusiasts, who have long been focusing on the advantages and disadvantages of hypertext and an electronic hypertext system vis-à-vis the text and the book. This article will discuss some of the problems of going from a book-based text to an electronic text on the WWW or, more precisely, a hypertext. It will discuss the following questions: What are the differences between a historical text and a historical hypertext? How did the students at Bergen meet the problems presented by a different environment? And what were their solutions? These questions are important, and they challenge our views about academic texts in general—whether they are student essays, research reports, master's theses, or professional monographs.

## The Main Challenges

Why should history students learn how to write hypertext on the World Wide Web in a history curriculum? In Norway, it has been a common belief that the hard sciences should be responsible for both developing and teaching new technology. Social sciences were allowed to study the impact of new technology on social life, and historians were allowed to study technology when it was put into use. Recently this belief has changed, at least under current government administration. The current four-year-plan for education[2] stresses that Information Technology must be integrated into every discipline at all levels of education. This is one of the current *political and educational challenges* confronting the discipline of history in Norway today.[3]

By one view, the Internet and the World Wide Web are just "hype" technologies, partly driven by commercial interests in the computing industry and by the infotainment and entertainment industries. However, the Internet can also be viewed as two-way communication between humans through new technology, unlike related technologies, such as radio, television, and print, that are clearly one-way, i.e., broadcasting. The Internet combines the broadcasting aspects of the audiovisual technologies with aspects of spoken, telephonic, and written communications. Using the Internet presents new ways to communicate.

The number of documents on the World Wide Web is already enormous. Several of these sites contain documents with historical content and they can be administered by a variety of persons and organizations: a John Doe telling the world about his family history, a tourist agency marketing a town, e.g., historical Bergen, or by extreme political organizations such as neo-Nazis rejecting the Holocaust. That groups outside the historical community are creating instructive historical content presents strong motivation for professional historians to use the WWW actively and to shape its content. By extension, this use gives historians an opportunity to communicate and to educate a broader audience in scholarly history. Exploring the new ways of communicating inside the history community and with a broader public is the *media challenge* facing the discipline of history.

The World Wide Web has become central in publishing primary historical material; structured sources like censuses and electronic text archives hold many historical texts, and aggregated historical statistics are also available. The World Wide Web is now a primary historical source itself: Net-newspapers with no paper counterpart appear daily. In Norway, *Netavisen* is a "newspaper" of this kind. These exclusively digital records create a *methodological challenge*.

These challenges, political, educational, media, and methodological, strongly affect historians as scholars and teachers. Historians will have to teach new students in their history programs how to use the Internet for gathering relevant information and train them in source criticism on the WWW, as we have for traditional print resources. We must also teach them how to use the Internet actively and to develop the content of the WWW. Students must learn to develop resources that can be read by other historians and by a broader public, as well as to create materials that can be used by teachers at all levels of history education. Many new skills will need to be cultivated, but there are also traditional historical skills that must be adapted to the new media.

Migrating to a hypertext system like the WWW is not straightforward. Writing hypertext is not necessarily like writing a print text, whether it is a student paper, research paper, or monograph. The differences and the problems created by the change in media and textual structure inflect both the way we read and the way we write. How can we ensure that what we as scholars try to communicate gets through to our readers, presumably scholars themselves? Is scholarly communication different through nonlinear text? This paper will show that this migration from the book to the Internet has three important impacts:

> On research: The Internet is/becomes a research tool for historians.
> On publishing: The WWW is/becomes central in publishing historical knowledge, both academic and popular.
> On teaching: History teachers will be using the Internet at different levels of the educational system, to find both texts and sources.

It is of crucial importance that we try to discover and discuss these challenges, else nonhistorians will set the course and make the paths. I do not think we as a community and a discipline want that to happen.

## Background: The Curriculum—History and Computing

History students in Norway have traditionally followed two career paths: one becomes either a professional historian or a history teacher in primary and secondary schools. To meet the challenges in the new educational reforms in Norway, the History Department of the University of Bergen created a new course or curriculum, *History and Computing*.

The length of this curriculum is one term and it constitutes the third and last term at the undergraduate level. The regular third-term curriculum has two parts, one subject common and mandatory for all students, like "Urbanization and Urban Society in Europe in the Nineteenth Century." The other part is a subject chosen by the student, which he or she specializes in. The subjects can be chosen from a variety offered by the faculty, and the course is the basis for a paper or essay (traditionally fifteen pages). The paper can be a discussion, based solely on historical literature, or can analyze relevant sources and present the results of this research. The students are encouraged to use original source material for their papers, and often the teachers prepare materials to be analyzed. In the new *History and Computing* curriculum, the common part is replaced by a computer course. The reading list for the computer section amounts to 1,200 pages and is divided into four main subjects:

Computers and History
Databases in Historical Research
Analyzing Computerized Sources
Internet Communication and Publishing

The second part of the reading list, the historical part, is the students' own responsibility and must be related to the subject of the paper. This part must be approved by the teacher/advisor. The "paper" can be written only as a hypertext on the World Wide Web, and it must have a historical topic, just like an ordinary paper in the parallel curriculum of the third term. The students in the History and Computing courses must write their "paper" as a WWW document, a "true" hypertext: the student cannot just convert or "dump" any ordinary word-processed document onto the Web. That would just be replacing the fifteen sheets of paper with fifteen digital pages of text, and this is not the course objective. A "paper" as a WWW document will contain hyperlinks between different parts of the text (internal links) or hyperlinks to other texts, like sources, on the Net (external links). WWW documents can also contain objects like pictures, diagrams, tables, maps, audio or videos—either included in the text—or these objects can be reached through hyperlinks and viewed in separate windows. The degree of "hypertextuality" will vary, of course, but so far this has not become a problem.

The students are also encouraged to use computerized sources. Digitalarkivet—The Digital Archive[4]—is one of the main collections of computerized sources in Norway. The Digital Archive is a collaboration between the National Archives of Norway and the Department of History in Bergen. The archives, thus, provide data, while the Department of History provides the tools for presenting and analyzing sources. The Digital Archive contains mostly list-based or structured, individually based sources like censuses, church records, birth records, death registers, marriage rolls, emigration lists from Norway, and immigration lists from across the Atlantic. Many of the students combine these computerized sources with other types of sources, like tax rolls, fire insurance policies, or property registers, which can be found either in the regional archive or the city archive. There are also several other institutions in Norway providing historical sources on the Web: Dokumentasjonsprosjektet at the University of Oslo has published 20,000 diplomas connected to Norway in the period 1050 to 1590 and a number of Court Proceedings and Protocols, court records from the 1600s and 1700s. And the National Library has placed a large collection of nineteenth-century photos, the Galleri Nor, on their Web archive.

Students thus have a variety of different sources, computerized and noncomputerized, to investigate, which opens many different subjects for study. The students can combine different databases with information from noncomputerized sources, or they can record part of these into a database. So far, however, the biases have been toward sources of a "quantitative" or statistical nature, coupled with maps, drawings, and pictures.

**Methods and Analytical Tools**

Most of the digitized data used in teaching is stored in DBASE III format. This may seem a bit out of date, but the advantage is straightforward: Almost every database, spreadsheet, or statistical package can import DBASE-files. We have chosen to use as few programs as possible, and accordingly students have courses in two different programs for analyzing the source material. Microsoft Access is used as the Database Management System (DBMS), and most of the basic combination and manipulation of data, querying, and aggregating functions can be dealt with very neatly in this powerful database package. The tables resulting from a database query also can easily be transferred to Microsoft Excel for making diagrams. Microsoft Excel is used to perform simple statistical computations (descriptive statistics). All students need to know these two software programs and also how to use the Digital Archive. Some students who need more specialized analysis tools are given separate training (e.g., students who want to do household analyses can use a special software program called CENSSYS, developed by Professor Jan Oldervoll of the department. CENSSYS is particularly well suited for household and demographic analysis).

**Hardware and Software for Internet Publication**

The area defined for study (topics), the source material, the methods, and the analytical tools comprise the basis for the student's paper. The next step is how to create the "paper" and make it public on the WWW. What software and hardware are needed to publish a student project on the WWW?

## Hardware

Bergen has a computer lab with Pentium PCs running Windows 95, and all are connected to the Internet. There are two Internet servers running Windows NT 4.0: a "production" server, where all the source materials for the Digital Archive are located, and a "student" server, which functions as a file server and a Web server for the students. The lab also includes four color scanners and a digital camera. The scanners are used to make digital images of maps, pictures, and copies of sources. The camera is used to create images of sources and pictures of houses and artifacts to avoid the copyright problems involved with many existing materials.

## Software

On the servers the Web server program is central. This is the program that publishes the documents on the WWW and makes them accessible to everyone on the Internet throughout the world. The computers connected to the scanners have two programs installed—Paint Shop Pro and Photoshop. Both these programs are used first for scanning or acquiring the pictures or maps, then for basic manipulation such as adjusting the contrast or zooming the scanned image. In the lab each student machine has Microsoft Access and Microsoft Excel for analyzing the source data files. Netscape Navigator is used for surfing the World Wide Web and for creating Web pages with Netscape Composer. But the students also have to understand the structure of the HTML,[5] so we also teach how to make HTML documents by doing the HTML tagging. Therefore we have used non-WYSIWYG HTML editors to develop the students' ability to do the HTML tagging manually or "by hand." We think this is important for understanding the basic structure of hypertext documents.

By the point students have learned HTML, they have also defined the topics of their papers, read existing books on their subject, identified some questions that need to be answered, and found some source material to answer the questions. They have learned how to use software to analyze the computerized sources, how to use software and hardware to scan additional sources like maps or pictures and to manipulate images of maps, and how to use software to write the paper as a Web document or hypertext. The tool used for writing the paper, Netscape Composer, very much resembles an ordinary word-processor. This final step, how to write a text for the Web, could be viewed as just simple word-processing and therefore the most trivial skill. This is not accurate, however, because problems arise from the structural differences between ordinary paper-based text and hypertext. What are these problems and what solutions have we found?

## Student Papers: Written Text Versus Hypertext "Papers"

Academic texts, like student papers, have a very simple structure. First, an introduction presenting the issue or discussion is required, followed by some questions to be answered or a hypothesis, some historiographical references, one part of source criticism, then a pro-et-contra discussion based on textbooks or interpretation of the sources where the aforementioned questions are answered, and, finally, a conclusion. The most striking feature is the linearity, a well-defined start and well-defined end—the conclusion. If the paper is *not* read sequentially, the reader can miss the line of arguments and, therefore, not fully understand the author's conclusion.

Hypertext, or true hypertext, is nonsequential. By using the feature of links, the reader can navigate through or to different parts of the text. There can be many sequences; there need not be one beginning point, but several; and there need not be just one ending. There can be several links out of the current block of text and into other hypertexts. These are the defining attributes of a hypertext.

The difference between a traditional academic text and a hypertext are striking: (1) traditional text is closed; hypertext is open or dynamic; and (2) academic texts are sequential, while hypertexts are nonsequential. Conversely, all types of academic texts—a paper, a thesis, or a monograph—share some hypertextual attributes:[6]

1. There are references to other articles or books and to printed or nonprinted sources. One also often finds discussions that do not "fit" in the text above, though this practice is generally discouraged.
2. There are references to the other parts of the same text, like "as mentioned in chapter four" or "this will be discussed later in chapter seven."
3. There are references to other texts within the same physical object, i.e., an appendix, like "see also source excerpt in appendix A.1" or "can be found in table 6 in appendix B.4."
4. Some publications also have a list of contents, list of figures, list of tables, and different indexes, like an "index of persons and places" or an "index of subjects."

These four classes of attributes in a paper-based text are hypertextual because they are links to other parts of the text or to other texts (books), but the process of realizing them or executing a link will often involve going to the library and borrowing a book. In a sense, we can say that most academic texts are filled with hypertextual links, but they are not exactly a mouse-click away. Can these two structures converge? Is it reasonable to say that we want to write academic papers that both are linear and nonlinear, like a true hypertext? Or must academic texts on the WWW just be "paper-based" text, replacing the paper sheets with a computer screen? Academic texts with the line of arguments of one interpretation, or a pro-et-contra discussion of interpretations, are fundamental to the academic tradition in the history discipline and to all academic disciplines. The linearity of an academic argument is independent of the media, whether it is spoken or written on sheets of paper or on the WWW. But is it possible to imagine a construction which combines the attributes of both forms? And would such a construction make academic papers better? Students at Bergen have found some answers to these problems, creating projects that do not break with the academic tradition, but that also use the flexibility of the WWW.

The problems that arise can be translated into simple questions:

How can I as an author ensure that the reader does not get lost in the paper?

How can I ensure that the reader knows what I wrote versus what is a hypertext written by somebody else?

How can I ensure that the reader can see the structure and the composition of the text? In what sequence(s) can this text be read and understood? It is of crucial importance that the reader understand the structure(s) of the text—both its main structures, and any substructures.

How many and what type of links should be in the paper?

How should different types of links be indicated? For instance, the reader should be encouraged to follow a link to a table for more detailed information on an argument, but need not follow a link to other hypertexts.

How can the reader return to the main text after following external links (the problem of backtracking)?

These questions indicate the main issues: How to indicate the author's structure of the text and how the text could be read to understand the content (arguments). I will briefly mention some results of the never-ending discussions we have on these questions. Take one scenario—the idea is to divide the computer screen into two columns using the HTML-tag called <FRAME> (see Figure 1). In the left column the text is held constant and in the right and widest column of the screen, the dependent part, the content will vary according to the reading process, i.e., actions in the right column. The outline of the paper (headings) will reside in the constant column to the left of the screen. The order from top to bottom indicates the sequence between different parts of the hyperpaper. This indicates the main structure of the text as

Figure 1. **Main Structure of a Hypertext "Paper"**

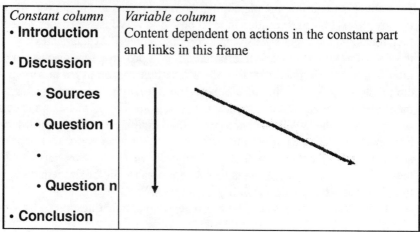

| *Constant column*<br>• **Introduction**<br><br>• **Discussion**<br><br>   • **Sources**<br><br>   • **Question 1**<br><br>      •<br><br>   • **Question n**<br><br>• **Conclusion** | *Variable column*<br>Content dependent on actions in the constant part and links in this frame |
|---|---|

the author sees it. In Figure 1, the main structure is put in the left frame. This is just one of several possibilities left, right, top, bottom. My point is that a constant column or window is needed to indicate both the structure and where in the hypertext structure the reader currently is. The outline at the left should also give some picture of the size and composition of the text. What I have referred to here as the "constant column" is also known as the "Scan Column."[7]

One way to indicate what text is included in one particular paper is to use a unique color for all the different blocks of text of one student. The constant column with the outline reduces the danger of losing the reader in cyberspace. Clicking on the *Introduction* link in the constant column will always bring the reader back to the Introduction in the variable part of the screen.

The other main problem is related to the use of hyperlinks in the different blocks of text. Should there be recommendations on whether hyperlinks could be placed anywhere in a block of text, or just in the beginning or end, or perhaps no links at all, expect those in the constant column. Too many hyperlinks can lead to fragmentation of the reading process and thereby confuse the reader. One possible recommendation is to not allow links other than those for navigation between the main parts of the text e.g. between chapters. This can be too rigid a requirement, however, because making links to tables with detailed information, links to footnotes, links to illustrations and links to sources can be useful. Common for these links are that they need not be followed unless the reader wants to get some extra information or to go in-depth. In this case the author does not want the reader to leave the main text to examine the subtext hidden behind the hyperlink, i.e., the author wants to present two separate blocks of text that should be viewed together. The

Figure 2. **Structure of the Reading Process—A Reading in Levels**

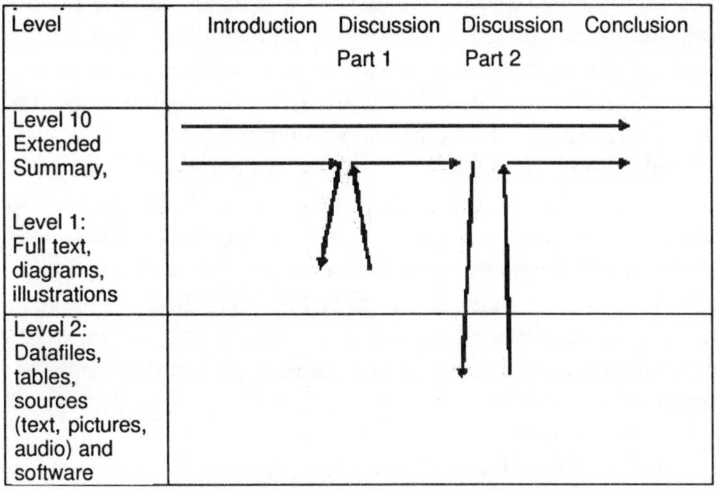

| Level | Introduction | Discussion Part 1 | Discussion Part 2 | Conclusion |
|---|---|---|---|---|
| Level 10 Extended Summary, | | | | |
| Level 1: Full text, diagrams, illustrations | | | | |
| Level 2: Datafiles, tables, sources (text, pictures, audio) and software | | | | |

students have solved this challenge by putting the linked text into a third frame, a secondary pop-up window using an extension to HTML called Javascript. The advantage with the second solution is that the reader can move and resize the secondary window.

The structure of the student texts—let us call it a hyperpaper—seems quite simple, yet it is flexible enough to handle different hypertextual aspects, like linking of blocks of text. Jumping to different parts of the text is simple, with additional information, illustrations, and sources brought forward and hidden with simple mouse-clicks. The reader can choose different ways of reading the paper by following the links. It is important that the structure of the hyperpaper is simple or at least explicit; otherwise the content of the text—the history, the discussion, the findings, the argument—cannot be easily understood.

**Reading a Hypertext—An Example**

Reading a hypertext can be quite different from reading an ordinary text. Figure 2 shows a sample of how a hypertext with several levels can be read. Reading the hypertext at level 0 will be like reading any text, and the hypertext system will allow you to read the text sequentially from the introduction, through the discussion, to the conclusion. In the text at level 0, there could also be some excerpts from sources, diagrams, illustrations, and simple tables. Level 0 could also be viewed as a kind of an extended summary, and then level 1 could be the full text.

We could also think of a more thorough reading process, where the reader chooses to investigate part of the text in more detail, reading excerpts from sources, definitions of terms, references, and additional tables of data that are sources of diagrams used at level 0. This is shown in Figure 2 by an arrow from level 0 into level 1. By investigating level one, the reader can check the arguments or find other interpretations.

In level 2, there could be more tables of data, more sources, different transcriptions of sources, data files for download, or software tools for analyzing the data files. At level two, the reader will be able to redo partly the analysis that supports a conclusion at level 0. In a hypertext system (e.g., WWW), these levels can be linked and integrated and the readers can adjust how the text is read according to their ambitions and wishes. Research publications structured and linked like this example could be termed a "virtual laboratory."[8]

### Hypertext: A Three-Dimensional Example—Time, Space, and Actors

The previous example is oversimplified because many historical problems have at least three dimensions: time, space, and actors (or social processes, or institutions). The analytical structure of historical research can therefore become quite complicated. Take an example: In studying the modernization process, it could be of interest to compare two or more regions over the same period of time and to analyze different social groups or classes. To present the results of this research in a book, one has to choose one single sequence. One must determine what should be presented first, in what sequence the regional differences should be discussed, and whether the social differences or the time variations should be emphasized. Would a chronological outline be best? The problem is to project or simplify the multidimensional analytical structure into a presentation that traditionally is one-dimensional and with a fixed sequence. In a hypertext it is possible to link each of these dimensions. The reader can choose to follow one path, for example, by following the links to read about the changes over time in one social group in one region. If this seems complicated, it is close to what one of our students did in a paper called *Handverkarar på Nordnes 1800–1875* [*Master Craftsmen and Apprentices at Nordnes, 1800–1875*]. It is possible to read this hypertext "paper" through different paths. As a reader you can choose to investigate changes over time in the households of the master craftsmen by following one set of links, or you can choose to read about both apprentices and masters at one point in time. The two different groups of apprentices (*Svein* and *Dreng*)[9] can be followed accordingly. By following some links, you will go back in time, contrary to the main structure or outline of the paper, which is chronological. And in each block of text you can go into other blocks of the text, where central terms or institutions are explained (e.g., modernization, the guilds) or additional tables are given to support the argumentation or as a "source" for diagrams. The structure of this hyperpaper can be described as a three-dimensional text: time as the first dimension, actor-groups as the second, and the sources/tables as the third.

A structure like this makes both the writing and the reading process more complex, but the process of reading resembles the research process in that the reader goes back and forth between variables and interpretative strands. Readers are free to choose their own paths through the text according to their interests. A text can have complex structure consisting of different layers (depth or levels) and dimensions (time, space, actors, institutions/phenomena). Because of this possibility of going easily into the depths of a project/study, one might ask whether hypertext perhaps supports a more critical reading.

Is the structure offered by the hypertext system something new and is it necessarily an advantage? In a book the reader is also free to choose paths through the text; however, it is not always specifically structured for making one's own way through the text. You, as a reader, can of course stop to read here and then jump to the next paragraph, so there is nothing "new" in that. Thus, there is no simple answer to this question, but hypertext is a new way of both presenting, structuring, and engaging historical knowledge. By exploring the possibilities of hypertext or hypermedia on the WWW, we may be able to give an answer to this question.

At Bergen, the students often experience two problems in their papers: overly elaborate presentation and overly complicated structure: The students become very preoccupied with layout or "look-and-feel"—their papers must have a personal "look" or "image." And by surfing on the Internet they find "cool" sites and want to copy different ideas into their own pages; as a result they emphasize the appearance of their work over its historical content. The second problem is one of structure: that is, a tendency to make the structure of hypertext too complex. For example, if the student uses too many hyperlinks, the reading process can become too convoluted and too complicated. To visualize the problem of structural complexity, just add two extra dimensions in Figure 2. The result can be a lack of evident sequence of reading with the reader very easily getting lost and asking: Where am I now? What am I reading? Why? These two problems, exaggerated layout and overly complex structures, should be taken very seriously. As historians, we cannot accept a project with a nice appearance or a flexible structure if the historical argumentation is muddled or unpersuasive.

## Conclusion

In this paper, I have tried to show how we have attempted to combine "traditional" and fundamental goals in the education of historians with the exploration of a new media.

The main goals are to view the WWW as an archive of sources and resources (The Digital Archive); to combine computerized sources and commercial software packages for analytical purposes; and to extend the traditional student paper by making it into a hypertext on the WWW.

These three elements allow us to focus on the crucial methodological questions of formalization when using computer technology in history. The ability to formalize and represent both sources and historical methods (e.g., quantitative methods) is an important skill that is transferable into less computerized history or subjects, because the student learns to generate abstractions. The students also learn to use computer technology to explore new ways to communicate, both in order to learn scholarly discourse and to disseminate historical knowledge.

The Internet has created new ways of communicating, and it challenges how we communicate, how we read and write. By letting students create their "papers" as hypertext in a history curriculum, we have tried to respond to this challenge actively and without raising too many critical questions at this juncture. There are still many questions to be answered, and we have tried to find some answers by using the technology itself. We do not yet know whether hypertext "papers" will improve the education of historians and history teachers or whether the students will learn both. But in any event, we want to use the media actively and to develop its content, not let other groups, whether they are academic or not, get far ahead of us. This is necessary since the new technology of media primarily deals with communication. As historians, we must explore and develop sensible ways of using the Internet in research, as a tool for communication and collaboration, and to make historical knowledge available to a wider audience.

### Notes

1. In this paper hypertext will also include the term *hypermedia.* Instead of *hypertext-papers*, the term *hypermedia-papers* would be more appropriate. Hypertext is nonlinear electronic text structured by using linking mechanisms. The linking mechanisms are analogous to the footnotes in a book.

2. *IT in Norwegian Education. A Plan for 1996–1999.* An English translation of the IT plan can be found at: http://odin.dep.no/kuf/publ/it-plan/eng/

3. The IT plan is a part of several reforms in the educational system issued in the last three years. The most important is the *Reform94* for secondary schools and

*Læreplan97* for primary schools—the Compulsory School Reform. An English translation of the reforms can be found at http://odin.dep.no/kuf/eng/index.html (Ministry of Education, Research and Church Affairs).

4. These sources can be found at: http://www.hist.uib.no/arkivverket/index-en.htm

5. Hypertext Markup Language.

6. These attributes are called *internal hypertextual functions* in contrast to *external hypertextual functions* like bibliographies and library registers. See George P. Landow and Paul Delany, *Hypermedia and Literary Studies* (Cambridge: MIT Press, 1994), 4.

7. See the "Yale Style Manual" Analyzing Page Grids: http://info.med.yale.edu/caim/manual/pages/design_grids.html

8. The term "virtual laboratory" is suggested by Jakob Nielsen in *Multimedia and Hypertext: The Internet and Beyond* (New York: AP Professional, 1996).

9. The Norwegian term *Svein* can be translated as *apprentice*, and the term *Dreng*, which literally means *boy*, can be translated as *journeyman*.

## Web Pages Cited

Department of History, University of Bergen, page in English: http://web.hist.uib.no/Admin/engelsk/
The 1801 census (English): http://www.uib.no/hi/1801page.html
The Digital Archive: http://www.hist.uib.no/arkivverket/index-en.htm
The WWW-"papers" (Norwegian/English): http://www.hist.uib.no/hit/studentarbeid.htm and http://www.hist.uib.no/dokkeveien/prosjekt.htm
Master thesis, semi-hypertext (Norwegian/English): http://www.uib.no/hi/hfag.html
The History and Computing Curriculum (Norwegian): http://www.hist.uib.no/hit/
The Ministry of Education, Research and Church Affairs: http://odin.dep.no/kuf/eng/index.html

# 4

# Linking History with Hypertext
## Rethinking the Process

### *Daniel Pfeifer*

The Internet is now a vital piece in the framework of the information society. At the foundation of the Internet is the World Wide Web. Many in higher education praise this information resource as a modern miracle. Proponents contend that the Web will help to democratize information.[1] Critics believe it is a waste of time and resources. Between the extremes, a growing number of instructors have decided that the Internet is an important tool for communicating information, and they are attempting to teach their students how to utilize the World Wide Web. It is reasonable to assume that any student in any discipline preparing to live in the information society should graduate from college knowing how to use the information and communication tools of the Web effectively. But why teach them in a history course? What specifically is there to gain for students of history?

Inherent in the communication of the past, and specifically within the conventions of narrative, are restrictions and boundaries imposed by authors. Consider the case of Western Civilization textbooks and the periodization of the Reformation and the Age of Discovery. In many textbooks, the two epochs are left unrelated, appearing separately and without textual connections. What are the implications for students? Given such disparate treatment, will students ever think of Hernando Cortés as a contemporary of Martin Luther? Or will they relate the Pilgrims' voyage to North America with the events of one hundred years before? Such are the confinements that print imposes and under which print authors work. It is difficult to relate events occurring in both time and space in any medium. Yet authors have to create boundaries to facilitate reader understanding, and this often requires sacrificing space for time, as in the case of the Reformation and the Age of Discovery.[2]

The World Wide Web and HTML coding provide a partial solution to this dilemma. Hypertext, one part of HTML, makes associations available through hyperlinks, allowing an author to connect more people and events across either space or time. Within a matrix of links, HTML has the further benefit of allowing the reader to decide which track to follow. Although multiple paths are available to the author and reader, however, the use of hypertext does not necessarily imply the complete elimination of time and space from the communication of history. This new capability to make unrestricted associations does not mean that links should be profuse or random. A developing part of the authoring process is to determine which links will produce the best paths for the reader.[3]

Given the need for computer literacy in modern society and the benefits of communicating with hypertext, a Web site project can be a valuable learning experience for history students. The goal of the project is to engage students in the process of drawing associations (links) and then communicating them on the Web coherently. The question for the professor is how to develop the assignment so that the students learn to make relevant and logical associations between many individuals and events. And in order to make hyperlinked materials, the professor has to teach the students HTML, requiring some addition or substitution in class content.

During the 1998 spring semester, two classes at Wake Forest University experimented with these issues. In Revolutionary and Early National America, twelve third- and fourth-year students, working in teams of two, created biographical Web sites about six people from the period. In the first-year seminar, Twentieth-Century World, fifteen students created a Web site around the theme of social transformations of the century.[4]

Before starting the project with the students in the classroom, the professors needed to address certain logistical issues involved in the computer assignment. In order to create a Web site, the students had to have access to computers, and they had to learn HTML. The first-year seminar students had laptops. The upperclassmen worked in the library computer lab. In both classes, most of the students had little or no knowledge of HTML.

During the first month of the Early America course, a technology trainer from the library taught three HTML classes. The upperclassmen also had five classes devoted to lab time at the end of the semester. A few sessions during the semester were used to discuss design and writing for the Web. Because the upperclassmen were not completely comfortable with the computer, they worked in teams and had more class sessions for computer training. The teams and lab sessions facilitated peer tutoring among the older students. The first-year students worked independently but received on-demand support through e-mail from the history department's Academic Computing Specialist (ACS).[5] They attended two training classes and several discussions on design and writing.

The discussions exposed the students to the difference between "programming" and layout. Although Web page authors do not always agree on what constitutes good design, the students found that the following principles led to an effective result. First, the opening page or home page is one of the most important parts of the site. Like the preface and table of contents of a book, the opening page should give the viewer an idea of what will follow. Visually, the student can give readers the sense that they are moving through the information with a subpage design that maintains continuity. Contiguous design may include things like a context-sensitive button bar (table of contents) at the top of the screen, an icon associated with a particular argument, or various but complementary backgrounds. Every page on the site must strike a balance between "sound and silence."[6] In other words, there must be well-placed white space on the page so the text, images, and any other elements do not look overcrowded or sparse.[7]

As mentioned previously, both classes had in-class training time for HTML. The upperclassmen met in the library computer lab, and the first-year students brought their laptops to a wired classroom. Both groups learned HTML quickly. After a brief in-class discussion about design, the upperclassmen, for homework, had to write a Web site review.[8] They also browsed the Web looking for a "best" site and a "worst" site; then they discussed their choices with the professor in private meetings. The first-year students had several classroom and on-line discussions about design. Interacting through a Lotus Notes cabinet, they evaluated each other's sites as they developed.[9] Several of the students also scheduled appointments with their professor or the history department ACS to inspect their work.

The content part of the assignment in both classes started with the students selecting a thesis (or a question), after which they were encouraged to draw relationships between their person or theme and the surrounding world. As the topics developed, however, the two classes proceeded in different directions for their research. The upperclassmen used the library and did mostly traditional research because their subjects were more obscure, while the first-year students studying the twentieth century chose topics more readily available on the Web.

Both classes found context-sensitive pictures, and some first-year students also found audio and video clips. Seeing pictures of their subjects made the experience more personal, particularly for the upperclassmen working on biographies. Moreover, accidental learning occurred as the students formulated historical questions about their pictures and discovered inaccuracies in some of them.

As part of the writing process, the upperclassmen needed to develop a "web of context" surrounding their individual, including writings, locale, religion, and so on. They were supposed to make links between the various areas, producing a coherent "web of interpretation."[10] A "web of interpretation" is analogous to the supporting arguments of a thesis in a research paper. In building their contexts, the students established something resembling a hierarchy of thought more than a linear argument.

Making links and creating paths requires recognizing relationships. Discussions, either as a class or individually, facilitated the students' learning to think historically about multiple connections. The classes also usually discussed parallels between their topics and events in the surrounding world. If the students did not perceive important relationships, they were given suggestive clues by their professor. The Web site assignment forced the students to look harder for associations between persons and events throughout the semester.

While developing their theses and research, the students needed to consider their audience as well. Because their sites would be "published," they were compelled to write for the general "Web public." The students had to assume that many surfers would know very little about their topics and, therefore, had to consider more details as they determined what information to include on their sites. The students also had to ascertain that their theses were clear to their readers. The assumption that their readers would know little about their themes forced them to be much more explicit, but without becoming turgid or confusing.

Following much learning and discovery, as well as many late nights, all of the students turned in a project at the end of the semester. Their Web pages showed that they grasped HTML and the related lessons about positional connections and causation that are key to historical thinking. Many also produced attractive and engagingly designed sites. Most of the students followed the layout suggestions given throughout the semester, which were the criteria for the technical grade on the assignment. There was no need to give a separate grade for HTML—after all, how many history professors give students a grade for knowing Microsoft Word or WordPerfect?

In both classes the students received some project objectives that were used as criteria for their grades. These goals were as specific as balancing white space and used space, generally by putting margins on a page, or as general as answering their thesis-question. The students were advised to produce relatively clear content and design outcomes. They also had latitude within those outcomes to be creative. The students' grades reflected their success or failure to meet these criteria.

In order to earn a good mark on content, the upperclassmen had to produce a fully elaborated "web of context" connected by a "web of interpretation." The students who developed their topic through pertinent links received the best grades. Less emphasis was placed upon the first-year students' Web design, and more weight was given to their answers to the posed question.

They needed to show the transformation of their twentieth-century themes, and those students who thoroughly answered their questions and produced quality Web site designs received the highest grades.

Upon the completion of the semester, the students were very pleased with their accomplishments. The upperclassmen suggested that the department should start a history seminar to teach Web site creation from a historical perspective. Almost all of the first-year students looked forward to another Web site project. The students in both groups went away from the classes with a more thoughtful judgment of the Web from an author's perspective as well as a viewer's. All participants involved consider the Web site project to be a valuable learning experience.

The general success of both classes was mixed. Some questions and difficulties appeared that might be avoided in future assignments. First, the logistical issues involved in the Web site project are of some concern, especially in institutions with small technology budgets. Second, most historians do not communicate in visual mediums. Third, most students are not accustomed to writing for a general audience. Fourth, many professors are not accustomed to grading projects that include hypertext or visual components. In short, the novelties of the various parts of the assignment are both opportunities and impediments.

A note on the logistics of this particular experiment may prove useful for those wishing to attempt similar courses. In retrospect, five interrelated factors appear repeatedly in any computer project—the learning goal, student access to computers, student technical skill level, the structure of the assignment, and the time available for the assignment. These factors influence the day-to-day procedures as well as the assignment's outcome. If they are handled well in the preparation stages, the assignment will progress smoothly in the classroom.

The first factor that obviously affects the assignment is the goal of the project. Some goals are suited to the new technology, while others require older methods. For the Web site project, the desired outcome was to teach students to draw associations (links) and then communicate them coherently on the Web.

The second factor is student access to computers. The mobility of the laptops gave the first-year students an advantage because they had more opportunity to experiment. The upperclassmen, however, working in the computer lab faced the disadvantage of having to develop their pages on diskettes, and more than a few disks went bad! This problem was overcome by stressing regular backups.

The third factor affecting a computer assignment is student skill level. Because the first-year students had laptops from the start of the fall semester, they had grown comfortable with the machine. The upperclassmen, who as a group were less computer literate, needed more in-class training.

Issues like training fall under the fourth category, the structure of the assignment. The students working in teams in the computer lab generally helped one another and learned together. Many of the students working independently, however, became more self-reliant. In fact, at midterm, the first-year students decided to cancel the remaining in-class lab periods. Although the younger students experimented more in the technical domain, the upperclassmen, not surprisingly, produced better content in their final projects.

The fifth factor, available time, required less of a commitment than anticipated, but it was a fair investment nonetheless. Most students will require about two hours of training to build intermediate Web pages with an HTML editor. At least an additional hour is generally necessary for introducing the student to visual design. In addition to the preparation time, toward the end of the assignment the students needed more technical support to add the finishing touches to their pages and to handle emergencies, like bad disks. The upperclassmen completed their projects during four "writing labs" where the professor and the department's ACS were available for consultation. The first-year students met independently outside of class with their instructors. Because the professors worked closely with their support person, the distributed workload may have seemed more light.

As each new wave of students enters the university, the factors above should become easier to address. Perhaps in the early years of the twenty-first century, a large number of professors will be able to give their students a choice between doing a historical Web page or paper without having to address student skill level or computer access. However, they will still have to deal with the difference between print and multimedia presentations.

As mentioned above, the students included pictures, audio, and video on their sites. On the one hand, the ability to incorporate new visual elements was exciting for the students. On the other, they spent a large amount of time adjusting to the new medium. They tinkered with image placement, colors, and fonts, which meant they spent less time working on researching or connecting information to support their thesis. A way to hasten the learning process might be to develop a Web stylebook to use as a layout guide. The students responded favorably to the idea, but also wanted to protect their freedom to be creative. Regardless of whether the students use a stylebook or not, they must produce designs that help their readers to navigate through the various paths of their sites.

Because the students were used to writing for a captive, expert reader, that is, their professor, and because Web surfers are known for their short attention spans, many felt anxiety concerning the amount of text on their sites. This anxiety forced several students to consider their topics and their writing more carefully. However, some students wrote for the least common denominator, producing summaries with few associations. Learning HTML, developing multiple paths, and writing for a general audience may have been more than the students could handle in one semester. All of those factors certainly produced many grading challenges.

When evaluating a Web site project, design and linking are the additional, essential considerations to "writing" for the Web. History teachers have always dealt with issues related to content such as a good speaking voice for oratory or good grammar and syntax for writing. It is appropriate to extrapolate such "design" considerations to multimedia projects. Professors need to become as comfortable grading Web page design as they are with writing styles today.

All in all, the students enjoyed making their Web sites, and, at the very least, they were exposed to important critical reasoning skills and to some of the issues surrounding communication on the Web. They learned the importance of maintaining high standards for Web page content and of balancing that content with a complementary design. Although professors do not need the Web to encourage their students to recognize relationships in history, the novelty of the assignment engaged the students in both classes.

The newness of the Web site project also meant an investment of more time and thought from the professor. As the assignment becomes more familiar, like the research paper, the planning requirements will lessen. As mentioned above, each time a professor deals with the five factors influencing computer-aided instruction, they are easier to handle. A growing number of students are arriving at universities with more advanced computer skills, making HTML easier to teach. Web page stylebooks may eventually emerge, helping professors to deal with design issues. As more professors use the capabilities of hypertext, examples will appear that students can follow. Grading Web site projects will become easier as outcomes are established, much as they have been for the research paper.

Because the Web site project was novel, the professors and the students had to rethink how they communicated history. The process was as much a part of the learning experience as the outcome.

## Notes

1. See the American Council of Learned Societies Occasional Paper No. 41, "Computing and the Humanities: Summary of a Roundtable Meeting" (National Research Council: http://www.acls.org/op41–toc.htm, 1998). For the discussion on access, see http://www.acls.org/op41–iv.htm

2. In *Western Civilization Since 1300*, 2nd ed. (New York: West, 1994), Jackson J.

Spielvogel discusses the Reformation in chapter 14 and the Age of Discovery in chapter 15. In Howard Spodek, *The World's History, Volume 2: Since 1100* (Upper Saddle River, NJ: Prentice Hall, 1998), the Reformation appears between the Spanish empire and the Portuguese empire in chapter 13. In William H. McNeill, *A History of the Human Community*, vol. 2 (Englewood Cliffs, NJ: Prentice Hall, 1990), chapter 15 deals with exploration, and chapter 16 deals with the Reformation.

3. For further information on hypertext, multilinearity, and linking, see George P. Landow, *Hypertext 2.0* (Baltimore: Johns Hopkins University Press, 1997).

4. Dr. David Libby taught the Revolutionary and Early National America course, and Dr. William Meyers taught Twentieth-Century World.

5. An Academic Computing Specialist at Wake Forest University is a full-time employee assigned to a particular department to assist faculty in the use of technology in the classroom.

6. Example adapted from the late composer John Cage.

7. Although somewhat commercial, a good discussion of design can be found in Roger C. Parker, *Guide to Web Content and Design* (New York: MIS Press, 1997).

8. The Web site review is similar to a regular book review, but it also includes design and technical skill questions. The Web site review form is available at http://www.wfu.edu/Academic-departments/History/reviews.html, and the students' Web site reviews are available at http://www.wfu.edu/Academic-departments/History/wreview.

9. The Lotus Notes cabinet is a computer collaboration and discussion tool.

10. "Web of context" and "web of interpretation" are terms used by David Libby in the manuscript "Context and Hypertext: The American Revolution Meets the Computer Revolution," 1998.

**Appendix: The Web Site Project**

*The Five Preparatory Factors*

*Learning Goal*

> In both classes, we wanted to teach students to draw associations (links) in history and communicate them on the Web coherently.

*Student Access to Computers*

> The first-year students in the Twentieth-Century World class had IBM laptops.

> The upperclassmen in the Revolutionary and Early National America course worked in a library computer lab on PC computers.

> Both classes used Netscape Navigator Gold to make Web pages.

*Student Skill Level*

> One student (out of twelve and fifteen) in each class had constructed a Web page.

> None of the students had considered the implications of visual design and linking on the communication of historical content.

> The least common denominator in both classes was e-mail and word processing skills, so we started building from that knowledge base.

*Assignment Structure*

> The first-year students worked independently and generally outside of class.

> The upperclassmen worked in teams of two with more computer lab sessions.

*Available Time*

> The first-year students had a total of three in-class computer training periods—two for HTML training and one for discussion of page and site design.

> The upperclassmen had three HTML classes with discussions of design included during each.

> In addition, the professor met with each student individually for thirty minutes to discuss design issues as they relate to communicating history. The final five classes of the semester were writing labs for the upperclassmen.

A basic understanding of the design considerations involved in constructing a Web page will also be helpful.

### Grading the Assignment

*Objectives*

Research paper writing standards applied, including proper grammar and spelling.

Research paper content standards also applied, including well-reasoned arguments and accurate descriptions of people or events.

*Design Standards*

The opening page should give readers an idea of what they will find in the site.

On the page level, the various items on a page need to be aligned to create active areas and white space. For example, the students added margins to a page of text.

On the site level, the design needs continuity. For example, all of the pages could have the same background color or navigation bar.

*Linking*

Links should give the reader an idea of what will follow.

Because of the summary nature of the Web, longer essays should be placed in the lower levels of the site for the more serious information "diggers."

Links should not be profuse or random.

# 5

# Reinventing the American History Survey

*Larry Easley and Steven Hoffman*

## Introduction

As we enter the twenty-first century, the number of reasons to reinvent the traditional American History survey is increasing. Not only does the research on effective teaching and learning at the university level suggest an increased use of active learning techniques and a greater emphasis on process skills rather than on content, but the reality of new technologies in the classroom virtually demands the attention of historians.[1] Over the course of the last year, a unique set of institutional changes at Southeast Missouri State University set the stage for a complete redesign of the U.S. History Survey that would combine the use of active learning techniques with the new technology of computers and the Internet. During academic year 1996–97, although the rest of the history faculty continued to teach traditional lecture-style surveys, the authors piloted several sections of "U.S. History II, 1900 to the Present." Based upon our initial experience, the increased use of technology in the classroom led to increased student interest in the course, as well as increased student learning. The introduction of new technology into the classroom was not painless, however, for either the students or the instructors, and a number of problems in implementation had to be overcome.

## Why Reinvent the Survey?

The desire to reinvent the American History Survey arose out of ongoing curricular change at the university, the desire to enhance student learning, a changing technological reality, and our own departmental collision with technology. For the fall of 1997 the Department of History at Southeast voted to change the U.S. History Survey from a course for majors to a nonmajors course in the "University Studies" program, thereby necessitating certain changes in format and delivery. Southeast's University Studies program emphasizes interactive learning, the ability to locate and gather information, and the development of critical thinking and communication skills. Although standard history courses are tailor-made for the University Studies program, since they emphasize these goals, with the exception of interactive learning, the change in designation led to a complete change in student audience. Instead of drawing only history majors, students in American History II would now represent the broad spectrum of students at the university, most of them uninterested in history and uninspired by the traditional history teaching technique of the lecture.

Although the lecture method is an effective means of communicating information and has a place in the history classroom, there are limitations to its effective use. Research on student learning suggests that while the lecture method is very effective at helping students learn information for recall, it is less effective than discussion for stimulating higher order thinking.[2] In part, this is the result of the passive role most students take in listening to lectures. As a result, for most students there is a steep decline in attention after the first ten minutes of lecture. Part of the problem results from the fact that not only do individual students have different learning styles, but most people respond better to visual clues than to spoken words. The increased effectiveness of using visual clues, however, opens the door for using technology to enhance student learning in the history classroom.[3]

Lectures can be made more interactive and hence more effective through the use of computer technology, both increasing students' attention and stimulating higher level thinking. Taking advantage of students' increased response to visual clues, computer-mediated slide lectures, also known as "enhanced lectures," make the presentation of material more interactive by illustrating major points and using movement to draw the attention of students. Using this technique, each major point of the lecture is emphasized both verbally and visually, thereby increasing students' response and attentiveness. We have gotten very positive student comments on the effectiveness of these presentations. When preparing enhanced lectures, however, the professor must design visually appealing materials to help maintain student interest.[4]

In addition to a desire to enhance student learning, another stimulus provoking a reinvention of the American History Survey was the recognition of changing technological realities. More and more students are arriving in college with computer skills vastly superior to those of their professors. Across the country, professors and students alike have increased access to computer technology and an increased desire to see it used effectively in the classroom.[5]

At Southeast, our own collision with technology combined with these other factors to move us from thinking about redesigning the survey to actually doing it. The Department of History is scheduled to move into a completely renovated building with full technology packages in all the classrooms. Outfitted with LCD projectors, Pentium computers, stereo VCRs, visualizers, and sound and light controls, the department's teaching facilities will be among the best in the world. Given the university's investment in these facilities, it is clear that if the historians fail to use the available technology, our classrooms will be turned over to departments that will. In order to prepare for the big move, the authors began teaching sections of the reinvented survey course using portable equipment that they brought to class each day. Although it will be easier in the new building, the changes we incorporated into the course work well even without the full technology packages that will be available in our new home.

## The American History Pilot

Reinventing the survey required changes both inside and outside the classroom. We developed computer-mediated lectures for all the course content, placed all course materials on the Internet, used group quizzes and discussions, and had students develop Web pages as their term research papers. We used an on-line syllabus as the central element of our course Web site to deliver all course information and materials to the students. The on-line syllabus contained basic course information, including explanations of all course policies, exam examples, class projects, and a course calendar. In addition to the information that would commonly be included in a paper syllabus, the on-line syllabus also provided additional resources for students to use in order to enhance their experience in the course.

One of the features we added to the course Web site was a way for students to check on their grades as the semester progressed. Although there are a number of programs available on our campus that allow password-protected grades for students, such as Maestro, we found them too restrictive. Instead, we opted for an Excel or Quattro Pro spreadsheet posted to the Web with student-selected PIN names. Most of the students liked being able to see their grades in the course at their own convenience and responded very favorably to this addition to the course materials.

Because the goal of the enhanced lecture is to stimulate student interaction and discussion, students sometimes find it more difficult to take notes than in a traditional lecture. In order to address this issue, we posted on the Web site a detailed outline listing the topics covered in class in our lecture/discussions. This outline formed the framework for our computer-mediated presentations in class, thus allowing students to know where we were going in class discussion and the important points that were supposed to be covered.[6]

In addition to providing students with the topical framework of the course, we hyperlinked the Web site outline to allow students to explore related topics or gather additional information. Although the outline was too detailed to provide hyperlinks for every listing, we were able to hyperlink approximately 50 to 75 percent of the items listed. We were always able to find and link to a variety of great resources out on the Web.

The outside sites we linked to our course outline tended to fall into five broad categories: government sites, institutional sites, nonhistory sites, private sites, and education sites. The government sites were among the best we located. The Library of Congress, for example, offers several excellent history sites in its American Memory series, including Voices of the Dustbowl[7] and the photographers of the FSA.[8] These sites provided solid information and good graphics. Other governmental agencies, such as the Social Security Administration and the White House, also provided good resources. Institutional resources outside the government, such as the CCC Museum and the Pennsylvania Turnpike Authority, also provided some interesting links. Although these sites were not as well developed as the Library of Congress sites, they did provide some additional perspectives on historical topics.

In order to use the capability of the Internet fully in our outline links, we included links to nonhistorical sites exploring issues that have historical relevance. Even though students would not gain any additional historical information from visiting the sites, they would develop further their understanding that many past issues continue into the present. For example, sites on urban poverty or volunteerism link especially well with Progressive Era or Hoover era topics. By exploring these sites, we hoped students would make connections between the past and their lives in the present.

Sites maintained by private individuals were probably the most problematic. There are many excellent privately maintained history sites on the Web, but there are also some of marginal quality. We made the conscious choice to utilize both kinds of sites on our course outline. The excellent sites posed little problem and provided great information, such as Trenches on the Web,[9] Old Time Radio,[10] or 1920s Flappers.[11] We also included sites that challenged the sensibility of our students (and perhaps some that challenged all right-thinking individuals), in order to make sure that students developed an understanding of the importance of site authorship. One of the sites we sent students to, for example, was the "Paranoid Politics" Web site, a link that is no longer operative. Students need to learn to evaluate Web sources the same as they would any other source, and by giving them examples that are less reliable than the Library of Congress, we hoped to provoke discussion.[12]

The last broad category of sites we included on our course outline comprised Web sites established by educational institutions. Universities and colleges are increasingly establishing sites placing primary documents on the Web and developing Internet-based history research sources to explore major issues, such as the Virginia Civil War Project established by the University of Virginia. Interestingly enough, for our purposes with the course outline, some of the best sites we found were developed by K–12 schools. These sites, such as the "We Made Do: Recalling the Great Depression"[13] site prepared by the Mooresville School District in Mooresville, Indiana, not only provided additional information on course topics, but also served to inspire our students in designing their own Web pages. We made it a point to send them to some of these sites, indicating that surely they could do as well as elementary and high school kids. It is hard to know whether this tactic worked or not, but it did serve to lessen some of the anxiety students felt about designing their own Web sites.

The on-line syllabus also contained links to our Group Discussion Questions along with additional readings that we scanned and posted on a separate site. On group discussion days, we assigned questions around topics that the students searched the Internet to find more information on or had them explore specific Web sites in-depth. For example, one of our more successful sites had students explore the "Ask Mrs. Roosevelt" Web site[14] and answer questions regarding the experience of ordinary people during the Depression. We also occasionally had students do readings beyond the textbook, which we scanned and made available in an unlinked Web site on the server. We used the unlinked site in order to restrict access to the readings, as only our students would know the location, and we removed the readings shortly after the assignment was due. Although this is an imperfect solution to the issue of copyright, we felt it reflected a good faith effort to restrict our use to a defensible position of "fair use." We are continuing to work to create a password-protected site so that only our students will have access to the material, but, given the ever present time constraints, this was the best solution that could be implemented quickly.

An additional resource we made available on the on-line syllabus was a link to the textbook Web site. The publisher, Prentice-Hall, maintains a Web site with a variety of features (most of which we did not use) such as the syllabus generator and a message board.[15] However, we found the on-line practice quizzes and the links to additional resources to be quite useful. In order to encourage students to explore the text Web site, we announced that we would include some of the Web site quiz questions for our in-class quizzes. We gave in-class quizzes on group discussion days, and students took the quiz first by themselves, then retook it with their group. Students' quiz grades were an average of their individual and group scores. We found that, in many instances, group grades were higher than any individual grade within the group, suggesting that some additional learning was occurring.

As a course project, instead of writing a term paper students developed a Web site. Each group was assigned a topic, such as World War II in the Pacific, the Vietnam War, or suburbanization, and the individual group members each developed a Web page on some aspect of the larger topic. Students selected graphics and wrote text. We helped the students scan their images on the departmental scanner or referred them to the numerous public labs on campus once they knew how to scan for themselves. The largest bottleneck occurred when we helped students convert their word-processed text into HTML and posted it to the Web, because they did not have independent access to the server. Although the one-on-one interaction between students and faculty was outstanding, this involved an inordinate amount of faculty time. Although we will continue to work with students designing their own Web pages, we have arranged to provide students with access to their own section of the server for next year. Many of our students found the opportunity to design their own Web pages the most exciting part of the course.[16]

## Measuring Results

The bottom line of any experiment on course design is whether or not it produces desirable outcomes. Although it is difficult to get an accurate measure of enhanced student learning, our initial experience indicates that most of our students enjoyed and profited from the redesigned course, despite a few problems in implementation. Following a model created by the Center for Scholarship in Teaching and Learning at Southeast, students were asked to respond to a series of questions about their experience in this course compared to others they had taken. In the anecdotal portion we received comments that ranged from "Web pages were cool!" to "Do away with the bells and whistles and teach."

When students were asked if the computer-mediated presentations aided their learning of course content, 36.6 percent indicated that the materials significantly improved their learning and 44.1 percent felt the enhanced lectures moderately increased their learning. Only 6.4 percent felt the heavy use of visuals and computer-assisted lectures made course materials moderately or significantly more difficult to learn. These numbers should improve as access to technology increases in the classroom.

The use of groups for discussion and quizzes resulted in a high degree of student energy and interest, increased test results on the quizzes, and a strong sense of community within the classroom. More than 94 percent of the respondents believed the group quizzes and discussions helped them learn course content. Concerning a sense of community in the classroom, 87.1 percent of student respondents found the class more comfortable while 1.1

percent expressed negative feelings about the group interaction. Verbal comments were also very positive, ranging from "the groups made me want to work harder, so I wouldn't let everyone else down" to "finally a class where I got to know people."

The heavy reliance on the Internet was a little more problematic, but most students responded favorably to the experience. A vocal minority of students, however, disliked the fact that the course materials were only available on-line, and so this year we will make hard copy printouts of all the material available as an adjunct to the Web site. Part of the problem for some students, particularly our commuting students, was inadequate access to computers to complete their assignments or to get needed course information. Even though computer labs are plentiful on campus, students reported long waits and inconvenient network down times, particularly when they waited until the last minute to complete assignments. Even so, 64.5 percent of students surveyed reported that having materials on-line made access to course materials more convenient.

We were most concerned about the creation of a Web site in lieu of the standard research project. Given the fact that most of our students have limited experience with computers and virtually no expertise with Web page development, we believed this aspect of the course would make or break our redesign efforts. In their responses, students were very favorable. In an evening class of nontraditional students, eleven of the twelve respondents indicated that the opportunity to create a Web page significantly increased their learning experience in the course. Since the majority of these students are not on campus during the day and typically have greater problems with access to computers, we took this as a significant vote of confidence. Though none of the day classes with traditional students were as favorable, 32.3 percent indicated the Web project significantly increased their learning experience and 38.7 percent reported a moderate increase in the learning experience.

**Problems in Implementation**

Overall, the authors judged the experimental redesign of the U.S. History Survey a success, although there were a number of obstacles to overcome. Difficulties arose in regard to student training, hardware malfunctions, presentation software, operating system platform, and finding appropriate graphics.

The most significant problem in implementation was the need for student training. We did not have a live Internet connection in the classroom, and, although we provided some how-to training manuals, it still required an enormous amount of time and energy to train students to perform the tasks they needed to perform in order to succeed in the class. For the coming year, we have modified our manual to make it more effective, and we will have Internet connections in the classroom, so we can train students during class time instead of outside of class in small groups or individually. Although we hope this will cut down the time we will need to spend with students, we still expect to spend more one-on-one time with our students than would occur in a more traditional survey class.[17]

Besides the enormous amount of time required to help students understand the technology, hardware malfunctions also consumed a great deal of time and energy. Difficulties with equipment ranged from minor irritations to someone dropping the departmental laptop and the LCD projector bulb exploding. Many advocates of technology-based instruction know well the motto "Live by technology, die by technology!" It was crucial to have a backup plan, from knowing where to find a spare LCD projector to keeping a slide projector with slides nearby or making overhead transparencies. Ironically, as we became more reliant on technology in the classroom, the success of the course sometimes depended upon our own flexibility and the willingness to do without it.

Choosing a program for designing the presentations was another issue we had to address. The basic choice in programs was between Corel Presentations and Microsoft PowerPoint. Although the university uses the Microsoft Suite, including PowerPoint, we decided to use Corel Presentations because we felt it gave us increased flexibility. The operating system also influenced what we could and could not do. The university still had Windows 3.1 as its platform, which meant that students couldn't use the latest Internet browsers, which led to problems accessing some sites, including the textbook authors' site. As a result, the Netscape browser frequently crashed, leading to many student complaints. We hope this problem will be resolved in the coming year when the university installs Windows 98. An additional constraint as a result of the operating system lies in the HTML editor program that can be used. Some of the easier to use editor programs, like Microsoft FrontPage, run only on Windows 95 or 98 machines. Until the university upgrades, we will have students use the built-in editor that comes with Netscape Navigator Gold 3.1.

The last problem we had to face involved finding appropriate graphics.[18] In order to stimulate interaction and highlight the material under consideration, appropriate photos, graphs, charts, and other visual materials are a necessity. To facilitate development and use of computer-mediated presentations, the Department of History allocated one graduate assistant specifically to aid faculty in developing materials. After the faculty developed ideas for presentations, our Technology Assistant handled the time-consuming chore of finding and digitizing appropriate visual materials. Many of these materials were located in photo collections or on other sites on the Web. Some materials that simply could not be located were, when possible, created using available software. This was particularly true when dealing with geographic concepts. If an appropriate "base map" could be located, it was changed to highlight the concept under discussion. If appropriate materials could not be located and edited, they were often created using Corel Presentations or Corel Draw.

## Conclusion

Although reinventing the American History Survey was neither painless nor problem-free, the authors remain convinced it was the right thing to do. The incorporation of technology in the service of learning caused only minor adjustments in content coverage and added an entirely new dimension to the course that excited students and, based on available evidence, enhanced student learning. Over the course of the last two decades, many academics have accepted the idea that every course offered at the university or college level should be a writing course and, as a result, we have witnessed the proliferation of programs advocating "writing across the curriculum." It is our belief that soon, sooner in fact than many of our colleagues realize, every course offered at the college level will need to be, at least to some degree, a "computer course." The reinvention of the American History Survey at Southeast Missouri State University is a step in that direction.

## Notes

1. Kyle L. Peck and Denise Dorricott, "Why Use Technology?" *Educational Leadership* (April 1994): 11–14. See also Carol J. Guardo and Scott Rivinius, "Save Before Closing: Bringing Technology to the Liberal Arts," *Liberal Education* (Summer 1995): 22–27, and Judith V. Boettcher, "Technology Classrooms, Teaching, and Tigers," *Syllabus* (October 1995): 10–12. It should be noted that the push among educators is not universal. For a list of concerns, see William M. Bulkeley, "Hard Lessons," *The Wall Street Journal*, 17 November 1997, R1–R35, and Colleen Cordes, "Information Technology," *The Chronicle of Higher Education*, 16 January 1998, A25–A26. The Cordes article is a summation of the concerns raised at the "Computers in Education: Seeking the Human Essentials" conference held at Columbia University in December 1997. See also, William H. Graves, "Learning as an Expedition, Technology as a Unifying Tool," *Syllabus* (August 1998): 20–22.

2. For discussions of the research and excellent bibliographies, see Thomas Cyrs, *Essential Skills for College Teaching: An Instructional Systems Approach* (Las Cruces: New Mexico State University Press, 1994), and Robert J. Menges and Maryellen Weimer, *Teaching on Solid Ground: Using Scholarship to Improve Practice* (San Francisco: Josey-Bass, 1996).

3. Steven Aukstakainis and Michael Mott, "Transforming Teaching and Learning Through Visualization," *Syllabus* (March 1996): 14–16.

4. Larry Easley, "The Enhanced Lecture: Bridge to Interactive Teaching," in *Writing, Teaching, and Researching History in the Electronic Age*, ed. Dennis A. Trinkle (Armonk, NY: M.E. Sharpe, 1998), 65–72. See also Reza Azarmsa, "Technology-Mediated Presentation in the Classroom," *Syllabus* (January, 1997): 10–12.

5. J. Terence Kelly and Robin Leckbee, "Reality Check: What Do We Really Know About Technology, and How Do We Know It?" *Syllabus* (August 1998): 24–26, 53–54. Discussing ingrained attitudes about teaching and technology, this article examines some models for change that might be instructive to others trying to move from lecture-based to learner-based teaching.

6. http://cstl.semo.edu/us107

7. http://lcWeb2.loc.gov/ammem/afctshtml/tshome.html

8. http://lcWeb2.loc.gov/ammem/fsahome.html

9. http://www.worldwar1.com/tlbtw.htm

10. http://www.otr.com/main.html

11. http://oldwww.dave-world.net/community/mchs/flapper.html

12. Traci E. Jacobson and Laura B. Cohen, "Teaching Students to Evaluate Internet Sites," *The Teaching Professor* (August 1997): 4.

13. http://ipad.mcsc.k12.in.us/mhs/social/madedo

14. http://newdeal.feri.org/eleanor/index.htm

15. http://beta.prenhall.com/. Note: The publisher recently came out with a new edition of the text and a new supporting Web site. The site we used has been moved to the url http://cw.prenhall.com/bookbind/pubbooks/faragher/

16. One disappointment for students creating the Web sites was that we could not keep them on-line permanently. We decided to remove them from the university site three months after the end of the semester due to copyright questions and server space. On our next attempt we will assign family/local history projects to make photo copyrights less a problem. We have established a department committee to review student-developed Web sites and plan to include the most effective ones in a Web site on local and family history.

17. Linda Wallinger, "Developing Technology Training for Teachers," *Kappa Delta Pi Record* (Fall 1997): 18–19. Though this article promotes technology training for teachers, the model discussed can be used for training students. See also Judith V. Boettcher, "How Many Students Are 'Just Right' in a Web Course?" *Syllabus* (August 1998): 45–47. Boettcher notes that faculty who get involved in Web-based courses should understand that their workload is going to increase and that there will be little compensation in the form of fewer students or contact hours.

18. For an interesting model in using graphics to help create an interactive environment, see Joseph M. Kirman, "Teaching About Local History Using Customized Photographs," *Social Education* (January 1995): 11–13.

# 6

# Computer-Generated Graphics and the Demise of the History Textbook

*Brian Plane*

It is a great irony that the encyclopedia, the most remarkable publishing project of the Enlightenment, may not survive the twenty-first century in print. To say this is not to embrace the notion that books will somehow become obsolete in an age of electronic publishing. It is to recognize the superior efficiency of computer and Internet technology in providing access to reference material. Indeed, Diderot's ambition to compile and centralize human knowledge in a single source still fascinates us today. How else can we explain, or justify, the tremendous investment of academic resources in the Internet—the information superhighway that critics dismiss as a glorified shopping mall? Internet hookups provide access to directories, dictionaries, and encyclopedias of every sort. Publishers are already developing a wide variety of alternatives to traditional bound reference materials. Personal computer makers even include encyclopedias on compact disks alongside standard operating system software, encouraging users to view the computer as the ultimate reference tool.

What will happen to the popular encyclopedia of historical knowledge, the standard, entry-level college textbook? History instructors have already begun to utilize alternatives to the traditional bound reference materials. This change is most pronounced in access to historical documents and documentary collections, which are increasingly available via the Internet. In the future, something akin to an electronic textbook may replace the traditional, bound lexicons that have dominated history instruction for decades. The obsolescence of conventional textbooks is rooted both in the computer's efficiency as a reference tool and in structural changes within higher education that encourage colleges and universities to offer educational services on-line and via electronic media. Even under a minimalist scenario, whereby classroom instruction remains the predominant model for education, educators will still seek to give their classes electronic and on-line components. Electronic history textbooks will help educators in this task. In addition to providing access to historical reference material, the twenty-first century text-book might supply instructors with richer classroom aids and attractive course Web sites, capable of facilitating testing, discussion, and teaching on-line. The development of alternative instructional media in history would be inconceivable without the democratization of images. Over the past decade, digital storage technology has democratized images, much as the printing presses of the sixteenth century brought about the diffusion of print. Part of the Internet's efficiency as a reference tool lies in its ability to transmit information in image form as easily as text. The extent to which conventional textbooks are image driven can astound: a one-thousand page textbook usually contains over one hundred historical maps, and over four hundred historical illustrations, not to mention tables, time lines, and text boxes, which bring colorful images to virtually every textbook page. Textbooks, in short, have long recognized the power of maps and other image documents as instructional tools. A provocative collection of maps, historical cartoons, artwork, posters, photographs, and other historical artifacts distinguishes a good textbook, often providing the impetus for its selection by an instructor. The democratization of images impacts the future of textbooks in at least two ways. First, it means that instructors need no longer rely on textbooks to illustrate historical material. Historians are now empowered to custom design a sequence of historical maps and illustrations tailored to the specific needs of their course. Second, it facilitates an easier transfer of images to a classroom setting.

The idea of customizing maps and illustrations to a particular course is foreign to most history instructors because image duplication technology has been either primitive or prohibitively expensive. But this has changed dramatically thanks to development of the Internet, digital scanners, oversized hard drives, and high-capacity storage disks. These technological changes invite history instructors to reconsider options for integrating images into their courses. (See Figure 1.) Paintings, cartoons, statistics, photographs, and posters—these are important primary documents that deserve consideration alongside text documents in designing a history curriculum. Instructors can now tailor images to the specific needs of a course as easily as reading assignments.

Moreover, the instructor can present attractive electronic maps and illustrations before classes of varying sizes at a fraction of the conventional cost. History departments have traditionally invested in expensive roll-down map sets, in which a single map may cost between $40 and $120. These cumbersome map archives are now becoming antiquated. Color inkjet printers can reproduce digital images on transparency film at little more than fifty cents per sheet. Computer projection systems can even eliminate the need for print-

**Figure 1.** The map on the top left showing the unification of Italy comes from a standard textbook collection. On the top right, simple photo editing has enlarged the legend to make it legible when projected before the class. Note also the addition of a map title and citations. The bottom left and right images represent a more sophisticated sample of photo editing. The image has been scanned from a textbook, the original scan cropped, small text erased, and large (color coded) text added. The resulting map would be a fine addition to any course on world history in the early modern period.

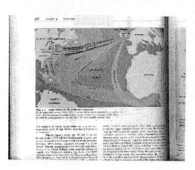

Anglo-American Transatlantic Commerce or
the "Triangle Trade"

ing altogether, although they require substantial investments in classroom infrastructure. In either case, instructors can vastly expand their access to visual classroom aids. An instructor's archive of classroom maps can approach—and even surpass—the sophistication of map collections in traditional textbooks. (See Figure 2.)

Often-neglected image documents can be brought before the class with equal ease. Historical images can dramatically enhance the quality of instruction and discussion. Entry-level students find image documents more accessible than text documents, making images a preferred means for introducing students to historical evidence and the practice of historical interpretation. Political cartoons and posters, for instance, present students with straightforward but intriguing riddles. What is the joke? To whom did this poster appeal? Instructors

**Figure 2.** The democratization of images allows instructors to assemble their own digital map archive. As shown below, this archive can supplant traditional classroom maps, as well as afford access to maps normally too specialized for classroom sets.

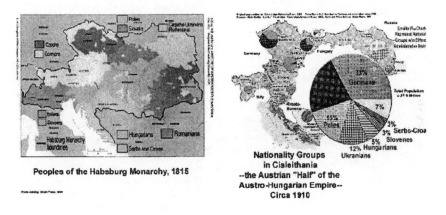

Peoples of the Habsburg Monarchy, 1815

Nationality Groups in Cisleithania
--the Austrian "Half" of the Austro-Hungarian Empire--
Circa 1910

can expand discussion to explore the historical dimensions of artwork and provocative photographs or challenge students to interpret historical statistics and maps. (See Figures 3 and 4.) Thus images can provide an alternative means of testing and enhance the value of any history course Web page.

The student's ability to access historical maps, images, and readings via the Internet further precipitates the demise of conventional textbooks. Alongside the class archive of images, a course Web site can include reading sequences tailored to support material covered in class. Like traditional course-packs, the Web site—or electronic textbook—contains primary text documents and scholarly articles, while placing greater emphasis on short, reference readings drawn from appropriate sections in conventional text-

**Figure 3.** A brief visual quiz illustrates how images of various sorts can be used to generate discussion, or to provide an alternative means of testing. The poster in Question One forces students to think about government propaganda and changing roles for women during World War I. Statistical evidence is powerful but not always easy to interpret or even comprehend. Question Two tests the student's ability to place the value of the German mark in historical context. The famous photographs in Question Three generate discussion over Stalin's rise to power and the rewriting of history during the Purges. Question Four integrates Romantic painting into the study of intellectual history in post-Napoleonic Europe.

Visual Quiz: Question One

How would you characterize
the political in this poster?

Visual Quiz: Question Two

What happened to the German Mark
between 1918-1923?

Visual Quiz: Question Three

Why were photographs this
falsified under Stalin's dictatorship?

Visual Quiz: Question Four

What elements of Romanticism
do you see in this painting?

books. Instructors can trim extraneous reading and focus on themes and topics most relevant to the class while retaining the maps and illustrations that give conventional textbooks much of their appeal. In this manner, an electronic textbook supplants traditional instructional aids by combining the advantages of customization inherent in course-packs with the advantages of illustration and presentation inherent in textbooks.

What might a customized, electronic textbook look like? The following examples are taken from a Web site I developed for a survey in modern European history while teaching at North Carolina State University. Stu-

**Figure 4.** Students also need help interpreting historical maps. Question Five asks students to explain the phenomenon of displaced peoples at the close of World War II. Question Six reminds that conventional text documents can also be attractively reproduced for classroom presentation and interpretation. David Low's grim cartoon in Question Seven provides an excellent window into deportation policies in Vichy France.

Visual Quiz: Question Five

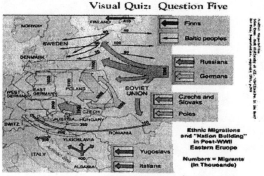

Interpret the information
presented in this map.

Visual Quiz: Question Six

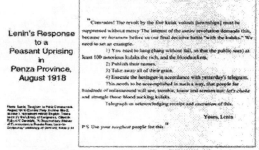

What does this document reveal
about Lenin's agricultural policy?

Visual Quiz: Question Seven

What does this cartoon say about
Western knowledge of the Holocaust
during WWII?

**Figure 5.** This sample Web page combines an academic syllabus of lecture topics, class assignments, and monograph readings with links to electronic readings and images.

| 5 | 7 | 9 |
|---|---|---|
| *Gender and Politics* | *Discussion of Freud I (Freud: Ch. IV, Va,b,d)* | *1900: Modernism and the Arts* |
| | | *Electronic Reading #18* |
| | **14** | **16** |
| | *Discussion of Freud II Report on Freud Due Electronic Reading #19* | *WWI and the Short War Illusion* |
| | | *(Allen: Ch. 1-6) Electronic Reading #20 Electronic Reading #21* |
| **19** | **21** | **23** |
| | *The Russian Revolution and the Collapse of Germany Electronic Reading #22* | *Electronic Reading #23* |
| **26** | **28** | **30** *(Allen: 7-15,* |
| *Peace and Demobilization* | *War Guilt, Reparations, and Depression* | *Conclusion) Discussion of Allen I Electronic Reading #26* |
| | *Electronic Reading #24* | |

*November*

| 2 | 4 | 6 |
|---|---|---|
| | *The Triumph of Fascism* | *Hitler in Power* |
| | *Electronic Reading #25 Electronic Reading #27* | *Report on Allen Due Electronic Reading #28* |
| **9** *( Schindler's List, Hill Library, 11/9, 7:00; Shoah, Hill Library, 11/10, 7:00)* | **11** *The Holocaust Electronic Reading #29* | **13** *Discussion of Shoah and Schindler's List Electronic Reading #30 Electronic Reading #31 Electronic Reading #32* |

dents access reference readings, maps, and illustrations through a simple interface, a hybrid of a class syllabus and an electronic table of contents. (See Figures 5 to 9.) This site allows students to access around 250 historical

**Figure 6.** This detail of the week of November 14–16 isolates the main features of the electronic textbook and syllabus. Students have discussion and an assignment due on November 14; November 16 introduces a new lecture topic (WWI) and asks students to read chapters 1–6 in William Sheridan Allen's *The Nazi Seizure of Power.* To access textbook reference readings electronically, students click on the hyperlinks at the bottom of each cell. To access historical maps and illustrations, students click on the lecture topic, "WWI and the Short War Illusion."

| **14** | **16** |
|---|---|
| Discussion of Freud II | WWI and the Short War |
| Report on Freud Due | Illusion |
| Electronic Reading | |
| #19 | (Allen: Ch. 1-6) Electronic |
| | Reading #20 Electronic |
| | Reading #21 |

maps and images, key lecture terms, study questions, and forums where students reconstruct class notes and share ideas.

The Internet provides an especially attractive medium for electronic textbooks due to its ability to facilitate student interaction outside the classroom. Student discussion forums center around problems of historical interpretation like those presented in the visual quiz above. (See Figures 3 and 4.) An analytical question accompanies each image—or sequence of images—as it is called up on the Web site. Students contribute responses to a selected number of images as part of the course requirement. If an answer has already been posted, students may review that response to reinforce their understanding of class material or contribute a critical review of responses already posted. (See Figure 10.) Students also study key terms (identifications) and study questions through the same process of contribution, review, and critical response. Such modest forums for interactivity accrue at least two major pedagogical advantages. First, historical knowledge no longer appears as a set of facts passed from instructor to student via a Web site; students themselves command responsibility for recreating points of historical emphasis and interpretation for the benefit of their peers. Second, a class Web site simplifies and facilitates the process of writing for—and being reviewed by—peers. The process of peer review enables students to view their own writing more critically because it requires them to establish firm criteria for judging good writing.

The electronic textbook, featuring visual classroom aids, reference readings, an image archive, and an interactive course Web site, yields three distinct advantages for the university. First, in a small class—like the one for

**Figure 7.** This bibliography shows the types of readings that are accessible through the electronic textbook (numbered items in the bibliography correspond to numbers as listed on the electronic reading hyperlinks—see Figure 6). Note that electronic readings are short so as to provide quick and easy reference to topics covered in class. Fair use guidelines allow university libraries to offer electronic access to discrete selections of readings such as those above.

---

19. Gilbert, Felix and David Clay Large, "The European Attitude Toward War in 1914" pp. 119-121, in Felix Gilbert and David Clay Large, The End of the European Era: 1890 to the Present, New York, 1991. Click here...

20. Paxton, Robert O. "A Longer View of the Causes of War" pp. 64-71 in Robert O. Paxton, Europe in the Twentieth Century (3rd Edition) Fort Worth, 1997 Click here to read

21. Paxton, Robert O. "The Impact of Total War" pp. 99-128 in Paxton Click here to read

22. Grenville, John A., "War and Revolution in the East" pp. 106-115 in Grenville, John A. History of the World in the 20th Century. Belknap: 1994. Click here to read

[...]
27. Paxton, Robert O. "A Closer Look at Fascism" pp. 231-240 in Paxton Click here to read

28. Spielvogel, Jackson. "Hitler and Nazi Germany" pp. 945-954 in Jackson Spielvogel, Western Civilization. Minneapolis/St. Paul, 1991 Click here...

29. Spielvogel, Jackson. "The Holocaust" pp. 987-990 in Spielvogel Click here to read

30. Wendt, Michael. "The Invented and the Real: Historiographical Notes on Schindler's List" in History Workshop 1996 (41): 240-249 Click here...

---

which this electronic textbook was designed—images can effectively generate discussion and promote critical thinking skills. Second, the use of digital maps and graphics can improve the quality of instruction in large introductory courses, exploiting the new instructional technology available in large lecture halls. In addition, the opportunity to participate in on-line forums compensates for the impersonal nature of large class sections. Third, this type of on-line textbook has potential applications for distance learning. It

**Figure 8.** The lecture topic hyperlinks (i.e., "WWI and the Short War Illusion") provide students with access to images, key terms (IDs), and study questions. All lecture topics immediately access the three-part menu shown below.

```
16
    WWI and the Short
       War Illusion
  (Allen: Ch. 1-6) ...




     •  Images
     •  IDs
     •  Study
        Questions
```

could be easily combined with distance learning software, such as test-grading programs, course comment or suggestion boxes, role-playing programs, electronic paper editors, syllabus makers, and electronic gradebooks.

Who is going to develop an "electronic textbook"? And who is going to pay for it? I foresee three scenarios for the development of sophisticated history course Web sites that may one day take the place of textbooks.

One possibility is the every-historian-their-own-publisher scenario, whereby instructors develop Web sites and electronic textbooks themselves. This boasts the advantage of producing a set of readings, maps, and other documents that are totally customized by the instructor to match course contents and objectives. The Fair Use Guidelines for Educational Media agreement, reached by key stakeholders in the intellectual property debate in 1996, establishes the instructor's right to use electronic media for educational purposes like classroom teaching and course Web sites.[1] This "fair use" agreement limits the number of images that can be taken from any particular source (not more than 10 percent or fifteen images, whichever is less), restricts access to course Web sites through passwords, and stipulates that guarantees be made to protect against copying. (See Figure 11.) Within these limits, history instructors are entitled to create an on-line image archive without fear of legal prosecution for copyright violation. Thus instructors reap the advantages of a customized textbook, save students the cost of textbook purchases, and assign a greater variety of historical monographs and other readings.

**Figure 9.** After selecting "Images," the student reviews a list of hyperlinks to image documents (like those discussed above in Figures 1–4).

- Poster (German)--German Woman Serves on the Home Front
- Poster (English)--Daddy What Did You Do?
- Poster--French Loan for National Defence
- Poster (German)--Buy Bonds--Show the English Bloodsuckers
- Poster (German)--Gold for the Fatherland
- Poster (Italian)--Help Us Win with a War Loan
- Poster (English)--I Only Wish I Were Young Enough
- Map---The Western Front
- Map--The collapse of the Ottoman Empire

**Figure 10.** The electronic textbook incorporates image documents into a course Web site that encourages students to continue the review and interpretation of historical evidence before their peers on-line. All images on the above site are paired with analytical questions and response options as shown below.

What does this poster reveal about the transformation of European society during WWI?

- Post a Response
- View Responses
- Go Back to Syllabus

Finding the time to compile, scan, copy, edit, cite, and write captions for an electronic archive, however, is not so easy. Moreover, the construction of interactive student forums requires additional time and advanced programming skills. Estimates for the amount of time needed to construct the prototype site described above are sobering. I spent around 250 hours collecting, editing, and organizing images; since then, HTML and Java programmers have expended another eighty hours' labor on the site. This considerable investment

**Figure 11.** A legislative agreement on copyright and electronic publishing has not been reached; however, the publishing industry has signed on to the Fair Use Guidelines discussed above, which are weighted to protect publishers' interests. Legitimate claims to intellectual property rights and professional standards amongst scholars demand that full citations be included with images, as seen here. According to the letter of the rather restrictive Fair Use Guidelines, the conventional means for posting image files on the Web violates copyright after fifteen days, due to the ease with which such images can be copied—even when instructors limit access to students via passwords or PINs. One means for avoiding concern about duplication and time limits is through watermarks, as shown below. Yet such precautions may be overly deferent to the interests of publishers and other copyright holders

The German Woman Serves on the Home Front !

Deutsche Frauen arbeitet im Heimat- heer!

Kriegsamtstelle Magdeburg

Taken From: Kishlarsky, Mark et al., "Civilization in the West" New York: HarperColins, 1991 p. 803    Credits: George Kirchbach, (1914-1918) Bowman Collection, Chapel Hill

of time clearly mitigates against the development of electronic textbooks via the every-historian-their-own-publisher scenario. If history departments want instructors to develop attractive course Web sites (as they often claim), they will have to honor Internet publication in hiring, tenure, and promotion decisions.

A second scenario for the advent of sophisticated history course Web sites involves active support from the department and the university. Under this scenario, departments would archive digital maps and images as they once archived rolls of classroom maps. They might purchase digital map collections–or a license to use such collections–directly from the publishers. Student workers and administrative assistants would assemble images under faculty guidance for the department's largest survey courses. Colleagues would exchange their favorite maps and documents electronically. The university, for its part, would provide programming assistance to the department, as well as developing educational software and other models for flexible educational Web sites. Students would reimburse the department and university for development costs through computer fees in Web-assisted classes, justifiable because students would be saved expensive textbook purchases. The problem with university development of sophisticated course sites is that it threatens to rob teachers of autonomy in the classroom, forcing them to conform to instructional models sanctioned by the department or university. Also, it is uncertain whether universities want to take on the added responsibility of developing instructional technologies, although a few history departments have created full-time positions in the area of technological development.

Ironically, I believe the textbook industry will ultimately offer the most viable alternatives to conventional textbooks. This scenario allows for publishers to offer in electronic format what they had once offered in print. Textbook publishers already offer instructors the ability via the Internet to customize document readers for classes. Many textbooks also offer compact discs as optional companions, although without an eye toward classroom presentation or Web-based instruction. In the future, instructors might choose to subscribe to a publisher's archive much as they once chose a text. From the publisher's archive, they will assemble collections of maps, images, documents, and texts appropriate for the specific needs of their courses. Instructors might also select interactive forums for their students, Web site prototypes, and other educational software that could help with class roll, grading, syllabus organization, and the tabulation of grades. In this manner, educational publishers could maintain their lucrative market for the sale of textbooks and expand into classroom maps, graphics, and Web-related software. Instructors could gain access to high-quality instructional aids appropriate for use in today's multimedia classroom and university—without substantial investment of time.

The challenge for instructors rests in developing new teaching methods in line with these new possibilities, while maintaining a well-warranted skepticism about the desirability of virtual universities. This means recognizing that the Internet can serve as a convenient and potentially superior reference tool. It also means exploiting the increased access to information in image form facilitated by computer technology.

### Note

1. A nonlegislative report adopted by the U.S. House of Representatives, Committee on the Judiciary, Subcommittee on Courts and Intellectual Property, September 27, 1996.

# 7

# Integrating Multimedia Technology into an Undergraduate History Curriculum

## Pedagogical Considerations and Practical Examples

*José E. Igartua*

## Introduction

Universities everywhere in North America are being confronted with the explosive impact of multimedia technology upon the way teachers teach and students learn. The combination of multimedia (nonlinear navigation among images, sound, and text) and networks embodied in the virtualities of the World Wide Web has stimulated the imaginations of teachers and university administrators. Access to richer pedagogical material and remote access by students are the two principal virtues ascribed to the Web. Some university administrators have waxed enthusiastic about the new technology in the belief that it will radically transform the learning process, while other commentators fear the commodification of university instruction and already speak of "digital diploma mills."[1]

History departments have to respond to the multimedia challenge. The Association for History and Computing has made it its task, over the last decade, to stimulate the development and the implementation of computer-based teaching tools for history. Well-designed multimedia packages, such as those developed by the Computers in Teaching Initiative Centre for History, Archaeology and Art History in the United Kingdom, the award-winning Valley of the Shadow Web site, or the promising Canadaian Confederation to Present CD-ROM being developed at the University of Alberta, offer exciting pedagogical opportunities. The question of the integration of these new pedagogical tools into general undergraduate history teaching, however, has received less attention than the new multimedia learning products themselves.

The aim of the present paper is to examine this question from the viewpoint of experience gained in the history department at the Université du Québec à Montréal (UQAM) and to offer some recommendations on the process of integrating multimedia technology into an undergraduate history curriculum. I first present the pedagogical context in which multimedia technology was introduced in our courses. I then outline three multimedia experiments in the teaching of history that we have conducted over the last years. In each case, the use of multimedia technology had specific pedagogical objectives geared to the nature of the course in which it was introduced. While we found clear pedagogical advantages to the use of multimedia technology in history teaching, we suggest that the introduction of the technology must be managed with prudence as well as enthusiasm. Pedagogy, rather than technology, must be the driving force.

## The Pedagogical Context—Characteristics of the Student Clientele

Any pedagogical endeavor has to take into account the characteristics of the student clientele at which it is aimed. These determine what can be attempted and what is beyond reach. For instance, students living on campus are in a different situation from students who commute and who work for a good part of the week. UQAM has an urban campus located in downtown Montreal, with next to no student housing. Its clientele is composed for the most part of students from modest socioeconomic backgrounds. Most students work part time to supplement their student loans. Thus their time and financial resources are limited.

Scheduling learning activities is therefore more difficult than on a residential campus. In order to keep travel between home and campus to a minimum, lectures at UQAM are done in three-hour blocks once a week. Some students hardly have time outside of classes to do course work on campus. Contact with instructors usually takes place once a week, around lecture time; problems that arise during the week can only be addressed the following week.

Given these constraints, access to computers for class work becomes a paramount issue. One way to solve the issue would be to require that students purchase a specific computer platform as part of the admission requirements. A few institutions in Canada (Acadia University in Nova Scotia, the École des Hautes Études commerciales in Montreal) have taken this route. Portable computers are brought to class and plugged into the school network as part of classroom activity. While this solves access problems and ensures that students all have the same computing platform, it does not automatically provide for improved pedagogy. There are indications (from colleagues in these institutions) that faculty are sometimes insufficiently prepared for a sudden, wholesale introduction of computers as a regular part of classroom activity. As a result, students are left wondering whether the mandatory expense has sufficient pedagogical justification.

At UQAM, requiring students to purchase computers (equipment that will be obsolete within two years) is not an option, given the socioeconomic characteristics of our students. This is one reason why UQAM has numerous computer labs. The faculty of social science, where the history department is located, has five computer rooms (three equipped with PCs, one with Macintoshes, and one mixed room) used for teaching and for student work. Yet using the labs to complete assignments and practice computer skills is inconvenient for many students for the logistical reasons outlined above.

Nevertheless, ownership of computers among UQAM students is becoming more widespread. There are two reasons for this. The first is that more and more students realize that computers are an essential tool for school work and for any future white-collar work. The second is financial assistance. The Québec provincial government offers a loan guarantee program for students who have successfully completed a semester of university study and who borrow or purchase a computer; loans can be repaid after graduation. Thus, while students would balk at being required to purchase computers, more and more see the benefit of owning a computer. In the future, students will own multimedia machines, since almost all new machines now come with a CD-ROM, a sound card, speakers, and a modem.

For the moment, however, we must deal with the fact that students have limited access to computing resources, whether at home or at school. This restricts the range of computer-based instructional activities that can be implemented in a mandatory manner or that can rely upon an up-to-date, standardized computing platform.

## Place of Multimedia Experiments in the Department— Faculty Resources

The introduction of multimedia teaching tools also depends upon faculty members familiar with the use of computer applications for teaching and willing to include these tools as a regular part of their pedagogical practice. At present, this is the case for a minority of staff in our department, as I suspect is the case in most history departments in North America. This minority provides examples and advice to colleagues intrigued by the pedagogical potential of multimedia tools.

Our institution encourages staff to develop their skills in this area by providing training workshops and modest financial help to integrate multimedia tools into teaching. Symbolic of the importance the administration attaches to this is its commitment to keep funding these activities in the face of substantial budget cutbacks that have led to larger class sizes, reduced library acquisition budgets, and a reduction of personnel among support staff.

The administration's enthusiasm for "innovative" teaching practices that make use of multimedia technology is not universally shared among faculty. One reason is that we do not yet have any conclusive assessment of the pedagogical effectiveness of multimedia technology within our institution, nor any measure of its cost-effectiveness in terms of equipment and time invested. Nevertheless, some faculty members are willing to experiment with multimedia teaching tools in order to arrive at a more informed judgment of their pedagogical usefulness.

## Program Objectives—The Place of Innovations in Departmental Priorities

The experiments described below took place while our undergraduate history program was being revised and restructured. In the course of this program revision, the systematic integration of multimedia technology into all undergraduate history courses was not envisioned. The department opted rather to mandate a committee to assess, in the light of the ongoing experiments, the place of the new technology within the range of departmental teaching practices and to make recommendations for the integration of multimedia technology into our teaching according to suitable pedagogical objectives. This prudence was based on the recognition of the importance of the experiments we were conducting, but also on the knowledge that substantial resources would be required for a sustained introduction of computer-assisted teaching into our undergraduate program.

## Course Objectives

Our multimedia experiments were designed to meet three different sets of pedagogical objectives. In the first instance, the objective was to make learning how to use bibliographical tools for historical research at once more systematic and less burdensome. To that end we created an on-line resource for a first-year course on historical methods. It seeks to offer more information than would be useful in a paper format, while at the same time making it easier for students to access information that is directly relevant to their pursuits.

The second experiment in multimedia technology was included in a course designed to train students to communicate history to the general public. The creation of Web sites by students has replaced the traditional term paper as the course's major assignment. It was intended to develop research skills, but also the analytical skills required to structure information and convey it clearly within the "space" of a Web site.

The third experiment was a history course delivered exclusively through multimedia channels. This was designed for students who, for various reasons, both personal and pedagogical, preferred this form of distance learning to the usual classroom-based course.

## An On-Line Teaching Resource: The Histoire-Hypermédia Project

The *Histoire-Hypermédia* project was set up in 1996 to produce on-line pedagogical resources to train undergraduate history majors in historical methods. The project team was made up of staff and research assistants from the history departments of Université Laval, Université de Montréal, and Université du Québec à Montréal, under my direction. During the first phase of the project, from 1996 to 1998, the team created a Web site that allows history students to learn how to conduct a bibliographical search systematically, using both traditional paper-based tools and electronic resources (on-line catalogues, CD-ROM bibliographies, Internet-based bibliographical databases). The Web site contains detailed analytical descriptions of eighty-four bibliographical tools (bibliographical guides, retrospective bibliographies, current bibliographies); access to these descriptions is provided by an alphabetical listing or by a "compass" that directs students to relevant bibliographical tools for each broad historical period.

### Reasons for the Project

The project arose from common concerns in the three participating history departments. The departments all require first-year students to take introductory courses in historical methods. These courses are designed to provide students with the methodological and technical skills they need in our undergraduate history programs. One of the essential methodological skills is the ability to carry out thorough bibliographical searches on a given topic and to find the relevant literature. While these skills have been taught for some time, the examples and the assignments used in teaching them depend upon the instructor's specific area of expertise. While we assumed that the skills developed in one area of history would be transferred to other areas, we offered little guidance on how to achieve this transfer of skills. The need for a more systematic approach was obvious.

Collaboration among the three history departments offered a way to achieve this more systematic approach. Pooling the collective knowledge and re-sources of colleagues in three history departments provides significant advantages in teaching historical methods. We have drawn on the collective wisdom of the faculty in the three departments in selecting bibliographical tools to be included in the project. Financially, project costs are shared by the three institutions: for a minimal investment of $5,000 a year over three years, each department has access to a teaching tool that cost $45,000 to develop. The advantages of co-operation, from all standpoints, are clear.

Another major reason for the project was the lack of class time in introductory historical methods courses to offer adequate training in the use of the various bibliographical tools available in the major areas of history. By offering an on-line multimedia self-teaching tool for this purpose, we wanted to give students a permanent resource to which they could come back as often as they liked for bibliographical guidance.

Finally, the *Histoire-Hypermédia* tool has practical benefits for our libraries. It will help in reducing wear and tear on bibliographical works. Each year, hundreds of students ransack the reference section of our libraries in order to complete the bibliographical research assignments required in our methods and survey courses. Because of manpower shortages, reference works used by students often end up in library sorting areas for days, sometimes weeks, before being put back on the shelves, thus being unavailable to other students. The physical handling of reference works will be reduced if students become familiar with the contents of bibliographical works and select those appropriate for a given research project before visiting the library.

## Pedagogical Objectives for the Project

From the outset, the project viewed technology as a means to attain clearly defined pedagogical objectives. The foremost objective was to develop in our students the ability to carry out systematic bibliographical searches. We spent a considerable amount of time working on an introductory text that explains the whys and wherefores of a systematic bibliographical search. The text includes examples from the major areas of history being taught in our institutions, definitions of bibliographical terms, and numerous research tips and warnings. A second introductory text explains the similarities and differences between bibliographical searches in paper-based reference works and searches of electronic materials.

We paid particular attention to the examples used to illustrate the process of systematic bibliographical searching. At each step of the search—from the choice of a general area to the framing of questions and the definition of special terms—specific topics in classical, medieval, modern (European), and contemporary history, as well as in Canadian history, are pursued systematically.[2]

The second major pedagogical objective of *Histoire-Hypermédia* was to provide guidance in selecting the appropriate bibliographical tools from the long list of available instruments. To that end, the description of each bibliographical tool begins with a summary that allows students to decide quickly whether a bibliography or bibliographical guide is relevant to the topic they are researching. This summary leads to a thorough description of the contents and structure of the bibliographical tool as well as to further remarks on use. (See Appendix A.)

The choice of multimedia environment followed from these objectives. The hierarchical, as opposed to linear, structure of a multimedia environment makes it possible to offer richer bibliographical information than a paper-based resource while avoiding information overload. Providing the same information in a print document would be so cumbersome that the bulk of the document would discourage its use. In past years, students at Université Laval, for example, received an extensive printed list of bibliographical tools as part of their course material. Yet little formal guidance was provided on how to select the appropriate tools for a given research task. So students usually ignored the list of bibliographies and proceeded more or less haphazardly in their search for bibliographical references.

We chose a Web site as the cheapest, most standardized multimedia environment format available. No software licensing is required; information can be accessed from a variety of computing platforms, both on campus and off campus; and there are no distribution costs, as UQAM provides a server for the Web site free of charge.

The *Histoire-Hypermédia* environment stresses the need for a systematic approach to bibliographical searching. Bibliographical tools can be selected using a "compass" that takes users directly to the instruments appropriate to a given historical period; bibliographies are further classified by type: guides, retrospective bibliographies, and current bibliographies. A click on the title brings up the summary description; scrolling down the page provides more detailed information, including links to scans of front matter and examples.

The Web site provides graphic materials that make information about each bibliographical tool more visual: for instance, each description of a bibliographical tool opens with a color reproduction of its cover. Appropriate sections of the front matter of each bibliographical tool and some examples of contents are reproduced; students can thus become familiar with the appearance, contents, and structure of a bibliographical instrument without physically handling it.

This on-line resource might be of little interest to students if they were not required to use it for assignments in historical methods courses. We have designed exercises to test students' understanding of the different types of bibliographical tools and to gauge their ability to select bibliographies relevant to a given research topic. However, we have not yet included these exercises on the Web site because assignments in the historical methods courses vary in format from department to department and from instructor to instructor.

## Assessment

Because *Histoire-Hypermédia* became operational only in February 1998, in the middle of the Winter term, we were not able to integrate it systematically into the historical methods courses offered during that term. We obtained feedback from about a third of the sixty or so students registered in the UQAM courses by means of a questionnaire form included in the site. With few exceptions, respondents were excited about this on-line learning resource. Some suggested enhancements to the graphical presentation of the site, which we had deliberately kept very plain. Students would also like to access bibliographical tools directly through the site, but of course this is only possible with on-line resources. Moreover, this is difficult to implement, since on-line resources have different interfaces (CD-ROMs on single machines or on networks, World Wide Web access) in different libraries. Each interface requires its own description, and access mechanisms vary, and are likely to change over time.

Respondents to the questionnaire most often complained that access to the site is restricted to users from the three universities. Copyright reasons have forced us to impose this restriction. Publishers have granted permission to reproduce material from their works without fees under the condition that the material be used only for teaching purposes and only for our students.[3] At present, the only technical means available to meet this obligation is to control access to the site by Internet Protocol address. Only addresses from the domains of the three participating universities are allowed to connect to the site.

This is not a very satisfactory solution, especially since one of the participating universities is phasing out its Internet Service Provider function in favor of a commercial Internet Service Provider. We are waiting for the implementation of a better technical solution. Access will be controlled by user IDs and passwords issued to students, regardless of the origin of their Internet connection. Given the size of the combined student population in the three universities—over 100,000—implementing this technical solution is a substantial task, undertaken by the university's computing services.

Overall, we are very pleased with the *Histoire-Hypermédia* site. Colleagues who have looked at it are also enthusiastic. Phase II of the project, for which modest funding has been obtained, will add descriptions and assessments of historical dictionaries and encyclopedias as well as textbooks and historical atlases.

## Putting History on the Web as a Term Paper

Another opportunity to use multimedia technology in teaching presented itself in the fall of 1997, within a semester course entitled "The Historian and Documentary Resources in Archives and Museums," which I was asked to teach. This is part of a set of advanced, optional historical methods courses, usually taken in the students' final year. The aim of the course is to make students familiar with the variety and richness of sources available in archives and in museum holdings.[4]

The Montreal area is particularly well endowed with archives and museums suitable for this purpose. The colleague with whom I team-taught the course, Marcel Caya, is a former archivist and museum director with excellent connections to local institutions. He and I decided that one of the major objectives of this course would be to train students in the art of *vulgarisation*, the popularization of historical knowledge, as we believed this would become an important component of any job requiring an undergraduate history degree.

## Reasons for the Project

The opening of a multimedia computer room within our Social Science Computing Laboratory, in September 1997, offered the opportunity to experiment with multimedia technology as a vehicle for *vulgarisation*. The room was equipped with Pentium II multimedia machines running Windows NT, scanners, a screen projector, Internet connections, color printers, and software to create multimedia and cartography applications. We believed the acquisition of a basic competency in the creation of Web sites would give our students valuable experience with multimedia technology besides the intellectual skills they were to develop in the course. Students were enthusiastic when we presented them with the idea.

## Pedagogical Objectives for the Project

We decided at the outset that the best way to attain the general aims of enabling students to work with primary sources and artifacts was to make them actually use archival and museum materials in their course assignments. They needed to become acquainted with the workings of archival institutions, with the way in which archival material is organized and catalogued, with the principle of provenance, and with legislation governing copyright, privacy, and access to information. They would also learn how museum collections are constituted, how they are catalogued, and how museum curators use their collections to mount exhibitions and present artifacts to the public.

**Course Organization**

For the instructors, the course was an experiment in a nontraditional pedagogical approach. Lectures were conducted in the multimedia lab and lecture materials as well as assignment specifications were placed on the course Web site. Students could access lecture outlines while we were lecturing, thus facilitating note-taking. Lecturing generally took place for about half the available class time. The other half was given over to hands-on experimentation. Students helped each other with design and technical problems, with the supervision and assistance of the instructors. Outside of class, a listserv and e-mail were used to answer specific queries and to draw students' attention to material posted on the course Web site. Besides class time, the multimedia lab was reserved for our students' use for two hours a week, during which I served as lab monitor.

The major assignment in the course was the production of Web sites on historical topics we suggested. The sites would showcase documents and artifacts, explaining how they help in understanding the chosen historical topic. As far as possible, students had to make use both of archival and of museum materials.

We wanted to equip students with two different sets of skills. The first set of skills was the ability to use the historical resources found in archives and museums. To acquire these skills, students were first given lectures and readings, and then taken on group visits to archives and museums, during which archivists and museum curators explained the nature of their work, described their major collections, and sketched the ways in which research was conducted within their institution.

After this exposure to the behind-the-scenes workings of archives and museums, students had to identify the institutions likely to hold materials related to their topic, become familiar with the various research tools available (catalogues, finding aids, etc.), and choose institutions and collections relevant to their topic. Students then had to select documents and artifacts to include in their Web site and to outline the thesis that their site was to convey through these artifacts. Arriving at a statement of purpose for the Web sites was sometimes difficult for students more used to summarizing other people's viewpoints in essays than coming up with viewpoints of their own, but most students were excited—if a little apprehensive—at the prospect of putting their creation on the Internet for all the world to see.

Students discovered that their selection of material was often contingent upon obtaining reproduction rights. While this was relatively straightforward in the case of archival material, it was much more difficult with museums, which were understandably reluctant to see some of their assets disseminated on the Web outside of their institutional control. Students were already aware of copyright issues from course lectures on Canadian copyright, privacy, and access to information laws and Quebec legislation governing archives. In negotiating reproduction rights with museums and other institutions, students learned that determination, resourcefulness, and persuasion are necessary components of the historian's toolbox!

The second set of skills involved training in the art of Web site design. This was conducted in parallel with the methodological research training. The first step was to make students aware of the qualities a good Web site should have, as well as to expose them to a variety of Web styles. For their first assignment, students had to find interesting museum and archive sites on the Web and assess them for form as well as for content. For this assignment we provided a questionnaire. (See Appendix B.)

We kept instruction on how to design Web sites very basic. A simple, common template was proposed, to ensure that all sites would contain essential information: statement of purpose, menu, e-mail address of creator, date of last update, annotated bibliography, and links back to the site's home page on each page. We also wanted to keep site structures as simple as possible in order to reduce the need for elaborate navigation aids.

We stressed the importance of planning a site structure according to the message one wanted the site to convey. Like any work of historical popularization, a Web site had to grab the attention of its visitors, tell them what the site was about, and provide a quick indication of its structure. Materials from archives or museums had to support the site's principal argument without overshadowing it. The rhetoric of Web site design was compared to that of traditional essay writing.

Students were then taught how to produce simple HTML pages. We countered their fear of technical hurdles by showing them that they could create Web pages with a word processor. (We used Word for Office 97.) We showed them how to insert visual material such as photographs or reproductions from newspapers on microfilm. Photographs were taken from the archives and museums collections or shot with a digital camera. Some students, already familiar with Web creation, included QuickTime VR panoramic shots, film, or audio clips.

Students quickly learned how to use Photoshop 4.0 to scan images and edit them. Surprisingly little formal instruction was necessary, though a fair amount of hands-on demonstration and assistance had to be provided. During the lab periods when I assisted students with the technical aspects of their assignments, I could observe that they enjoyed exploring the features of Photoshop. They discovered that cropping and digital manipulating of images have a lot in common with selecting written documents and extracting citations from them: they are forms of argument in support of a thesis.

The greatest technical hurdle students faced was uploading HTML pages and image and sound files to Web servers. Creating the appropriate directories on the university Unix server and using FTP to upload files to it required understanding the workings of Unix directory and file systems, something not immediately obvious to most students. (New FTP software now makes this a lot easier.)

Students produced sites on a wide variety of topics,[5] ranging from the symbolic meaning of military uniforms, the evolution of beer advertising, and wartime propaganda films to the *vie mondaine* of Montreal's bourgeois women. Each site had its own flavor. Students put a lot of effort into creating presentable sites; some even asked their parents to proofread their work! As a keepsake from the course, a CD-ROM containing the students' Web sites was produced by the instructor and a student with strong technical expertise.

The final assignment was an oral presentation by each student of his or her Web site. The presentation had to include a self-assessment of the student's learning experience. Most students were very excited by what they had learned about archives and museums and about their own creative abilities but found the course demanding of their time. At the end of the course, a final exam required students to reflect critically on the role of archives and museums in the historian's work.

### Assessment

The formal student assessment of the course confirmed the students' interest in the course matter and in the pedagogical formula used, but pointed to the need to improve instruction in the technical aspects of Web design. This was not unexpected, since lab equipment, the design of Web sites, and the requisite software were all new to the instructors as well as the students when the course began! Another measure of the course's success was that interest in museums and archives was sustained into the next semester for about half the students,[6] who enrolled in a practical course on exhibition design.

## Teaching Entirely by Electronic Means

Our department's most ambitious experiment was a course taught entirely on the Web. Over the last ten years, my colleague Michel Guay had developed considerable technical skills in producing multimedia material for his survey courses on ancient Egypt. He was approached by our administration to design a history course to be given entirely through multimedia channels. After nearly a year's preparatory work, a course on Pharaonic Egypt was offered in the fall of 1997 and a second time in the fall 1998 term.[7]

## Reasons for the Project

The goal of the project was to gain experience in the design and teaching of courses exclusively through multimedia channels and in testing students' reaction to this mode of instructional delivery. The multimedia channels consisted of a Web site containing various documentary resources, live broadcast radio lectures (made available on the Web site afterwards), a discussion list, e-mail, and reading materials.

## Pedagogical Objectives for the Project

The course aimed at creating a highly structured, resource-rich learning environment for students who could not attend regular university courses or preferred not to do so. It sought to make full use of the time students are expected to spend on a three-credit semester course.[8] Students would determine their own pace within the fifteen weeks of the regular semester. They would be responsible for their own learning; the course materials provided all the required resources. The course can be considered a variant of the distance learning approach. The major innovation was the provision of on-demand audio and visual materials through the Web, as well as asynchronous access to the instructor via e-mail and a discussion list.

## Structure of the Course

The course was divided into nine general *modules* or segments. Each segment included five themes, and each theme was comprised of four sections. Each of the 180 sections was meant to represent thirty minutes' work on the students' part. Included in this total was lecture material provided in the form of forty-five hours of audio recordings of interviews between a radio host and the course lecturer. The remaining forty-five hours were allotted for off-line student work. Two textbooks were required reading. Students had to write nine short papers (three to four pages), one for each segment of the course. Papers had to be submitted electronically, and grades were sent back the same way. A discussion list gave students the opportunity to put general questions, whether of a technical or of a substantive nature, to the whole group.

The site also provided a wide variety of documentary resources, including a glossary, chronologies, bibliographies, and excerpts from written documents. But the Web format also made it possible to offer pictures, computer-generated images and maps, 3D animations, and links to other Web sites of interest. Within each section, course material offered appropriate hyperlinks to these resources. On-line quizzes allowed students to check on their mastery of the factual knowledge required in the course.

**First Uses**

Enrollment in the course (around fifty students at the beginning of the fall 1997 term, thirty of whom completed the course) was roughly the same as in the regular version of the course offered during the same term. Thus the course did not attract the masses that the administration had hoped for, in spite of the exposure the course gained on Canada's national French-language radio network, which broadcast the lecture part of the course. For the instructor, course preparation required systematic, elaborate planning, with precise pedagogical objectives for each segment of the course. Interaction with students through e-mail also demanded much time.

For the fall 1998 term, the course was offered on a CD-ROM. This medium makes it possible to provide a greater range of documentary resources without the technical impediments of Web delivery (long download times for audio or graphic files). The CD-ROM links to the course Web site for freshly updated material.

**Assessment**

This course has provided the university with some favorable media attention and given it some valuable insight into the resources required to mount such courses. But it is difficult at this time to judge whether it has reached the clientele it was aiming for and whether it has achieved its pedagogical objectives to the students' satisfaction, for we do not yet have a systematic assessment of the course from the students. The instructor notes that most students were enthusiastic about the format, as is to be expected of early adopters of any given technology. But it appears obvious that this type of course is suited only to a fraction of the student population and that it cannot replace traditional forms of course delivery. From a pedagogical standpoint, it has the virtue of requiring the instructor to do meticulous planning and tracking of the students' progress. The other side of the coin is that such courses are often faced with technical difficulties outside the control of either instructor or students: networks go down, Internet links disappear or move, students' machines break down.

Did the course reach its intended target, namely students who otherwise could not attend classes or who prefer to be free of the time constraints of the classroom? The course drew about a quarter of its enrollment from outside regular university programs. A third of the students were from other programs than history, and a little over a third were enrolled in the history program. Registration for the fall 1998 offering of the course was eighty-seven; almost three quarters of students came from other programs than history, but only four were from outside the university. The course appears to be drawing to history a wider constituency than the traditional format. Conversely, it has drawn a smaller proportion of its enrollment from history majors, which is a concern for the department. Whatever the shifts in clientele, it is clear that this teaching formula has yet to gain mass appeal.

How the Internet version of the course will fit within the regular history undergraduate curriculum remains to be seen. The department's position is that the course cannot be given exclusively on the Web as part of its regular course offerings. Its normal rotation on our calendar is every two years, though the experiment has allowed us to offer it more frequently because of financial support from the administration. Yet the course has also involved extra costs for the department and it is unknown how long it can bear these costs when enrollments remain small compared to the traditional format of the course, which can range from 100 to 120. These issues need to be addressed in the coming year.

### The Place of Multimedia Technology in the History Curriculum: Assessment and Recommendations

As with any pedagogical innovation, the integration of multimedia technology into an undergraduate history curriculum requires a suitable mixture of enthusiasm and prudence. Enthusiasm is necessary to generate support and student acceptance. Prudence is required to ensure that the introduction of multimedia technology answers specific and explicit pedagogical needs and that the resources required for a successful implementation are available.

A significant benefit of the process of integrating multimedia technology into the history curriculum is that it will trigger a review of existing pedagogical objectives and practices. At the program level, making training in multimedia technology a general objective of an undergraduate history program should be considered, in order to equip students with the technical skills required in today's labor markets. At the course level, defining a clear pedagogical objective for the use of technology is essential and this objective has to be congruent with the overall objectives of the course. These in turn will help in determining the appropriate multimedia content to include in the course.

The experience with multimedia technology gained over the last years has made us aware of the need to include basic training in the use of electronic resources for historical research in our first-year methods course. This was done in the fall 1998 semester.

The inclusion of multimedia literacy in upper level courses should gradually become a natural part of assignments. Most students quickly learn the rudiments of Web navigation and many, if not most, have done so prior to university. This will increasingly be the case. Most students will soon be more technologically fluent than most of their instructors. What history faculty can offer students as part of an undergraduate education is training in how to use electronic resources, and the Web in particular, for scholarly purposes. Our department is proceeding in that direction. We are making use of the Web as an efficient, quick, and cheap method of dissemination for course materials. The Web has also been used as a means of turning individual student work into a common class resource.[9] Students can readily see how the Web opens up new communications channels between faculty and students and among students.

Turning students from consumers to producers on the Web can yield clear pedagogical benefits as long as students are not overwhelmed by technical hurdles. Students can compare their work with that of others and more easily recognize their own strengths and weaknesses. Students will be also very much aware that their productions have a potential worldwide audience and that their work will be judged not only by their instructor, but by anyone who happens onto their site. This is a strong motivator to produce the best possible work.

It is also important that the introduction of multimedia technology in a given history curriculum proceed gradually. Experience is best gained in cumulative short steps, particularly if resources are hard to come by. Another reason is that technology changes rapidly and technological choices made at the outset of a long-term project may not be optimal once the project is nearing completion. And projects always do take longer than estimated! So it is important to keep the focus on content. The experience we gained with the *Histoire-Hypermédia* project is instructive in this regard. We worked first on content and waited until content was almost complete before committing to a delivery platform. This proved wise, since, when the project began, Web browsers had limited navigational capabilities and we had envisioned using a proprietary—and expensive—hypermedia environment. We changed our minds when Web browsers improved. It is also crucial to choose as simple a multimedia environment as is compatible with course objectives. Students and staff often lack the resources to keep their computing platforms up to date with the latest technological advances. Fancy animation, video, and sound usually require computing and network facilities that are beyond these users' resources. There is no point creating these types of multimedia documents if few people can access them!

## Conclusion

It is worth stressing once more that any multimedia implementation in the history curriculum must focus on pedagogical objectives and on the contents required to achieve those objectives. This is what we as historians are best suited to define, however great our technical skills and fondness for technology may be. Let us remember that content has a much longer half-life than any given technology, and that the efforts expended in making sure of its quality will bring longer-term benefits than efforts expended at mastering technology.

## Notes

1. See David F. Noble's alarming description of the coming of digital diploma mills at http://www.journet.com/twu/deplomamills.html. A better multimedia rendering of the article is available at http://www.firstmonday.dk/issues/issue3_1/noble/index.html

2. We have an example in American history ready for inclusion and intend to include one in Latin American history as well; this will cover the major fields taught in our departments.

3. Only one publisher out of about seventy refused us permission. The publisher is the *Presses universitaires de France*, which argued that copyright legislation regarding the Internet is "uncertain."

4. Here is the official course description: *Examen de l'ensemble des ressources documentaires utiles à l'historien en insistant particulièrement sur la diversité et la richesse des sources premières des archives et des musées, y compris les ressources audiovisuelles. Sensibilisation aux rôles et aux exigences de la recherche dans ces institutions. Les contraintes spécifiques susceptibles d'être rencontrées en matière de classement, d'indexation, ou d'inventaire d'archives. La question de la mission de ces institutions en tant qu'élément essentiel à la définition d'une mémoire collective et de leurs rapports avec les historiens.* The course examines the breadth of documentary sources of use to historians, with emphasis on the range and depth of primary sources, including audiovisual documents found in museums and archives. It introduces students to the nature and function of historical research in museums and ar-

chives. It deals with the research issues involved in classifying, indexing, and creating and finding aids for archival documents. It discusses the relationships between historians and archives and museums and outlines the role of these institutions as vital components in the construction of collective memory.

5. See the list of sites prepared for the course at http://www.er.uqam.ca/nobel/r12270/cours/a9_his4017/sitesetud_menu.htm. Some of the sites were removed by students for copyright reasons or because they felt their site was not presentable enough.

6. The course began with thirty-one students and ended with twenty-six.

7. The address for the current version is http://www.unites.uqam.ca/egypte2. Since most of the material for this year's course is on a CD-ROM, one should consult last year's version of the course, where all the multimedia material is on the Web, to obtain a better idea of course structure and contents. The address is: http://www.unites.uqam.ca/egypte

8. For each of the forty-five hours of class time, students are expected to do two hours' work, for a total of 135 hours.

9. I have taught a Canadian history course to education majors in which one of the assignments was a critical assessment of audiovisual or computer resources for teaching Canadian history at the high school level. Students were required to fill a common template, available on the course Web site, and to submit it either by e-mail or on a disk. I then put all the assessments on the course Web site (http://www.er.uqam.ca/nobel/r12270/cours/his4505BES/) as a resource for current and future students.

**Appendix A**

**Bibliography of European Economic and Social History**

*Summary*

| | |
|---|---|
| Type of Bibliography | Historical bibliography |
| Dates of Publication for | |
|   Listed Documents | To c. 1989 for the second edition |
| Historical Period | 1700–1939 |
| Geographic Area | Europe, other than British Isles |
| Topics | Economic and social history; historical demography |
| Usage Notes | * This tool is directed primarily at students and teachers (Anglophone), rather than to senior researchers. |
| | * For Great Britain, one should consult *Bibliography of British Economic and Social History* (Manchester, 1984). |
| | * Limited to English-language publications |

*Detailed Description*

*Identification*

| | |
|---|---|
| Formal Title | *Bibliography of European Economic and Social History* |
| Author | ALDCROFT, Derek H., and Richard RODGER |
| Publication Details | |
| | * 1 ed.: Manchester, Manchester University Press |
| | * 2 ed.: Manchester and New York, Manchester University Press |
| Type of Bibliography | Historical bibliography |

| | |
|---|---|
| Dates of Publication | 1984 and 1993 |
| Frequency of Publication | Two editions |

*Location*

| | |
|---|---|
| UQAM Call Number | Z7165 E88 A4 |
| Inventory Description | A copy of the first edition (1984) |
| Laval University Call Number | Z7165 E89 A357 |
| Laval University Inventory | A copy of each edition |
| University of Montreal Call Number | [ REF. ] Z7165 E95 A42 |
| University of Montreal Inventory | A copy of each edition |

*Field*

Topics
Economic and social history; including also works of historical demography and, for certain countries, the history of education, sciences, and technology

Excluded Topics

Geographical Area
Europe (including Turkey, Iceland, Russia, and the Baltic States); Great Britain and Ireland, however, are excluded (see *Other Comments*).

Period
1700–1939 (see 1 or 2 ed., p. ix); some of the listed publications extend past these dates.

Types of Listed Documents
Works of synthesis; monographs; periodical articles; collective works (mixtures, acts, etc.); editions of sources; bibliographies; some official publications (statistics emanating from a government, an organization, or an association)

Excluded Documents

Places of Publication
Primarily English-speaking countries

| | |
|---|---|
| Dates of Publication of the Listed Documents | From 1300 to 1982 (1 ed.) or up to 1989 (2 ed.) |
| Language of the Documents | English exclusively |

## Contents

| | |
|---|---|
| Summaries | None |
| Other Precise Details | |
| | The titles considered to be too vague are briefly clarified |
| List Stripped Publications | None |
| Instructions | Yes |
| Diagram of the notes | None |
| Abbreviations | None |
| Other | None |

## Usage

Principal Means of Classification

*The first section comprises works of more general range.
*The remaining works are classified by area (e.g., Southernmost Europe).
*Subclassification (e.g., Spain)
    *Subdivided by themes, which are relatively uniform from one country to another.
    *Under each heading, the notes are classified by authors and directors.

Index
Index of the authors
References
Notes

---

## OTHER COMMENTS

*This tool is directed primarily at students and teachers (Anglophone), rather than to senior researchers.

*The first edition comprises a little more than 6,000 entries; the second, approximately 9,000. In the latter, works considered to be superseded or no longer relevant have been replaced by more recent (see 2 ed., p. x).

*The economic and social history of Great Britain was deliberately excluded by the authors, in order to avoid double coverage with *Bibliography of British Economic and Social History* (Manchester, 1984), by W.H. Chaloner and R.C. Richardson.

*In general, the volumes give the reference for the first edition of a work, except when the subsequent editions involved a substantial revision of its contents (see p. ix of each edition).

*Caution: Those works covering two countries are indicated in the section corresponding to each country, whereas those works covering more than two countries are gathered in the general section (e.g., a work covering France, Belgium, and Germany will be indexed in the section on Europe) (see pp. ix–x each edition).

**Appendix B**

**HIS4017–30 The Historian and Documentary Resources in Archives and Museums (A97)**

*Evaluation Matrix for Web Sites*

*Your name:*

*Identification of the Site*

Name of the site:
Address (URL):
Topic of the site:
I found this site via . . .
I retained this site because . . .
This site is addressed mainly to . . .

*Contents*

Are the encountered contents the expected contents?
Principal elements of the contents:
Quality of the contents:
Information available about the origin of the contents (provenance):
Does the site contain audiovisual elements (sound, video, or animation)?

*Structure and Operation*

Is the structure of the information contained in the site apparent to the user?
Are the hypertext links relevant and obvious?
Do the pages load quickly?
Is the page length appropriate for reading on the computer screen?
Does the site offer indications of size for large files?
Can the site be navigated in an intuitive way?

*Quality of the Graphic Presentation*

Does the site have a graphical coherence (arrangement, fonts, colors, position of the buttons, etc.) throughout?
Are the aesthetics of the colors, backgrounds, and images pleasing?

*General Assessment*

In a few words, indicate your appraisal of the site and provide a rating.

# 8

## "Doing History"
### Evaluating Technologies That Promote Active Learning in the History Classroom

*Margaret M. Manchester*

### Introduction

As historians, we are concerned with primary sources, historical methodology, and historiography. As teachers of history, our goal is to expose students to a variety of historical sources, both primary and secondary, to encourage them to form and defend their conclusions, and to compare these with what other historians have concluded. In short, we strive to get our students to think and act as historians by helping them develop the research, critical thinking, and analytical tools to construct a usable past. Additionally, many faculty today are seeking ways to expose their students to a variety and multiplicity of sources inexpensively and to promote active learning by designing problem- and/or project-based learning activities that provide increased opportunities for students to explore their interests and develop their skills. As educators, we seek to encourage habits of the mind that will contribute to lifelong learning. What role can technology, especially software programs and the World Wide Web, play in helping educators achieve these goals? Given the different levels of preparedness to use the technology among both students and faculty, are there any programs that can facilitate the process? This essay will examine a number of options available to educators to promote more active learning in the history classroom, including textbooks whose publishers provide Web-based supplementary materials and Web Course in a Box, a software program that provides an electronic environment for the classroom, and will suggest ways to use these materials in designing classroom activities.

### Ancillary Materials Available from Textbook Publishers

Most textbook publishers today have developed ancillary materials for adopters of their texts. These range from electronic versions of the text on a CD-

ROM or accessible through the publisher's Web site to full-service Web sites that allow students to test their comprehension, develop their mapping skills, examine additional primary sources, and link to related materials on the World Wide Web. Other materials include test and presentation makers, electronic lesson planners, and discussion forum sites.

For a U.S. History Survey to 1865, I selected the George Brown Tindall/ David E. Shi text, *America: A Narrative History*, fourth edition, published by W.W. Norton. This text is now in the fifth edition. Norton maintains a Web site at http://www.wwnorton.com/college/history/twelcome.htm. Access for both students and faculty is password-protected. For each chapter, Norton provides three modules: Resources, Review, and Research.

Resources include maps, primary sources, and illustrations. For example, for the period before 1600, students can click on a map of Columbus's explorations, read excerpts from his account of the discovery of America, and read selections from De las Casas's description of the slaughter of natives in Cuba. The Review section for chapter 1, "Collision of Cultures," includes a chapter outline, a list of key words (People, Places, and Events), study questions, links to the primary documents listed in the Resources, and a Reading Quiz. The Research section is a useful tool for students and teachers alike. Each module exposes students to a different historical problem and helps them develop specific skills, such as analyzing primary versus secondary sources, distinguishing between fact and fiction, limiting focus, reconstructing past world views, analyzing disparate positions, analyzing literature for its social/historical content and doing research. Each research module provides a section that introduces the problem and provides instructions, a source list that links the students to various primary and secondary sources on the Internet, and a help section. The topics of the modules include Pocahontas: Evidence and Conjecture, The Salem Witch Trials, The Opposing Sides in the American Revolution, The American Renaissance, The Alamo, Slavery, and The Coming of the Civil War. Research topics for the second half of the U.S. survey include the Lives of African-Americans from Reconstruction to 1960, the Women's Rights Movement until 1920, the Decision to Drop the Atomic Bomb, Decision-Making during the Cuban Missile Crisis, and Media Coverage of the Persian Gulf War.

Each module is well designed and constructed to engage students directly with historical materials. The modules can serve as the basis of short position papers, longer research papers, group projects, oral reports, and other class activities. They can be used as is or modified to meet specific class goals and objectives. Students found the topics interesting. Several students had followed some of the links and, unexpectedly, spent time reading sources that were not directly related to the essay or project, but which they found fascinating nevertheless.

The module Revolution or Rebellion was an excellent assignment that provoked a great discussion on analyzing disparate positions and looking at events from "their" historical perspective rather than "our" modern perspective. The Norton site provided links to a collection of primary documents, including speeches and petitions by both Loyalists and Patriots. Students were asked to write a three- to four-page essay defending Britain's right to tax and rebutting at least three claims made by the American revolutionaries. The module provided help on organizing the material. In their essays, students were required to provide specific examples from the primary sources to support each type of objection made by the Americans. During class, students referred to their essays to help them argue their position. To spark debate, I asked students to classify the objections as economic, constitutional, or social. By being forced to examine the American Revolution from the British point of view, students gained a new perspective on the reasons for the Declaration of Independence. In their oral arguments, students quoted not only traditional sources, such as the Stamp Act Congress petitions and the Declaration of Independence, but also Edmund Burke, Soames Jenyns, David Dulaney, and William Pitt. Of the twenty-six students in the class, at least twenty-four contributed at least once to the discussion. My role was to write the students' arguments on the board, to help them to classify the position, and to ask leading questions that helped them to make the connections. Students also speculated on when the point of no return had been reached and compromise was no longer a viable option. One student commented that "[the assignment] brings history to life through illustrations and primary sources from real people's lives."

The Norton Presentation Maker, a software program that enables the user to create slide shows, is a useful tool for teachers. Norton provides this program free of charge to textbook adopters. It is relatively easy to use and provides maps, political cartoons, drawings, paintings, advertisements, and other kinds of primary sources. Faculty can develop a short presentation to introduce a topic, a slide show to accompany a lecture, or simply use the sources as needed to illustrate a point or spark class discussion. One drawback is that, with the exception of the maps, the sources are all in black and white. I supplemented the materials from the CD-ROM with color images, especially of artwork, found on the WWW.

Since many students today are visually oriented, the images projected on the screen during class were a great tool to get students to observe and report details, to draw conclusions, and to make connections between facts and concepts. For example, I started a class on the North and South in the Antebellum period by showing slides of materials from the CD-ROM and photographs from the Matthew Brady Collection at the Library of Congress. The slides included maps of the United States in both 1820 and 1860, showing cotton culture, railroads, industrial production, and major cities. After this visual presentation, students were asked to compare and contrast the two regions on the eve of the Civil War. Students were clear and focused in their responses, making frequent cross-references between the assigned readings and the electronic sources. The focus in the class thus shifted from the instructor who provided this material in a lecture format to the students drawing and defending their own conclusions. My role was to facilitate the discussion by asking questions that helped the students establish the linkages between the sources and the readings, filling in the blanks, and pulling it all together at the end by relating it to materials we had already covered and setting the stage for the events to come. Again, the access provided by the technology made it possible for students to be actively engaged with the historical materials and to become aware of the methodology and historiography as well. On the course evaluation, one student commented, "These materials have given many and varied perspectives on subjects that were previously mostly one-sided. They teach the student discernment in judging opinions and searching for truth."

**Web Course in a Box**

Web Course in a Box (WCB) is a course creation and management tool for Web-based or Web-assisted delivery of instruction. It enables creation of basic course pages, such as syllabus, class schedule, and personal home pages. It also permits interactive functions, such as a discussion forum and self-correcting exercises. The developers of this product maintain a Web site and practice area at http://www.madduck.com. Although I already had some experience with creating HTML documents and Web pages and had experimented with a discussion forum for a previous class, WCB was attractive because of its short learning curve, its ease of use, and its low cost (it is free to institutions except for a nominal technical support fee). With the use of templates that do not require any knowledge of HTML or other technical skills, faculty can begin to create course Web sites, set up discussion forums for their classes, and provide links to Web sites useful for a particular class. WCB provides a safe, self-contained environment for students as well. A course is accessible anywhere in the world, as long as the student has access to the Internet and a Web browser. It is also easy to find one's way home without getting lost on the World Wide Web.

The WCB main menu includes Class Information, Announcements, Schedule, Students, Help/Utilities, and Learning Links sections. Additionally, faculty members can create a personal Web page or link to an existing one.

The Class Information Section allows students to visit the instructor's Web page or send him or her an e-mail message. This section is the electronic version of the syllabus, containing information on goals and objectives, policies and procedures, required texts, office hours, and so on. At the bottom of the page, faculty can provide the addresses for Web sites of particular interest. WCB provides the option of automatic hot-linking to the site. The options are endless: faculty can link students to electronic news sources, on-line academic journals, on-line collections of primary sources, such as the Smithsonian or the American Memory Collection of the Library of Congress, research collections, or sites on the Internet specific to the topic and themes of the course.

The Announcements section enables faculty to post last-minute changes and revisions, announcements about events on and off campus, new Web sites of interest, and other materials. Students are encouraged to check out the course Web site frequently to be apprized of any important information, which is available to students twenty-four hours a day. The Schedule allows students to check a particular date for required readings, work due, topics, and so on. Students noted convenience as a positive feature of this section of WCB. One student commented, "Being able to access your professor and classmates is a good way to 'group study.' I feel it's easier to stay on top of this when I have the twenty-four hour access to the class."

The Student's section allows students to create their own Web page that they can personalize with their choice of colors. They can also add graphics and images, and provide links to their favorite Web sites. Although this section is somewhat limited, it does enable students to get to know one another in a nonacademic way. It contributes to the creation of a learning community and makes it easy for students to contact one another by e-mail from within WCB. This section is also useful when students need to work together for group projects or presentations. The Help/Utilities section provides students with the ability to change passwords and to create or revise their personal Web pages.

From the instructor's point of view, the Learning Links section of WCB offers the most exciting possibilities. It is from this menu that students can link to lessons, discussion forums, quizzes, or Web links provided by the instructor. WCB provides a lesson builder, forum builder, and quiz builder. Students can access instructions, link to primary sources on the World Wide Web, link to word-processing documents, spreadsheets, and other files uploaded by the instructor, participate in a discussion, and take a quiz, all from within a lesson. WCB provides templates and step-by-step instructions. Images, graphics, sound files, and other types of multimedia can also be added. For example, in a recent lesson on Women and Families for a History of the

Modern Middle East class, students read an assigned text and browsed some related Web sites. They were then asked to respond to the following question in the discussion forum, "Why is feminism a double-edged sword for women in the Middle East?" Students then included these ancillary materials in their comments during the class discussion of the readings. In another class, Women and the American Experience, students were asked to write a two- to three-page essay answering the question, "What happened to the women's movement after 1920?" In responding to the questions, they had to make specific references to primary evidence available at Web sites ranging from one provided by the League of Women Voters, to the Jazz Age, the Harlem Renaissance, and American Prohibition. (See Appendix.)

## Student Feedback

I surveyed fifty-nine students during the spring semester of the 1997/98 academic year on their assessment of the impact of WCB and other technologies on their learning. Eighty-six percent (51) of the students responded to the survey question, "Assess the impact of electronic sources, the class Web site, and other forms of technology on your learning experience. Which were most helpful? Least helpful?"

|  | Total | % |
| --- | --- | --- |
| Respondents | 51 | 86 |
| Positive | 42 | 82 |
| Negative | 3 | 6 |
| Mixed | 5 | 9 |

(NOTE: One student responded to the survey but did not answer this question.)

The most frequent responses given for a positive impact on learning included the following:

Access to class materials (8)
Access to information through Web links (28)
Break from traditional assignments (3)
Increased knowledge about WWW and technology in general (7)
Discussion forums (2)

Twenty-six percent (11 of the 42) of the students who responded positively to the question listed the class Web site as the most helpful feature. Sixty-four percent (27 of the 42) who responded positively to the question listed the class Web links as the most useful feature. "The electronic sources were great. I found myself spending a lot of time trying to get into the different sites to find as much information as possible," one student commented.

The most frequent reasons given for a negative response included the problem of access (4), lack of time (2), and lack of knowledge about the Web and technology in general (3). One student wrote that the technology was a "gimmick" that "wasted time in the classroom," while another student "felt overwhelmed."

Of the mixed responses, one student was "unfamiliar with the Web and did not take full advantage of the materials available." While another student thought the technology was a good idea, it "needed to be integrated into the classroom."

These student responses raise interesting issues for instructors. Noteworthy is that the overwhelming majority of the students who responded positively to the use of technology, in this case a combination of the Norton text and Web site and Web Course in a Box, noted the access to a greater number and variety of sources as the chief reason for their positive evaluation of the impact of technology on their learning. Equally important is that it works best when it is an integral part of the learning experience. The technology and the classroom are integrated; the focus is on the students becoming actively engaged in the historical process. This means that a balance must be established between opportunities to read, research, write, and discuss.

**Faculty Feedback**

Faculty response has been overwhelmingly positive. More than thirty faculty members now offer courses through our WCB Web site at Providence College. The courses range from the humanities to the social sciences and from hard sciences to business courses. Although the evidence is primarily anecdotal, it is revealing nevertheless. Many instructors have noted that not only class participation has improved, but also the quality of the discussion. Others have commented on improved quality in writing assignments. One faculty member stated that he had become much better organized and had clarified the linkage between his teaching objectives and the pedagogical tools he used to achieve those objectives.

WCB is relatively easy to learn. Most faculty users attended a half-day workshop sponsored by the Providence College Center for Teaching Excellence. Each participant came to the computer workshop with a diskette containing the syllabus, bookmarks, and other class materials. By the end of the session, most had at least partially completed courses on-line. Other users simply used the manual (available on-line in either PDF or WordPerfect versions) and learned to post their course materials following the step-by-step instructions provided by the WCB program. While the program has some limitations, most agreed that WCB was a good tool for those faculty who do not know and do not wish to learn HTML. Faculty can create courses, discussion forums, and upload files all within the program. They do not have to use FTP or any other protocols. Problems always exist so long as students and faculty have differing levels of expertise in the use of computers, the Internet, e-mail, and other technology. Few want to use technology simply for the sake of using technology. However, tools like ancillary materials provided by the publishers and software programs like Web Course in a Box make it easier for faculty to promote their teaching and learning objectives, especially those concerned with active learning in the history classroom.

**Appendix**

**HIS 225: Women and the American Experience Web Project: Feminists and Flappers**

**Assignment: Write a two- to three-page essay answering the question:** *"What happened to the women's movement after 1920?"*

**Be sure to make specific references to the primary evidence to support your arguments.**

**Web sites:**

**Flapper Culture**
http://www.pandorasbox.com/flapper.html

**The Roaring Twenties**
http://www.users.interport.net/~ahajnal/20s.html

**American Prohibition**
http://www.history.ohio-state.edu/projects/prohibition/default.htm

**League of Women Voters**
http://lwv.org/

**Equal Rights Amendment**
http://now.org/issues/economic/cea/history.html

**Women's Rights Links**
http://www.inform.umd.edu/EdRes/Topic/WomensStudies/ReadingRoom/History/

**The Jazz Age**
http://arachnid.colgate.edu/tmaikels/jazz.html

**Harlem Renaissance**
http://www.yahoo.com/Arts/Humanities/History/U_S__History/20th_Century/1920s/Jazz_Age/Harlem_Renaissance/

# 9

# Matter, Method, and Machine

## The Synergy of World History, Active Learning, and Computer Technology

*Douglas J. Cremer*

## Introduction

The traditional first-year world history survey, like many other survey courses, usually consists of broad attempts to cover content: the first cities and empires, the origins of religious belief, the development of social and economic structures, and so on. The structure of the course is usually determined by formal lectures by professors, examinations using Scantron and blue books, and perhaps a short writing assignment consisting of a book review or an essay. This model places the emphasis on the transmission of knowledge by a highly trained specialist to a group of apparently passive recipients who are asked to memorize and synthesize the knowledge dispensed through lectures and readings. It is the way many of those reading this essay were educated and the way many of us teach. In our time it was (and in some respects it remains) an effective and useful model of higher education in history.

This model, however, is challenged by a number of developments in and out of academia. These three areas I categorize as: (1) the development of active learning philosophies and techniques; (2) the exponential increases in cultural diversity on many college and university campuses; and (3) the explosion in the use of personal computing technologies. The development of various active learning techniques, such as student-professor collaborations, group work projects, and student-driven discussions, has transformed many university classrooms from lecture halls into workshops. Increasing classroom diversity on multiple levels in one's classroom—not just gender, ethnicity, and race, but also class, family, disability, and past education— challenges any professor to find the right intellectual and cultural level at which to pitch one's lectures. Lastly, the potential presented by newer generations of personal computers—word processing and Internet capabilities, e-mail communications and World Wide Web research—has increasingly removed the professor from the center of the students' learning experience and turned them toward the library and the computer lab. The combination of these factors opens the possibility for a major rethinking and redesign of the first-year world history survey.

## Active Learning

A large quantity of research dating back to 1981 on critical thinking, collaborative work, and active learning[1] forms the foundation of this reconceptualization and redesign. The idea usually subsumed under the short phrase "active learning" involves the following principles:

1. the discovery rather than the transmission of knowledge, or, put another way, the development of questions rather than the delivery of answers;
2. the professor as facilitator rather than dispenser; alternately, "student-driven" rather than "professor-driven" classroom work;
3. the emphasis on both a disciplinary method of critical interpretation and a defined body of disciplinary knowledge;
4. the use of collaborative group learning and projects that are subjected to frequent public assessment and critique.[2]

In terms of world history, these principles work themselves out as an equal emphasis on how historical knowledge is gathered, evaluated, judged, and processed, as well as on the substance of the historical record.

The philosophical challenge of active learning strikes at the heart of what many instructors have experienced as students: the tedium of a poorly done lecture and the thrill of discovering the historical world for ourselves. Practically, it means reconceptualizing the first-year survey in terms of the introductory courses offered in the other social sciences, which focus as much on methods of inquiry as on content knowledge. The use of active learning principles means no longer reserving historiography for history majors, but introducing all students into the pleasures and frustrations of doing historical research. This includes training them to form historical questions, seek answers to their own historical curiosity, explore the limitations of historical materials, and collaborate together to extend historical knowledge.

## Cultural Diversity

These basic concepts of active learning also enable the professor to tailor much of the course to the specific needs and situations of often very diverse students. The challenge of increased diversity—understood here as encompassing not only issues of ethnicity and gender, but also such experiential factors as socioeconomic status, quality of educational preparation, familial responsibilities, and income-producing workloads—is not new by any means. However, the power of multiculturalism, the ideal of the open university, the expansion of student aid and loan programs, and the sweeping globalization of the American economy have transformed the American university. The heterogeneous population of any classroom makes assumptions about prior learning, shared perspectives, and common cultures difficult at best.[3] Similarly, assumptions about what motivates and energizes students to involve themselves in the study of history are subject to the same challenges. One can no longer focus on "a" tradition because both the world and the classroom contain many traditions.

This diversity leads to another challenge, presenting the entirety of world history in just one year in a way that does not fall back on tired Eurocentric themes. Early attempts at world history surveys made the related mistake of emphasizing the marginal, the exotic, and the different, keeping a now-absent Europe at the center of the discourse. The transition from western to world history on many campuses has occasioned a major "reimagining of the world as history"[4]—a major intellectual undertaking that is still in progress after more than twenty years of work in the field of world history. The solution to these issues, approaching diverse students and creating non-Eurocentric world history courses, lies in inviting the students to become actors in their own historical education. The diversity of the student body itself tends toward decentering any particular part of the world or intellectual discourse, and the active involvement of the students militates against making false assumptions about their knowledge and values.

**Personal Computing**

All of this activity, so far, can be done without the necessity of introducing complex technology into one's interactions with students. What the advent of inexpensive, reliable, and fast personal computers has done is to open up an entirely new arena for historical investigation and education that builds on the previous two areas discussed. For example, multimedia-based Web sites such as "The Valley of the Shadow," "Victorian Web," and "Cybrary of the Holocaust" have created significant opportunities for students to explore their own historical questions through the Internet (Ayers 1997; Landow 1996; Dunn 1998). Similarly, the tremendous growth of on-line indexes and collections of documents such as the "Historical Text Archive," "EuroDocs," and the "World History Compass" have increased the amount of historical information available for students' own analyses (Mabry 1998; Hacken 1998; Schiller Computing 1997). These two changes alone have sent many instructors to the Internet as a principle resource in the construction of their courses, as can be seen in the "World Lecture Hall."[5]

If students and professors are turning in increasing numbers to electronic resources, the kind of rethinking or reimagining around issues of active learning and cultural diversity as outlined above is essential as a foundation for the introduction of computer tools into the classroom. If one looks at the efforts to introduce writing across the curriculum and the submission of drafts and revisions facilitated by word processing, one finds that the move to active learning predates the introduction of technology. Similarly, efforts toward incorporating active learning and multiculturalism preceded the introduction of computers in the classroom. The technology enables more and faster applications of active learning techniques, but has not created them in and of itself. Nevertheless, without this preparation in critical thinking, the "flying merge" necessary to enter fully and readily onto the information superhighway would be most difficult.[6] All three challenges can therefore be recharacterized as new foundational concepts for the practice of a new kind of first-year world history course.

## Schedule Construction

The strategy I wish to outline here responds to all three of these challenges. It includes students in the course design process from beginning to end, starting with a collaboratively designed course schedule covering the topics to be discussed and their sequence. It continues with a weekly e-mail or Web-based discussion forum and finishes with the construction of student-designed Web pages. Both the forum and the Web pages become part of the overall course content. The process of collaborating with students on the design of the course schedule is actually much easier and less risky than it sounds. A professor undoubtedly knows more about the subject and its methods than the students and can be more or less directive in this process as might be necessary, insisting on a few topics if the students do not come up with them. This process necessitates spending the first two weeks of class exploring the meanings of basic historical concepts such as memory, significance, perspective, and judgment through a variety of group activities. For example, one could ask students to introduce themselves to fifteen people in the room, find out something "historically significant" about each one of them, place all the names of the people in the class on the board, and list what others found significant about them. This often leads to an interesting discussion of the meaning of memory, significance, perspective, and judgment.

Through a review of the course Web site, the course text, or other resources the professor may wish to utilize, the students are asked to chose ten topics, however they may define them, by the third week of class. Students can be further engaged by referring them to the relevant Web sites that contain indexes and collections to make suggestions for class reading. Their ideas generally fall into the obvious categories of persons, events, movements, or political entities such as Moses, the Conquest of the Americas, Christianity, or the Han Dynasty. By listing these topics on the board in the classroom and beginning to group, organize, connect, and refine them into a final collective list of ten or more topics, the professor uncovers the general curiosity and issues of a particular class of students. Most of that third week is thus taken with the work necessary to brainstorm, outline, assign, and schedule relevant readings or other resources in order to cover the topics selected, a process that produces a finished course schedule. In collaboration with the professor, then, the students have helped to create their own course and taken the first steps in formulating their own approaches to historical study.

**Electronic Discussion**

The preparation for the brainstorming needed to construct the course syllabus is thus also the first opportunity to introduce an electronic discussion. Either a Web-based discussion forum or an e-mail listserv community can serve well. Each week, beginning with the third week, students can be asked to post a message or send in an e-mail journal entry based on the reading or work they have done in the class. Each entry (approximately one full paragraph in length) identifies and discusses at least one major point, observation, story, or criticism they found or formed during the week. These entries are distributed unedited to all the other members of the course, with the professor (or an Internet discussion forum program) acting solely as the moderator of the discussion, occasionally adding an opinion as one of the participants. The aim of these exercises is fourfold.

First, they keep students writing, knowing that constant practice and the critical feedback from others on the list will help sharpen their skills. As early as 1987, educators were noticing that word processing was enabling a whole new culture centered around the frequent rewriting and rethinking stimulated by many drafts; this process is facilitated even more by electronic discussions.[7] Second, the professor is able to keep up with what students are learning, seeing, finding, and thinking on a constant basis. The feedback among the students and with the professor is thus continuous, allowing for adjustments to be made in the course rather quickly. This is an essential element in effective active learning.[8] Third, the mailing list format is a good supplement to the main work of the course, serving much as a teacher-assistant-led discussion section can in a course with three hours already devoted to lecture. It provides an open and relatively safe forum that is more secure and less intimidating for many students who otherwise might refrain from contributing in a more traditional forum.[9] Finally, the e-mail journal allows students to become comfortable with the frequent use of the computer and the resources of the Internet for learning, thinking, and communicating.[10] This is crucial in that all of their research work must be submitted in the form of Web pages.

**Student Web Pages**

Much of the success of active learning comes from its open nature. Student work is not just privately critiqued by the professor, but publicly by the students. It means the work traditionally done by a student for a research paper can now be seen and profitably used by all the students as part of the course itself. This of course necessitates some training in evaluation, both of sources and of student work, but the goals of critical thinking about historical sources and about student projects are remarkably similar. It also means that the research projects have to be carefully guided and limited in scope to fit the objectives of a first-year history course. An essay of one thousand to twelve-hundred words with supporting images, bibliography, and Internet links has worked well in my courses. No specific training in writing Hypertext Markup Language (HTML) is necessary, providing the students have access to current Web editing programs that function much like word processors and to a staff of computer lab technicians willing to assist with problems that may arise.

The students' Web page projects can be posted on commercially available or university maintained Web sites and then linked to the course's main page. Students can be asked to submit a preliminary draft of their Web pages in their midterm review, during which two weeks of the course are taken up with brief oral presentations of the Web pages to the class and a collaborative critique. These weeks give students the opportunity to share the fruits of their own research with the class, as well as to receive constructive suggestions for improving the work, objectives that hold true in all levels of professional historical production. All midterm and subsequent drafts are posted to the students' own Web sites for discussion, but only those pages that meet the evaluative standards worked on in the course are transferred to the course Web site and maintained after the course concludes. They thus can become part of subsequent courses as models of successful Web projects. For an example of this process in its entirety, see the pages for my own World Civilization II course.[11]

## Conclusion

Most history professors began teaching world history in the way we had been taught ourselves: they develop the syllabus and readings independently, lecture and direct discussion after their own agenda, and assign and read term papers on topics they provide. The transition to a course with collaboratively developed course schedules, student-generated e-mail discussions, and projects based around the individual construction of multimedia Web pages is a process with a number of intervening stages, the majority of which are actually *sans* technology. The Internet can play a vital role in a world history course by enabling and expanding the active learning environment. It does not bring it into being by itself; rather the technology is another tool–a highly effective one when properly used—to add to the array of intellectual, pedagogical, textual, and analytical implements that history professors use in the classroom. The resulting synergy can be exciting, at times unpredictable, but above all invigorating to both students and professors.

## Notes

1. Dean Hammer, "The Interactive Journal: Creating a Learning Space," *PS: Political Science and Politics* 30, no. 1 (1997): 70–73.
2. Hammer, "The Interactive Journal"; Lee R. Alley, "Technology Precipitates Reflective Teaching: An Instructional Epiphany," *Change* 28, no. 2 (1996): 48, 54, 56–57; Stephen C. Ehrmann, "Asking the Right Questions: What Does Research Tell Us about Technology and Higher Education?" *Change* 27, no. 2 (1995): 20–27; Elizabeth Anne Yeager and James W. Morris, "History and Computers: The Views from Selected Social Studies Journals," *The Social Studies* 86, no. 6 (1995): 277–283.
3. Marcus Klein, "Multiculturalism and Its Discontents," *New England Review* 18, no. 4 (1997): 75.
4. Michael Geyer and Michael Bright, "World History in a Global Age," *The American Historical Review* 100, no. 4 (1995): 1034.
5. ACITS, "World Lecture Hall," http://www.utexas.edu/world/lecture/his/
6. Trent Batson and Randy Brass, "Primacy of Process: Teachings and Learning in the Computer Age," *Change* 28, no. 2 (1996): 42–47.
7. Ehrmann, "Asking the Right Questions."
8. Alley, "Technology Precipitates Reflective Teaching."
9. Hammer, "The Interactive Journal."
10. Everett M. Rogers, William H. Georghegan, Jane Marcus, and Larry Johnson, "In Response: Four Viewpoints," *Change* 28, no. 2 (1996): 29.
11. Douglas J. Cremer, "World Civilization II," http://remember.org/index.html

## Bibliography

ACITS, University of Texas. 1998. "World Lecture Hall." http://www.utexas.edu/world/lecture/his/

Alley, Lee R. 1996. "Technology Precipitates Reflective Teaching: An Instructional Epiphany." *Change* 28 , no. 2: 48ff.

Ayers, Edward. 1997. "The Valley of the Shadow." http://jefferson.village.virginia.edu/vshadow2/reception.html

Batson, Trent, and Randy Bass. 1996. "Primacy of Process: Teaching and Learning in the Computer Age." *Change* 28, no. 2: 42.

Cremer, Douglas J. 1998. "World Civilization II." http://www.woodburyu.edu/dcremer/courses/wldciv2/wldciv2.htm

Dunn, Michael Declan. 1998. "Cybrary of the Holocaust." http://remember.org/index.html

Ehrmann, Stephen C. 1995. "Asking the Right Questions: What Does Research Tell Us about Technology and Higher Education?" *Change* 27, no. 2: 20.

Geyer, Michael, and Michael Bright. 1995. "World History in a Global Age." *The American Historical Review* 100, no. 4: 1034.

Hacken, Richard. 1998. "EuroDocs." http://www.lib.byu.edu/~rdh/eurodocs/

Hammer, Dean. 1997. "The Interactive Journal: Creating a Learning Space." *PS: Political Science and Politics* 30, no. 1: 70.

Klein, Marcus. 1997. "Multiculturalism and Its Discontents." *New England Review* 18, no. 4: 75.

Landow, George P. 1996. "Victorian Web." http://www.stg.brown.edu/projects/hypertext/landow/victorian/victov.html

Mabry, Don. 1998. "Historical Text Archive." http://www.msstate.edu/Archives/History/index.html

Rogers, Everett M., William H. Georghegan, Jane Marcus, and Larry Johnson. 1996. "In Response: Four Viewpoints." *Change* 28, no. 2: 29.

Schiller Computing. 1997. "World History Compass." http://www.lexiconn.com/lis/schcomp/whl/index.htm

Yeager, Elizabeth Anne, and James W. Morris. 1995. "History and Computers: The Views from Selected Social Studies Journals." *The Social Studies* 86, no. 6: 27.

# 10

# The Bay Area National Digital Library Project and the Library of Congress

## A Case Study in Enriching History Classes with the Riches of the Internet

### Kathleen Ferenz

## Introduction

When I was working as a middle school teacher in 1998, if I had wanted to introduce my students to the riches of the Library of Congress, I would have had to travel to Washington, D.C., and apply for what the Library calls a "reader's card." Today, any citizen can view over a half million digital objects in the Library's American Memory historical collections via a Web browser. In theory at least, students and teachers can digitally sift through George Washington's papers or Walt Whitman's hospital notebooks, listen to recordings from ethnic Northern California communities of the 1930s, explore Matthew Brady's Civil War photos, or view films of San Francisco between 1897 and 1916.

Even though more than 78 percent of all United States public schools and 27 percent of all classrooms now have Internet access, few teachers use these resources. As schools acquire digital technologies, they often find that the challenge is not access to information, but what to do with it all! Ultimately, all kindergarten through twelfth-grade schools will need to ask: Who can manage digital-age information? What role should the librarian play? How can teachers use information technologies effectively? And how will all this result in meaningful learning for our students?

The Bay Area National Digital Library project (BANDL) seeks to answer those questions while posing two others for teachers of humanities: How can we best harness the power of new and emerging information technologies in support of learning? How can schools use curricular and pedagogical changes to transform core relationships between teachers and the ideas that connect them?

## Fremont High: A Typical California School with No Librarian

Like many public schools in California, Sunnyvale's Fremont High does not have a librarian. That position was eliminated in 1981 due to declining enrollment and Proposition 13, which drastically reduced California tax revenues to schools. But library assistance will be essential as Fremont begins to work with the Bay Area National Digital Library, a project that is creating inquiry-based lessons based on the resources of the Library of Congress. To ensure that BANDL has the necessary library support, Fremont plans to ask a full-time teacher to enroll in evening and weekend classes at San Jose State University, one of the nation's few remaining library science programs. Fremont is having to "grow its own" in part because California has so few qualified librarians. Although about half of the state's schools have access to the Internet, California ranks last among the fifty states in the number of students per librarian. Positions for librarians have been scarce here for over a decade, and many candidates have moved away or found new careers.

Moreover, across the nation, the job of school librarian has changed. Today, the school librarian needs teaching and technological skills because the library has been transformed from a room full of books into a central network that reaches beyond physical boundaries, connecting classrooms and students working in their homes to resources across the nation.

To support BANDL at Fremont, the librarian will need to be an information literacy and media specialist who can actively collaborate in curriculum design, provide technology training and coaching to teachers, and redesign the school library to accommodate computerized resources. "We need to reestablish the role of the librarian," says Fremont High principal Pete Tuana. "We need to grow into it. If we don't do a good job of this we will absolutely shortchange the school." If the job is done right, however, Fremont and its students stand to reap benefits that reach far beyond the library into the school's career academics and other course work.

## Connecting Digital Age Library Science and School Reform

Fremont High and the Fremont Union High School District, which has been without school-based librarians for eight years, see the expense of hiring a digital-age librarian as part of a long-term commitment to school reform. Fremont High is a Hewlett-Annenberg Leadership school and part of the Bay Area School Reform Collaborative (BASRC), the Northern California affiliate of the Annenberg Challenge, a nationwide effort to revitalize public schools. The Annenberg Challenge began in 1993, when former U.S. ambassador Walter Annenberg announced the largest private gift to public education in U.S. history, half a billion dollars in matching grants for public schools. The Annenberg Challenge is a public-private partnership that now serves over 1.3 million urban and rural students in over thirty states.

Fremont is participating in BANDL along with two other BASRC schools: Garden Village Elementary and Ben Franklin Intermediate, both in Daly City. At all three schools, the goal is to teach social studies by connecting students' personal lives to the "big ideas" of history. Using Internet-based collections, specifically the American Memory Collection at the Library of Congress and the California Heritage Collection of University of California Berkeley, teachers are coaching students to "be historians." This means that students are learning to find and critically evaluate primary and secondary sources, to present information in ways appropriate to their audiences, and to support their conclusions and ideas.

## What Research Has Discovered about Technology in the Classroom

In traditional classrooms, textbooks and other secondary resources constitute the bulk of all lessons. Teachers and students use primary source materials mostly for show and tell. Similarly, in traditional curricula, teachers use information technology primarily for enrichment or to publish student reports. But, as a recent study in *Edweek* Magazine has shown that's not an effective way to use technology—or to teach students.[1]

Used correctly, technology can serve as a catalyst that improves teaching not only in classes that use technology, but throughout the school. What has now been shown to be most effective is teaching that engages student interest and builds higher level thinking skills. This was shown empirically through recent research commissioned by *Edweek* Magazine, which asked the Educational Testing Service to analyze National Assessment of Education Progress (NAEP) data. They were looking for evidence of whether the use of computers in schools helped or hindered students' achievement. *Edweek* looked at the 1996 NAEP data on a state-by-state basis and correlated computer use with academic scores. Research director Harold Wenglinsky found that computers can both help and hinder: "Used in the right way, technology can stimulate better teaching and learning. Used in the wrong way, it can backfire."

What is correct and incorrect use? Wenglinsky found that eighth-grade students who used computers mostly for "simulations and applications" performed better—two-fifths of a grade level higher—on NAEP tests than students who did not use technology. When teachers gave students "drill and practice" work to do on their computers, they performed half a grade level worse on the NAEP. Similarly, fourth graders whose teachers used the computer mainly for "math and learning games" performed better than students whose teachers did not. Moreover, students whose teachers had received professional development classes in computer use outperformed students whose teachers had not received such instruction.[2] BANDL draws on all these lessons by fully integrating technology into the teaching and learning of humanities in ways that interest and motivate the students, by pushing students to develop higher level literacy skills, and by providing ongoing professional development opportunities for teachers.

## Curricular Considerations

To develop BANDL curricula, teachers must fundamentally change three facets of their teaching: curriculum, assessment, and instruction. Classroom lessons must encourage students to apply knowledge in a meaningful and interesting way, and lessons must be designed to lead to the learning results expected from students. Those results must, in turn, be tied to academic standards, to the essential questions that the unit of study is trying to answer and to whatever curricular big ideas might be worthy of understanding. Finally, teachers need to devise assessments that will clearly show how well students understand the material. Considering this complex interplay of standards, assessment, and curriculum design, it is not surprising that two BANDL schools are involved in reform efforts that focus on those areas.

BANDL's curriculum design is rooted in principles developed by noted authors Grant Wiggins and Jay McTighe, who advocate planning the curriculum "backwards." Wiggins and McTighe argue that teachers should wait to develop specific lessons and to select teaching strategies "until the last phase of the process." Specifically, they write, "Until we have specified the targeted understanding, the assessment tasks implied, and the enabling knowledge and skill necessary to master such tasks and display understandings, a discussion of learning activities and teaching strategy is premature. Teaching 'moves' must be made in light of our goals and what they require."[3]

Drawing on those "backward-to-forward" design principles, BANDL teachers develop their lessons in three separate steps. The first step is for teachers to determine what results they expect from students: to define the academic standards, verbalize what "essential questions" the unit of study will try to answer, and define what "big ideas" are "worthy of understanding." The next step is to devise ongoing assessments that can be integrated into the teaching and into lesson design by asking, "What evidence will we have of how well students understand the material?" The final step is to design classroom activities and learning experiences that will encourage students to apply their knowledge in a meaningful and interesting way. This requires the teacher to undertake a considerable amount of planning, asking, "What activities and resources will students need to make meaning and to understand what is being taught?" There's an adage among technology educators that sums all this up: "It's not about the technology, but more about the learning."

To effectively integrate technology into curriculum, assessment, and instruction, teachers will need the assistance of a digital-age librarian and an up-to-date school library, but they will also require a solid grasp of their subject matter and an understanding of how to teach key information literacy skills. Information technology, guided by a certified professional school librarian, can help teachers to gain skills in both areas.

## The Challenge at the Three Schools

Each of the three schools participating in the Bay Area National Digital Library project—Fremont High, Garden Village Elementary, and Ben Franklin Intermediate school—has a BANDL curriculum and technology design team comprised of several teachers, an administrator, and (at the middle school) a librarian/media specialist. These resources are written into the schools' grants, which are underwritten by a two-year grant from the William and Flora Hewlett Foundation. The schools' teams develop curriculum and pedagogy to draw on new and emerging technology resources and, importantly, to also transform core relationships between teachers and students.

Teams of teachers at all three schools have begun to work with new models of humanities curriculum design and technology integration. They collaborate with each other and receive on-site support from the BANDL coaching staff. Since distance and time are a factor in providing on-demand support for participants, the BANDL coaching staff moderates a Web site for participants as well as a listserv. To jump-start the project, team members from all three schools met in August 1998 at a residential summer institute to promote collaboration among schools, develop an understanding of inquiry curriculum design, sharpen technology skills, and learn what was available in Web-based primary resources.

Garden Village Elementary and Ben Franklin Intermediate, which are located across the street from each other, are now in the second year of a coordinated four-year school reform project. BANDL teams are designing inquiry-based, technology-rich lessons based on the new standards and assessments. Teachers are designing standards and assessments and fully articulating them across all grade levels, K–8.

This year, at Garden Village Elementary, teachers in two upper-grade classrooms—one combined fourth and fifth grade class and a separate sixth grade class—have redesigned the way they teach social studies. Students are creating a history museum that will demonstrate what they have learned about the past and show it is connected to their own lives. In creating the museum, students learn to use primary and secondary sources as well as to analyze and organize what they have learned. In the late spring, when these students serve as docents to other students who tour their classroom museums, they will also be learning to present what they have learned.

At Ben Franklin, interdisciplinary teams of eighth grade Language Arts and Social Studies teachers began the 1998–1999 school year with a unit based on their social studies standard. The unit, entitled "What's Worth Fighting For?" first steeped students in the ideas of the American Revolution. Students then analyzed digitized copies of the Declaration of Independence, early papers from the Constitutional Convention, and other on-line sources. Although the unit was successful, the school faced multiple hurdles in implementing it. Even though Ben Franklin does have a full-time librarian and part-time support staff, the library's print collection is not automated. It also lacks the depth needed to support full-scale inquiries on many topics. To help make up for this, the librarian has received several grants to upgrade information technology in the library. She also collaborates in planning and delivering lessons and teaches information literacy skills to students and staff.

Fremont High has also worked intensively on planning. After attending a summer institute with teachers from the two other BANDL schools, team members developed a year-long plan that included coaching, time for classroom lesson design, and outreach to involve the rest of the school. Veteran teacher Grace Voss, who had never used e-mail prior to the summer institute, surprised her colleagues by opening the school year with a literary unit based on the Civil War–era novel *Killer Angels*.[4] Voss's students successfully developed inquiry skills by locating primary resources that could verify the accuracy of events in the novel.

### Lessons for Other Digital-Age History Teachers

Drawing on what teachers at these three schools have learned, it's clear to me as director and coach of BANDL that teachers will need to grapple with two new skills before they and their students can benefit from lessons developed around primary resources like those of the American Memory collection. First, teachers need to learn to find appropriate technological resources for their classrooms. Second, they need to develop curriculum that successfully draws on those resources. To learn both skills, they will need timely support in the classroom, collaboration at multiple levels, and, above all, time.

All three BANDL schools receive on-site support from the BANDL coaching staff. In each school, a classroom curriculum/technology coach and a librarian consultant meet regularly with teachers and school library staff, and the coach maintains close contact with each school's administrators and district officials. As mentioned earlier, the BANDL coaching staff also provides a Web site for participants and moderates the BANDL listserv. BANDL has also established the Bay Area National Digital Library Librarians Network (BANDLL.net), an additional outreach program that offers staff development opportunities for sixteen school librarians who teach in Bay Area member schools. Through BANDLL.net, librarian professionals and the BANDL coach are working together to take on new roles associated with both emerging information technologies and whole-school change efforts. This group is supported by a moderated listserv and meets for at least four full workdays per year.

## Conclusion

The BANDL project has taught the faculty and staff at its member schools a number of lessons that are applicable to all K–12 schools as they move the teaching and learning of humanities into the digital age:

1. Upgrade your library and invest in on-going training for your librarian and support staff. The librarian should be a skillful user of information technologies, should teach information literacy to both teachers and students, and should provide leadership for school-site curriculum development.
2. Provide opportunities for your librarian and teachers to collaborate on curriculum design. An inquiry-based curriculum demands that humanities teachers have a solid grasp of the subject students will investigate. The librarian can help teachers to upgrade both their subject knowledge and their information literacy skills.
3. Start small and devise a plan to grow out to the rest of your school. When shifting away from traditional curriculum and staff development, a school is implementing a change of norms and culture. By growing skills in-house, a school will create a sustainable change.
4. Support your staff by embedding curriculum design, technology training, and related staff development opportunities into school operations. Teachers need coaching and time for peer collaboration as well as developed strategies for using primary source materials well.
5. Allow more time for planning and management. BANDL teachers say that time is the factor most critical for implementing a shift from

a traditional to an inquiry-based curriculum. Each BANDL school has embedded collaborative planning blocks into its master schedule, and coaching time occurs in addition to regular planning time with peers.

## Notes

1. Jeff Archer, "The Link to Higher Test Scores." *Education Weekly*. Available on-line from http://www.edweek.org/sreports/tc98/ets/ets-n.htm
2. Ibid.
3. Grant Wiggins and Jay McTighe. *Understanding by Design*. (Alexandria, VA: Association for Supervision and Curriculum Development [ACSD], 1998).
4. Michael Shaara. *The Killer Angels: A Novel*. (New York: Ballantine Books, 1996).

## Further Reading

### *Web Sites*

Bay Area National Digital Library Project (BANDL), http://www.wested.org/basrc/bandl/
The Bay Area School Reform Collaborative, http://www.wested.org/basrc/
American Memory Collections, The Library of Congress, http://memory.loc.gov
National Archives and Records Administration, http://www.nara.gov/
California Heritage Collection, The Bancroft Library, http://sunsite.Berkeley.EDU/CalHeritage/
Education Week on the Web. *The Link to Higher Test Scores* by Jeff Archer, http://www.edweek.org/sreports/tc98/ets/ets-n.htm
The Insider's Guide for Preparing your Digital High School Application, http://ctap.k12.ca.us/dhs/

### *Print Materials*

American Library Association. *Information Literacy Standards for Student Learning*. American Library Association, 1998.
International Society for Technology in Education. *National Education Technology Standards for Students*. Eugene, OR: International Society for Technology (ISTE), June 1998.
Loertscher, David V. *Reinvent Your School's Library in the Age of Technology: A Guide for Principals & Superintendents*. San Jose, CA: Hi Willow Research and Publishing, 1998.
Loertscher, David V. *From Library Skills to Information Literacy—A Hand-*

*book for the 21st Century, California School Library Association*. San Jose, CA: Hi Willow Research and Publishing,1997.

Wiggins, Grant, and Jay McTighe. *Understanding by Design*. Alexandria, VA: Association for Supervision and Curriculum Development (ASCD), 1998.

# 11

# Heuristics for the Educational Use and Evaluation of Electronic Information

## Searching for Shaker History on the World Wide Web

### *Deborah Lines Andersen*

**Introduction**

Traditional teaching of history at the high school and undergraduate level has focused on primary and secondary source documents in print format. This focus was out of necessity. These sources, the grist of historical research, were available only in paper formats because of the dominance of print as an information-transfer medium and the sophistication (or lack thereof) of high-quality reproduction and transmission technologies. In the last several years, that tradition has been challenged by information on the World Wide Web. Not only are there secondary source documents available at Web sites, but, with the advent of high-quality scanning technologies, primary source documents are also becoming available electronically.

Electronic access changes the very way in which history students go about doing research. Card catalogs and archival records have been augmented by search engines and Boolean logic. Thus, information access services have been expanded rather than replaced, creating more choice for researchers. Traditional, paper-based research required traveling to libraries or archives in order to have access to primary and secondary documents. The advent of the World Wide Web and scanning technologies has brought about the luxury of being able to sit at one's desk and request that information be delivered via the user's personal computer. Of course, the user no longer holds the book or manuscript in hand. If the document is a primary source, it is not possible to feel the paper, or check for various types of ink, or examine the binding of the pages. Nonetheless, if the information seems pertinent to the research, the user can make an informed decision about whether or not to visit the document many hours away—a great improvement in savings of research time, dollars, and frustration.

The use of the term "augment" is critical to this discussion. Not all information critical to any research project will be found on the World Wide Web. There is little incentive for individuals to put esoteric or rare manuscripts through a scanning process if they are not going to have wide appeal. Research institutes and governmental organizations have started to make historically pertinent materials available on the Web, but the volume of that information is small compared with records available in print formats in repositories (or unmarked, brown paper boxes) all over the world.

The idea for this paper originally surfaced in response to several e-mail messages that circulated among the editors of the *Journal of the Association of History & Computing*. An initial e-mail noted that a junior high school teacher had forbidden the use of on-line resources for a class assignment. "Books only from the library" were the information sources required of students. Responding e-mail related that the same kind of electronic prohibition had been enforced by professors of undergraduate history as well as by a doctoral dissertation committee. These stories raised numerous issues concerning pedagogy at all levels of education. With various academics taking policy stands on whether or not students should be allowed to use electronic sources in their research and writing, it seemed worthwhile to examine these issues in greater detail.[1]

In order to accomplish this goal, this researcher proposed an experiment to search the World Wide Web for materials about the Shakers, as if it were an assignment for a high school or undergraduate class. Using three search engines linked to the University at Albany library home page, the researcher gave herself three hours, perhaps more time than a student would actually use, to find primary and secondary source documents on the World Wide Web that could form the basis for a paper on the Shakers.[2]

The experiment was complicated by the fact that not all materials that appear on the World Wide Web have had the same kind of peer review and editing that one expects from traditional print journals and monographs. This electronic experiment therefore highlighted the need to evaluate the information found on the Web.[3] To this end, the researcher also looked at sources (see "Evaluation of Information" in this chapter) on the Web that would provide guidelines as to how to value information found there. The insights gained from looking at both primary and secondary sources, and at evaluation tools, form a case study of skills, issues, and policy concerns for instructors, librarians, and students. Additionally, the Appendix of this paper presents a technology skills continuum and specific exercises to help students and faculty members become more critical users of World Wide Web materials.

## The Shakers

In Mantissa, England, in 1747, a small group of Quakers led by James and Jane Wardley formed a separate religious society based upon the Quaker beliefs of meekness, simplicity, and pacifism and adopted the seizures, trances, and dancing practiced by the Camisards or French Prophets. They evolved their own patterns of worship, which led to their being derisively called Shaking Quakers and later Shakers (also known as the United Society of Believers in Christ's Second Coming).[4]

Eleven years later, Ann Lee joined the society, and by 1774, with eight other individuals, she sailed to New York to form Shaker communities first in Niskayuna and New Lebanon, New York, and then in Hancock, Massachusetts.[5] Mother Ann, as she became known, held two tenets central to the Shaker religion. The first was that the godhead was both masculine and feminine. The second was that Adam and Eve were lost through their original sin, that God was free from original sin and thus, that the members of the Shaker community would remain celibate—"Hands to work and hearts to God."[6]

Although only a small number of Shakers are alive today, there are Shaker museums throughout the eastern part of the United States, all boasting collections of tools, furniture, and household goods invented and produced by the Shakers, along with archival collections of diaries, journals, and ledgers kept by the various Shaker communities. The number of sources available about the Shakers, their inventions, and their lifestyle makes for plentiful research opportunities. Numerous monograph and journal articles have been written about the Shakers. The challenge for this project was to see how much material was available on the Internet and how difficult it would be to find. Would it be enough to preclude turning to print sources?

## The Experiment

Given three hours and a connection to the World Wide Web, this researcher's plan was to find three search engines, look for any electronically accessed primary and secondary materials on the Shakers, and see if that information would be sufficient to explore topics and write a high school or college level paper.[7] For the purposes of this experiment, the researcher first went to the University at Albany, State University of New York library home page since it has links to over fifteen search engines that a student might use.[8] "Electric Monk," "Direct Hit," and "AltaVista" were all listed on the library Web site. The first two search engines were new to this researcher. "AltaVista" had been on the library Web site for an extended period of time and was familiar.

This was a haphazard selection process, but probably no more hit-and-miss than what a student would do when first selecting a search engine.

## Electric Monk

Electric Monk claimed to be "the first search engine that understands what you're looking for," allowing the searcher to type in a sentence as if asking for information from a reference librarian.[9] This researcher started with the query, "I need any information on Shakers." The results of this ill-formed, "natural language" search were all inappropriate, but they were at least humorous. Of the top ten answers, all rated as "probably contains your answer," there were salt and pepper shakers (in several different patterns including Kate Greenaway dolls, fruit, and Bart Simpson), movers and shakers, the Blues Shakers (a music group), hand shakers (percussion instruments), and cocktail shakers. None of the top ten had any relation to Ann Lee and her Shakers.

Refining the query for Electric Monk resulted in asking for "Shakers as a religious community." This search yielded another ten sites, with several of them (but not all) pertaining to the correct Shakers. Nonetheless, since the purpose of this exercise was to find primary and secondary sources that could be used for a basic paper on the Shakers, the search was not a success. The four sites that were perhaps appropriate were

1. Exhibit: Eleanor Parmenter Churchill: Canterbury Shaker Child (http://wwwsc.library.unh.edu/specoll/exhibits/chrchill)*
2. An HTML version of SHAKER.DOC: A special collection of historical materials at the Dayton and Montgomery County Public Library (http://www.dayton.lib.oh.us/~ads_elli/shakers.htm)
3. About the Shakers: Hancock Shaker Village. About the Shakers. The Shakers, or United Society of Believers in Christ's Second Coming (http://www.hancockshakervillage.org/old/shakers.html)
4. A Brief History. A Brief History of the Shaker Oval Box. The Shaker community has been around since 1774 and is still following the original . . . (http://www.enter.net/~schunsbe/shaker.html)*

Of these four sites, the first was rated as "probably contains your answer" while the last three were rated "might not contain your answer."

Three issues emerged from this query of a randomly selected search engine.

1. It is important to be as specific as possible in constructing search terms.

2. Search engine rating schemes do not necessarily surface the best sites.
3. The sites that do surface will not necessarily meet the needs of the researcher in providing useable primary and secondary resources.

### Direct Hit

The next search engine results were more promising. When the search terms "Religions Shakers" were used, Direct Hit listed its top three sites with a promise to send "an e-mail when the top 10 list changes" if the researcher would subscribe to Direct Hit.[10] Of the top three sites listed, the first was about Quakers. The next two were:

1. Shakers: Priscilla C. Butler. Origins of the Shakers: The Heresy of Mother Ann Lee. Vassar College Department of Religion. Senior Thesis. Fall Semester, 1982. (http://www.ziplink.net/~pcb/and/nat00121.htm)*
2. Shakers—Research Guide: Center for the Humanities. Shakers and Shakerism. A Research Guide. The Research Libraries of the New York Public Library (http://www.nypl.org/research/chss/grd/resguides/shaker.html)*

The senior thesis could be used both for the information that it provided in its text and for the bibliography that it contained (all print, paper materials). The New York Public Library guide was just that—a guide to what was available, but with no primary or secondary documents available on-line.

As with the Electric Monk search, several lessons could be learned from searching Direct Hit.

1. More specific search terms yield a higher percentage of useful results.
2. Results that concern the correct topic do not necessarily contain usable documents.
3. Some sites will lead the researcher to print sources that will have to be examined in a library or archives.
4. Primary source documents appear elusive, or at least hard to identify given the way that information is listed by the search engines (usually just a repeat of the opening lines of the Web page).

### AltaVista

Having used up an hour of the three hours at this point, with only one document, a senior thesis, "in hand," the researcher looked for a more familiar search engine, AltaVista, and entered "Shakers Massachusetts" to see if a geographic location would yield information about the Shaker communities in question. Of the ten results that were retrieved (with 2,432,590 Web pages found!), some were just about Massachusetts, others were about cocktail or salt and pepper shakers, and two seemed to be to the point:

1. Columbia Berkshire Regional Net—Hancock Shaker Village: A National Treasure! Twenty restored buildings, Shaker furniture and crafts, historic farm and gardens, and activities for all ages. (http://www.regionnet.com/colberk.shakervillage.html)*
2. Reminiscences about the Shakers—The Shaker Meeting: "I don't want to be remembered as a chair!" Reminiscences. Nineteenth-Century Shaker Meeting. (http://www.shakerworkshops.com/19th_sm.htm)

This final site at last contained primary source documents about the Shakers. The title "Nineteenth-Century Shaker Meeting" was one of eight "reminiscences" listed at this Web site, each with a citation to the original source. These were not scanned documents, but retyped copies of original letters and diaries. One could read the words but not see the original manuscript. Finding and reading these took up an additional forty-five minutes.

### AltaVista—Again

Having come up with a good source on AltaVista, the researcher requeried the same search engine, this time asking for "Shakers Hancock," another geographic refinement of the search. Again, the search engine found thousands of Web pages and displayed the first ten. These yielded one potentially useful site.

1. Directory Index: Hancock Shaker Village, Pittsfield, MA. Canterbury Shaker Village, Canterbury, NH United Society of Shakers, Sabbathday Lake, ME. (http://www.shakerworkshops.com/dirindex.htm)

This particular site did create additional search terms—other locations that the researcher could use as search commands. It was also from a site that had come up previously in the AltaVista search (Shaker Workshops) so that particular site might be worth searching in more detail. It did not, however, produce any primary or secondary source documents that could be used for a high school or college research paper. After three hours spent on the assignment, several additional lessons and questions emerged:

1. Sites that do not yield useful documents might suggest additional search terms.
2. It takes a long time to examine a hit list to find relevant materials.
3. How long should one spend searching for materials?
4. How many search engines should one look at? This researcher had used three engines, with little time left for additional searching.
5. How does any researcher evaluate the worth of different search engines? Why select one over another?

Given that more than fifteen search engines are available through the University at Albany library home page, it would have been possible to spend several more hours trying out search terms on a variety of engines, going back when new terms emerged, and, it would appear, not finding too much information that would be helpful. This was a frustrating process that did not yield particularly good results. Given the amount of time spent, there was little return on the investment. On the other hand, before the World Wide Web existed, three hours of research time would have been hardly enough to travel to a major research library or archives, to check card catalogs for information on the Shakers, and then examine that information. The potential of the technology appears to have made this researcher much more impatient for immediate information delivery!

**Information for Research and Writing**

In a traditional research environment, historians use primary and secondary source documents to create a historical argument. These documents differ in their origin, authenticity, and reliability as sources of information. It is usually assumed that print information found in libraries has undergone some kind of rigorous review before it appears on the shelves. Either peer review or heavy editorial process "validates" the information so that researchers can assume a certain amount of reliability.[11] Archival materials and other primary source documents do not have that level of review. In fact, the historian's job is to assess the worth of these documents and to see how they support or add to historical arguments and discussion. Part of teaching students history is teaching them to evaluate these primary sources.

The advent of materials on the World Wide Web has created a real dilemma for seasoned historians as well as neophyte students of history. The same level of peer review or editorial process does not necessarily exist on the Web. It is often not clear if an electronic document has undergone serious peer review. Primary source documents often come without adequate provenance, so it is again hard to judge how "good" or reliable they are. The user must be much more cautious and evaluative in an electronic environment. The teacher of history must guard against students' believing that all electronic documents are of the same caliber or, indeed, that all information they need can be found electronically.

## Evaluation of Information

Information sources can be evaluated based upon a large number of criteria.[12] As previously mentioned, peer review and editorial practice have been the usual benchmarks for good practice in print publication. Furthermore, various journals and publishing houses have developed reputations for printing high-quality scholarly works. Scholars in any academic field additionally have internal "editors"—that is, their familiarity with the subject matter, their knowledge of individual scholars, their predisposition about the interpretation of the subject matter, and their basic spelling, grammar, and logic checking—that allow them to evaluate information and its presentation. These are the skills faculties work to instill in high school and college students in academic classes.

The addition of electronic information to this mix means that more evaluation skills need to be passed on to high school and college students. These skills fall into two general classes. First, there is the ability to evaluate the quality of a Web page and how well it presents information. Although this is not the interest of this paper, it is a very important skill for those students who have reached the stage of developing their own home pages.

The second skill, and pertinent to this paper, is the ability to evaluate information that appears on a Web page. Standard criteria for electronic information evaluation include the last date of update and the source of the material. Other criteria include examining the reliability, credibility, perspective, and purpose of the information.[13] More ephemeral is the "face validity" test, in which readers decide if the information seems reasonable, based upon their world view and previous experience with the subject matter.[14]

This last skill takes experience and time. There is, however, a series of recently developed Web sites that attempt to teach students about evaluating electronic material. A query of various search engines on the World Wide Web (April 8, 1999), using the search terms "information evaluation," led to a variety of sources that would help faculty and students understand how to evaluate electronic information. Two of these sources are bibliographies with hypertext links to evaluation literature:

1.  Evaluation of information sources (part of Information Quality on the WWW Virtual Library) at (http://www.vuw.ac.nz/~agsmith/ evaln/evaln.htm). Last updated November 13, 1998.

> 2. Evaluating Web sites and information (http://www.namss.org.uk/evaluate.htm). Last updated May 2, 1999.

These two sources, one from New Zealand and the other from the United Kingdom, include tutorials for students on how to evaluate Web information.

Although there are many examples of Web page evaluation sites (and one can go to the sites listed above to find them), one site was particularly useful for this discussion. EvalWEB, Evaluating WWW Resources was designed as "a tutorial on evaluating Web pages to determine their suitability for use as research sources for middle and high school research."[15] Although last updated on November 30, 1997, the material is such that the concepts have not gone out of date. These concepts include evaluating the address, content, author, revision date, and links, and then drawing a conclusion. For each concept there is a short paragraph describing the issue under discussion. Finally, there are sample sites for the student to evaluate, with subsequent pages that can be used to compare the student's conclusions with those of the "expert." The text of the site ends with information worth repeating:

> Despite all of the media hype, sometimes the internet is not the best resource to use for research. Depending on your topic there may be thousands of reliable pages or none at all. Knowing when to use the internet is part of the challenge of doing research.
>
> You should be responsible enough to recognize when a Web page does not meet your needs, and when it shouldn't be used. By applying these rules to the pages you find, you can help avoid the problem of inaccurate, unreliable information finding its way into your work.

Other sites for faculty and teaching assistants to learn about Web information abound across the Web. In particular, the University of Washington computer training workshop, "Teaching Students to Think Critically about Internet Resources,"[16] and Purdue University's "Evaluating World Wide Web Information"[17] present Web tutorials for helping students and faculty learn the critical points of Web site evaluation.

## Recommendations

From the previous discussion it seems apparent that faculty and students need extensive training about the uses and misuses of electronic information for their research and teaching. Technological illiteracy can lead to assignments that demand no use of the World Wide Web. The ability to find relevant information and evaluate its usefulness is a necessary skill for faculty and students in today's technologically advanced world. Students need to be able to evaluate primary source documents if they are to be good historians. That evaluation now needs to be extended to include electronic information as well as material found in attics and archives.

## A Technology Skills Continuum

There is no one-size-fits-all skill required for acquiring and manipulating information on the World Wide Web. Both faculty and students need to make distinctions about the various skills that individuals need to acquire, both to use the Web for research and teaching and to trust the Web for providing appropriate information. Closely related to skills and trust is the need for careful evaluation of what is provided on the World Wide Web.

A technology skills continuum takes into account a necessary linear progression of abilities as well as several variations on those abilities. The following outline presents those skills:

A Technology Skills Continuum for
WWW Information Acquisition

A. Generic knowledge about computers (windows; word processing)
B. Internet access capabilities (modem or Ethernet technologies, e-mail, Web access skills)
C. World Wide Web access capabilities
   1. Ability to locate a URL on the Web
   2. Ability to locate search engines
   3. Ability to use a variety of search engines
   4. Ability to refine a search to find relevant topics
   5. Ability to evaluate the information found and select appropriate sources
D. Web page development expertise (knowledge of software for creation of Web pages)

The first two items are skills that librarians and instructors are starting to assume of all students. Since various initiatives at the junior and senior high school level have brought computing skills into the general curriculum, students arrive in classes prepared to turn on computers and use them to create text documents. Similarly, it is becoming more and more common for junior and senior high school students to have skills and software that allow them to access the Internet for e-mail. Libraries and home computers have made access potentially available to students. Additionally, students have become sensitized to the quality and reliability of information on the Internet through realization that chat rooms and e-mail pen pal correspondence do not necessarily yield truthful information about others!

World Wide Web access capabilities (see item C above) are not necessarily a tidy package of skills. A student may be able to bring up a Web page, given a specific URL, but inept at searching for additional materials on the Web. One must be able first to locate and then to identify appropriate search engines for the topic in question (C2). One must then be able to use those search engines to perform a fruitful search, keeping in mind that each search engine has its unique set of search algorithms (C3). Using a reasonable set of key words in one engine might not yield equally valuable results in subsequent searches of other engines. Thus, another necessary skill is the ability to adapt and refine a search depending upon which search engine is being used (C4). Finally, a researcher must be able to evaluate the information that surfaces through these searchers (C5). The ability to actually create a Web page (D), which obviously goes beyond the scope of this paper, does not necessarily guarantee the ability to appropriately search for and locate others.

One cannot assume that any high school or college student (or any faculty member in a college or university) has a full complement of the skills just mentioned. Inadequate or partial understanding of electronic information can lead to poor choices not only in using materials on the Web, but also in not using that information for teaching and research.

**Teaching about the World Wide Web**

As the previous discussion suggests, it seems absurd to throw students onto the Web and ask them to find information that meets their research needs. Not only is pertinent information hard to find, but unclear searching is a frustrating waste of teaching time. Students need to be "checked out" on a variety of the skills listed above before they are cast out into cyberspace. Such skills also need to be taught to faculty members who have not developed a fine set of distinctions among the various skills necessary for using the World Wide Web.

In particular, the following suggestions for creating research competencies on the Web should go hand in hand with teaching information evaluations skills, both for print and electronic documents. (See the Appendix, which presents a set of exercises that makes use of the hierarchy of skills listed below.)

1. *Locate a known item.* The simplest of Web skills is being given a site and going to it. This skill includes the ability to move through

links on a site, get back to the home page, and print out or electronically download pertinent materials for future reference.

2. *Visit best practice sites.* Students should be given a set of URLs for sites that the instructor feels are truly excellent. Students should then exercise the skill of finding these sites as well as creating their own evaluation criteria.

3. *Create criteria for evaluation of Web-based materials.* At a certain point students should be able to list their own criteria that lead to good or poor practice in electronic dissemination of information.

4. *Use criteria to evaluate a given item.* Based upon criteria developed by students and faculty, students move to the next level of evaluating an item, or set of items, given to them by their instructor.

5. *Complete a search for a known term.* As a first step in searching the World Wide Web, students should be given a search term for which the instructor knows the results. Ideally, the assignment would provide lessons in what happens when searching a particular engine or engines, with useful as well as humorously useless results.

6. *Compare results from several search engines.* Again, using a controlled vocabulary, where students are given search terms, they should be able to evaluate the results from two or more search engines. (Note that this list has yet to contain an assignment that sends students out to do free-form searching of any topic. The next item finally does this.)

7. *Conduct a free search.* Finally, students should be ready to do research on the World Wide Web using topics and search engines of their own choice. This level of search does not preclude the use of paper-based documents. In fact, by the time students have reached this level, they should be aware of the inadequacies of information on the World Wide Web and the need to conduct research in a variety of formats.

8. *Master sophisticated free searching skills.* Certain skills greatly improve a searcher's ability to find useful information on the World Wide Web, although it is possible to search blindly, using whatever previously acquired skills one has. These high-level skills start with an adequate understanding of one's subject matter in order to create appropriate search terms. Here is the place for dictionary and thesaurus work before spending time on the World Wide Web. Subsequent high-level skills include Boolean logic, and truncation and restriction algorithms.[18] Perhaps equally important is an understanding of the hidden algorithms that various search engines use to create their results. The rating systems of various sites are not

transparent. It is worth having students try to uncover how they work or, very often, do not work to unearth valuable information.[19]

9. *Be sensitive to cost/benefit assessment.* In addition to these specific steps in locating information on the World Wide Web, students (and faculty) need to consider Web time management and information overload. Students might be asked to keep track of how much time they spend doing particular searches, running a cost/benefit analysis of this method compared to traditional library and archival research. They need to be aware of when they have enough information ("satisficing"), rather than increasing research time by doing just one more search before stopping an open-ended research project.[20] Similarly, students should have a set of coping skills that will help them deal with information overload, sifting through masses of information to find what is pertinent and appropriate to their work without having this task consume valuable time that should be spent on creation of insights, synthesis, and historical interpretation.

## Conclusion

It seems quite apparent that the World Wide Web and electronic information are not going to disappear in the foreseeable future. Research and education need to teach students the skills to make critical judgments about information, learn about a wide variety of information sources, efficiently find those sources, and balance the mix of electronic and paper to best meet the needs of historical analysis. These skills are not just about information in electronic format, but about information evaluation in general. We need to be careful about rejecting the message—the information—just because the new medium has created additional challenges for faculty, librarians, and students.

## Notes

\* = Underlining the ephemeral nature of World Wide Web documents, several of the sites that were accessible when checked in March 1999 were no longer accessible in April 1999. It is possible that some documents are permanently lost or others have been changed to different domains.

1. Richard Varn, "Paying Off Faculty Development Deficit Technology," in *Converge* (electronic journal) 2, no. 3 (1999): 42–43; available from http://www.convergemag.com

2. This research dealt with print records. There is an entirely different area of research that deals with nonprint media. The World Wide Web can transmit both audio and video. Thus, the argument about whether or not electronic information access is appropriate could be broadened to ask if a photograph or speech could be experienced adequately over the Internet so that it could form the basis for a historical

discussion. Further, a second broad question asks if any form of access is better than no access if the item is unavailable to the researcher because of travel distance or accessibility restrictions.

3. Throughout this discussion a distinction must be made between student and faculty research. Most of what a serious historical researcher (faculty and graduate students) is looking for would not be found on the World Wide Web. There is little incentive to scan and make available the unique documents that support historical arguments for these researchers. Documents that do appear on the Web are of general interest and thus appropriate for high school or undergraduate researchers.

4. John Harlow Ott, *Hancock Shaker Village: A Guidebook and History*, rev. ed. (Hancock, MA: Shaker Community, 1976), 11.

5. Ibid., 14–15.

6. Ibid., 11.

7. It should be perfectly clear at this point that this research was not designed to duplicate the behaviors of a high school or undergraduate student. The author holds a master's degree in library science, teaches information science, and has worked at a Shaker museum. The experiment was designed to uncover the sorts of materials and challenges that a student might face in this endeavor.

8. See http://www.albany.edu/library/

9. Electric Monk may be found at http://www.electricmonk.com/

10. Direct Hit may be found at http://www.directhit.com/

11. Scott D. Brandt, "Evaluating Information on the Internet" (West Lafayette, IN: Purdue University Libraries, 1996); available from http://thorplus.lib.purdue.edu/~techman/evaluate.htm

12. See Sarah Hinman (http://www.albany.edu/sisp/student.html) under student projects for a discussion of evaluation criteria for Web sites and Deborah Lines Andersen (http://mcel.pacificu.edu/history/jahc/jahcindex.htm) for a discussion of history department sites. Also see John Morkes and Jakob Nielsen for "Concise, Scannable, and Objective: How to Write for the Web" (1997), a summary of four years of Web usability studies (http://www.useit.com/papers/webwriting/writing.html)

13. Brandt, "Evaluating Information on the Internet."

14. Genie Tyburski, "Publishers Wanted, No Experience Necessary: Information Quality on the Web" (Philadelphia: Ballard Spahr Andrews & Ingersoll, Law Library Resource Exchange, 1997); available from http://www.llrx.com/columns/quality.htm

15. EvalWEB may be found at http://www.hudson.edu/hms.comp/evalweb/ *

16. See http://weber.u.washington.edu/~lib560/NETVAL/index.html *

17. See http://thorplus.lib.purdue.edu/rese...lasses/gs175/3gs175/evaluation.html *

18. Boolean logic requires understanding the terms that search engines "understand" to combine multiple search terms. An "and" usually indicates sources that include information on two subjects (Shakers and religion), whereas an "or" requires that only one of these terms be present in a source (Shakers or religion). The default search algorithm for search engines is usually of the "or" variety. Truncation allows one to enter only part of a word, with some symbol such as "*" after it. The truncation should pick up the root with various suffixes (e.g., relig* for religion, religions, religious). Restriction allows one to narrow a search by adding items, often dates, that will target a particular topic or time period. There is no standard method of accomplishing these search strategies across various search engines—one must learn the search system for each of them.

19. See http://www.albany.edu/library/internet/#search for a series of tutorials in World Wide Web search strategies.

20. Herbert A. Simon (1955). A behavioral model of rational choice. *Quarterly Journal of Economics* 69 no. 1, 99–188. Herbert A. Simon used the term "satificing" in the context of the private sector firm, looking at how managers made information choices. A variety of constraints were central to his notion of satisficing—individuals did not look for the optimal solution but a solution that was good enough given various feasible possibilities. Time, funding, or personnel resources could all create constraints on finding an optimal solution. Arguably the same holds true for individuals searching the Web.

21. Edward D. Andrews (1953). *The People Called Shakers: A Search for a Perfect Society* New York: Oxford University Press, and New York: Dover Publications. Kathleen Mahoney. *Simple Wisdom: Shaker Sayings, Poems, and Songs*, (1963); New York: Penguin Press. Clara Endicott Sears. *Gleaning from Old Shaker Journals*, (1916) Boston: Houghton Mifflin Co.

22. See http://www.albany.edu/library/internet/#search for a series of tutorials that will improve users' ability to conduct more and more sophisticated searches on the Web.

## Appendix

### *Exercises in World Wide Web Use: Shaker Museum Sites*

Shaker museums and related Web sites contain a wealth of information about the Shakers and their history. Often mounted and updated by volunteers, these Web pages form a good information base for teaching about the use and evaluation of Web information.

The following exercises follow the text of the paper presented here, suggesting ways in which high school and college instructors could guide their students in the use of Web resources. The exercises are progressive, allowing individuals the chance to develop one set of skills before moving on to the next. In a high school class, it is expected that each skill set would take one or two class periods to acquire if students had access to an electronic lab for their work during class time. In a college setting, students might set out on their own to do several of the assignments at a time. The Web sites listed in these exercises were all active as of April 8, 1999.

*Known Item: (http://www.shakers.org/history.html)*

A first step in acquiring WWW skills is simply going to a known site and then following the links that exist at that site. The URL listed for this exercise gives not only a history of the Shakers, but also links to a variety of other information and sources about the Shakers. In particular, the acknowledgments link gives a list of sources that students could look for in the library. Humorously, a link to "recipes" from the original URL is actually a link to a tour of Canterbury Shaker Village in Canterbury, New Hampshire. That Web site is notable because it gives descriptions and pictures of the buildings at that particular museum.

Along with creating a brief history of the Shakers based upon this secondary source material, students could also create a list of potential search terms for finding additional information about the Shakers on the World Wide Web and in local library databases (for journal articles) and catalogs (for monographs).[21]

*Best Practice: (http://www.passtheword.org/*
*SHAKER-MANUSCRIPTS/)*

This site gives links to copies of six original Shaker manuscripts, either excerpted versions or the complete text. In particular, http://www.passtheword.org/SHAKER-MANUSCRIPTS/Shakers-Compendium/

compndm.htm gives the complete text of the "Compendium," published in 1859 by the Shakers in order to help others outside their community understand more about them. Included are sections on history, settlement, belief, doctrines, and biographies of the founders.

This particular site lends itself to searching for more information about the Shakers than could be found in the "known item" search above and it is a primary source document. For high school students, this site could form the basis for a series of document-based questions (DBQ) about the Shakers. The distinction between primary and secondary sources is quite apparent after looking at the "known item" and "best practice" sites. This site contains a retyped (digital), not scanned (bit-mapped) document.

There are sites that do contain bit-mapped documents of the Shakers. Students still cannot touch the paper or examine the ink, but they are one step closer to the original. At http://www.hancockshakervillage.org/brdsidlg.html, there is a one-page broadside titled "The American Shakers" from circa 1880. No provenance is given for the broadside, although one could probably contact Hancock Shaker Village for more information. The broadside, which gives basic information about the Shakers, was an advertising piece.

Another site contains not only a scanned, primary source Shaker document, but also a transcription of that document. See http://www.logantele.com/~shakmus/journal5a.htm for the scanned document and http://www.logantele.com/~shakmus/journal5.htm for the transcription.

***Item Evaluation:*** *(http://www.hancockshakervillage.org/)*

Having already explored the site for the Canterbury, New Hampshire, Shaker Museum, students should have the opportunity to compare the information presentation of a variety of sites, deciding what criteria a researcher should use when looking at Web information. The URL given in this section is to a guided tour of the Hancock Shaker Village in western Massachusetts. Both sites use pictures and descriptions of various buildings to give the searcher a feel for the museum site and structures.

The Hancock Web site also contains a "Shaker Link" to other sources of information about the Shakers and about Shaker museums. Depending upon the sophistication of the students, a variety of assignments could ask them to evaluate the content and presentation of information at one, two, or more of the sites listed here. Some of these sites are commercial, listing information about programs, hours, and gift shops, while others have more information on buildings, history, and additional sources of information.

1. Canterbury Shaker Village, http://www.shakers.org/index.shtml

2. Shaker Village of Pleasant Hill, Kentucky, http://www.shaker villageky.org/
3. Shaker Museum of South Union, Kentucky, http://www.logantele.com/~shakmus/index.htm
4. http://www.logantele.com/~shakmus/othersites.htm (links to other Shaker sites)
5. Shaker Heritage Society, Albany, New York, http://www.crisny.org/not-for-profit/shakerwv/
6. Sabbathday Lake Shaker Village, Maine, http://www.shaker.lib.me.us/
7. Enfield Shaker Museum, Connecticut, http://www.valley.net/~esm/ This site has a link to several pages of bibliographic materials on the Shakers, for adults and children. All the books listed are available at the museum shop.

## Evaluation Criteria

Having looked at a large number of sites, students should be able to generate a list of criteria they would use if trying to decide the "goodness" of any individual site. This particular exercise could be done as a homework problem or generated with a lot of class discussion and brainstorming. The museum sites listed in the previous section are more than enough to form examples of best practice and sites that could perhaps use some adjustment. (See "Evaluation of Information" in the body of the paper for a listing of evaluation sites.)

## Known Search Term

After having come this far, students will be ready to use one or more search engines. There are so many search engines available today that individuals or pairs of individuals could be sent out to search using a specific term and then come back to the class to report their results. As seen in the body of this paper, "Shakers" as a search term yields more false hits than not, but the instructor might start there. Using specific sites or names will yield more usable results for students.

## Comparison of Results

Having done the "known search term" exercise, students will be ready to compare the results of their searches for materials on the Shakers. Again, this step would lend itself to in-class discussion.

*Free Searching*

Finally, having gone this far in the search process, instructors might send students out to do their own searching and evaluation of Web materials. This assignment could be directed toward a more narrow paper or presentation topic on the Shakers that a student wished to pursue.

*Sophisticated Free Search*

As mentioned in the body of this paper, each search engine has its own peculiarities. Some engines have help links for individuals who want to narrow their topics. Others set up sidebars of related topics or categorize related areas for the researcher. Still others use particular methods of Boolean logic to limit or restrict searches. A sophisticated class of students could analyze the search algorithms apparent, or not so apparent, in various search engine procedures and test to determine which methods give the best results.[22]

*Cost/Benefit Assessment*

Finally, it is no surprise to most people who have used the World Wide Web that it is potentially an enormous time sink. Students might be required to keep a log of time in/time out while working on the projects suggested here, at the same time keeping track of how many useful items, or useful pages of information, were acquired through electronic means. They might also keep track of how many nonelectronic bibliographic citations they found. Undergirding this entire assignment set is the very real possibility that it might be faster or more beneficial to do unknown item searching in a library, rather than spend enormous amounts of time surfing the Web with little research benefit in return.

*Web Page Design*

The discussion of assignments to this point has totally avoided the issue of students' creation of their own Web pages. There is pedagogical value to students in having to create and organize information for hypertext display. Nonetheless, all the exercises proposed in this paper could be accomplished without this last skill.

# 12

# Bringing the Internet and World Wide Web into the History Classroom

## Stephen Kneeshaw

### Introduction

I remember one time reading an early definition of the Internet, including the World Wide Web: "It is the world's largest library, but all the books are spread across the floor." Perhaps at one time that was true—or, at least, close to fact. But while the part about it being a large library remains true, today the WWW is indexed and cataloged and cross-referenced in ways that make it accessible for novices as well as experts. "The information super-highway" seems to be everywhere. Parents introduce their children to the Web at young ages; friends show friends new Web sites; teachers at all levels incorporate Web-based materials into their teaching, and they spend more and more time each day staring at computer screens, trying to stay one or two hits ahead of their students.

History teachers who want to use the World Wide Web for research, for course materials, even for ideas about teaching methods are fortunate to have a wealth of Web sites within a few keystrokes. Small schools and colleges with limited money and space for traditional library-based materials can increase their store of materials hundreds and thousands of times over by using Web resources. They can find out-of-print texts, documents buried in archives, and much more to enliven and energize the teaching and learning process.

But teachers need to exercise care when they bring the World Wide Web into their classrooms. Teachers who encourage students to use the WWW for research can tell you about students' successes. But they are also quick to share horror stories about misinformation their students found and the warped projects that resulted.

One high school social studies teacher tells about the time one-third of his students completed Web-based research on the Holocaust that led them to believe that the Holocaust never happened. A college history teacher writes about a young African-American student whose research on the Ku Klux Klan, much of it based on Klan-created Web sites, led him to present "the KKK as a white equivalent of the Southern Christian Leadership Conference and David Duke as the equivalent of Martin Luther King Jr." These are real problems that might cause some people to question the value of the World Wide Web. But teachers and students can stay clear of these kinds of problems if they understand that they must treat Web-based materials as they would printed matter.

It is important, for example, to ask questions about Web sites and Web-based materials just as you would about a book or an article that you order for class or find in the library. Who created the site? Is the Web site author connected to a reputable institution? Does the author have some standing in the academic or professional community? Note the domain in the URL. Sites in the "dot edu" domain tend to have been through some scrutiny. But even that is not a guarantee—I can show you plagiarism (or what appears to be plagiarism) on at least one major university Web site.

When you get into the "dot com" and "dot org" domains, the same questions apply that you used for "dot edu" sites. But here you also want to look at the leanings (or "agendas") of the Web sites and their creators or the public reputation of the organizations connected to the site. This is something that teachers might want to monitor, especially when younger students begin to use Web sites. Some students believe everything they read in books, and they likely will accept as fact whatever they find on the World Wide Web. This is not a call for censorship, but a recognition that understanding comes with experience. We can use our classrooms and our lessons to teach students to ask the right questions and then to make their own decisions about the value and credibility of Web-based materials.

Experienced users of the World Wide Web might know how to begin a search for ideas and materials for their classrooms. But for novices the first questions is "Where should I start?" One relatively simple way to begin to look for information is to use search engines and directories. Among search engines there are old standards, such as AltaVista, Infoseek, Excite, HotBot, and Lycos, and relative newcomers, such as Dogpile and Google. For directories, the best place to begin remains Yahoo. These all offer user-friendly ways to search for information. Type in a keyword or topic and hit "search" or "fetch" or "go get it" or some other such button, and the computer will do the rest.

If you want to start a little deeper into the World Wide Web and build on research that others have done, you can get right into Web sites keyed to your main areas of interest. These can be broadly defined fields such as "history" or more specialized topics such as "Holocaust" or "Vietnam War" and the like. The annotated list that follows can send a teacher or researcher off in any number of directions.

The list opens with three metasites, moves to ten "best sites" for history teachers and then six sites run by history organizations, and finishes with a lengthy list of WWW sites for history teachers. Here you will find lesson plans, course materials, documents, biographies. Some emphasize the needs of elementary or secondary teachers, while others work best for college and university faculty. Somewhere in this list there will be something for everyone.

## Metasites

### Academic Info
http://www.academicinfo.net/table.html

Academic Info is a subject directory designed for college-level use that provides both annotated listings of Internet sites and gateways to specialized materials. The site offers meta-indexes, general directories, and teaching materials to serve needs at many academic levels. Especially useful is the section on U.S. history—Academic Info United States History—at http://www.academic.net/histus.html, with an annotated directory of Internet resources in American history.

### Index of Resources for Historians
http://www.ukans.edu/history/VL

Maintained by the University of Kansas and "Lehrstuhlfur Altere deutsche" at the University of Regensburg in Germany, the Index of Resources for Historians is an exceptional metasite with more than 3,000 connections arranged alphabetically by subject and name. There are no annotations, but subject breakdowns make this an easily usable site. The list emphasizes college- and university-level history, but some sites are geared specifically to K–12 audiences.

Designed originally as a lynx site accessible by telnet, with text rather than graphics, the index is effective with text-to-speech and text-to-braille, making it friendly to the visually handicapped.

### Lesson Plans and Resources for Social Studies Teachers
http://www.csun.edu/~hcedu013/index.html

This site, maintained by Marty Levine in secondary education at California State University, Northridge, should be the first gateway accessed by elementary and secondary history teachers who want to sample the wealth of the World Wide Web. A clickable table of contents on the opening page leads to nine areas such as "Lesson Plans and Teaching Strategies," "Other Social Studies Resources" (including government and museum sites), "Teaching Current Events," and "Newsgroups and Mailing Lists." The lengthy lists of links are alphabetized and annotated for a quick reading of contents.

## Ten Best Sites for the Classroom

### *American Memory*
http://rs6.loc.gov

The rich collections of the Library of Congress come to life in words and pictures in American Memory. This rapidly growing site, now with forty-two collections on-line, includes documents, maps, photos and prints, motion pictures, and sound recordings. An easy-to-use search engine and a list of entries alphabetized by both keywords and titles provide entry to topics ranging from baseball cards, Civil War photographs, and the conservation movement (one of my favorites) to presidents and first ladies, the Spanish-American War, and "Voices from the Dust Bowl."

### *The Digital Classroom*
http://www.nara.gov/education

The Digital Classroom, from the National Archives and Records Administration (NARA), encourages teachers at all levels to use documents in their classrooms. This is NARA's complement to American Memory from the Library of Congress. The site delivers documentary materials from the National Archives, lesson plans, and suggested methods for teaching with primary documents. The topics already available on-line span a wide range from the *Amistad* case to the Zimmerman Telegram. NARA also provides a reproducible set of document analysis worksheets for written documents, photographs, cartoons, posters, maps, artifacts, sound recordings, and motion pictures that history teachers will find easy to use and attractive for their students.

### *Digital Librarian: A Librarian's Choice of the Best of the Web— History*
http://www.servtech.com/~mvail/history.html

Self-described as "a librarian's choice of the best of the Web" (and run by Margaret Vail Anderson of Cortland, New York), the Digital Librarian covers virtually every academic discipline, many of which are linked to the History page. This site provides an entry point for such diverse topics as the ancient world, genealogy, Judaica, Latin America, the Middle East, and women's resources. For elementary teachers, there are useful connections to children's literature and resources. Lists are alphabetized and annotated briefly, but there is no internal search mechanism.

### History Matters
http://historymatters.gmu.edu

Designed for secondary and college teachers in American history, History Matters combines the efforts of the American Social History Project at the City University of New York and the Center for History and New Media at George Mason University. With an express "focus on the lives of ordinary Americans," this site offers teaching materials, first-person documents (from the Knights of Labor to Sacco and Vanzetti), interactive exercises, electronic essays, "syllabus central," and threaded discussions on teaching history. The current focus is on the years 1876–1946, but eventually the site will grow to cover all of the American experience. A keyword search option allows users easy access to materials in the site.

### History/Social Studies Web Site for K–12 Teachers
http://www.execpc.com/~dboals/boals.html

As the name suggests, this site focuses on the needs of K–12 classroom teachers in locating and using the resources of the Internet. A clickable table opens a wide range of topics, including K–12 resources, archeology, genealogy, geography, American history and non-Western history. This site provides a gateway to some 600 locations, including lesson, commercial, project, and general sites. The one downside is that the lists are not alphabetized, although they do provide brief but useful annotations.

### Kathy Schrock's Guide for Educators
http://school.discovery.com/schrockguide

Maintained by Kathy Schrock, technology coordinator for the Dennis-Yarmouth Regional School District in Massachusetts, this is one of the best-known Web sites for educators. This "categorized list of sites on the Internet," which is updated daily, covers the whole span of academic subjects. Clicking the link for history and social studies opens connections to American and world history as well as "general history and social studies sites." The site also provides links to several search engines, bulletin board ideas, and critical evaluation tools.

### Learning Space—Washington Social Studies Home Page
http://www.learningspace.org/socialstudies

The Learning Space provides many links specific to a single state, here Washington state, but the site has great value for all history teachers with links for history, geography, museums, Holocaust resources, K–12 education, and much more. Each connection provides lengthy alphabetized and annotated lists of Web sites for history teachers at all levels everywhere.

### SCORE History-Social Science Resources
http://score.rims.k12.ca.us

This site, designed primarily for K–12 teachers, comes from Schools of California Online Resources for Education (SCORE). Links include resources and lessons by grade level, resources by theme and topic, virtual projects and field trips, and more. Although one objective of SCORE is to link WWW resources to California's curriculum, this site will be useful to teachers in all states. All of the materials have been evaluated and rated on a 1 to 5 scale by a team of educators, assuring some quality control in such areas as accuracy, grade appropriateness, depth, and variety.

### Studying and Teaching History
http://www.tntech.edu/www/acad/hist/study.html

This fine Web site from Tennessee Technological University aims to create a database of syllabi and suggestions for history teachers and students. Currently available are study guides for history classes from several universities, reference works, guides for research and writing, and links for oral history, maps and audiovisual materials, portfolios, living history and reenactments, studying and teaching history at K–12 levels, and graduate schools.

### Teaching History: A Journal of Methods
http://www.emporia.edu/socsci/journal/main.htm

Designed and maintained at Emporia State University by the publication team for the journal *Teaching History*, this site reflects the main objective of the journal, to provide teachers at all academic levels "with the best and newest teaching ideas for their classrooms." Besides information on the journal, this site provides links to a rich list of resources in ten history-related categories, from American and world history to genealogy, maps, writing and editing, and teaching resources.

## History and Social Studies Organizations

### American Historical Association
http://www.theaha.org

The home page for the American Historical Association provides information on the AHA and on more than 100 affiliated societies, selected articles from the newsletter *Perspectives*, a calendar of historical events, and "a primer" on how the AHA serves K–12 teachers in history.

### H-NCC—National Coordinating Committee for the Promotion of History
http://www.h-net.msu.edu/~ncc

Run through the H-Net group out of Michigan State University, H-NCC is "the official electronic voice" of the National Coordinating Committee for the Promotion of History, which supports history and historians in the political circles of Washington, D.C., and the American states. Included at the site is a connection to past issues of *Washington Updates* that describe the work of the NCC and its lobbying successes. A keyword search mechanism allows easy use of materials in the H-NCC site.

### National Council for History Education
http://www.history.org/nche

The NCHE Web site is more useful than many organizational sites because it goes well beyond descriptions of NCHE and its programs. For example, "History Links" sends a user to a diverse mix of sites: Web sites for historical organizations; history education sites; links of interest to social studies educators; and repositories of primary sources, "a listing of some 3,000 Web sites . . . for the research scholar."

### NCSS Online—National Council for the Social Studies
http://www.ncss.org

NCSS Online offers Web-based information services for the National Council for the Social Studies, the largest "umbrella organization" for social studies educators. This site promotes NCSS, which is to be expected, but it also provides links for professional development, standards and curriculum, and teaching resources.

### Organization of American Historians
http://www.indiana.edu/~oah

The Organization of American Historians is the premier professional association for United States history. But beyond its service to college and university teachers and researchers, OAH serves precollegiate history teachers through such means as the *OAH Magazine of History* and outreach programs, which are described at this site. A link to "History Teaching Units" introduces lesson plans for grades 6–12 based on primary documents developed by the OAH in concert with the National Center for History in the Schools at UCLA.

### Society for History Education—The History Teacher
http://www.csulb.edu/~agunns/relprm/tht01.html

This site, now under construction, will feature the Society for History Education, which publishes *The History Teacher*. The two entities will be linked together through the Web server at California State University at Long Beach, where the journal is housed.

### WWW Resources for History Teachers

### AMDOCS—Documents for the Study of American History
http://history.cc.ukans.edu/carrie/docs/amdocs_index.html

This Web site, managed at the University of Kansas, provides users with one of the richest lists of documents on American history available on the Web. Running from the fifteenth century through the twentieth century, the documents range from Columbus's letter to Ferdinand and Isabella in 1494 to Bill Clinton's inaugural address in 1993. The list is strongest in the eighteenth and twentieth centuries, but the whole of U.S. history gets good coverage. This kind of Web site removes the need to buy document collections for the classroom when such good materials are available at a click.

### AskERIC Virtual Library
http://www.askeric.org/Virtual/

The AskERIC Virtual Library archives hundreds of lesson plans in a variety of disciplines, informational guides on topics of interest to K–12 educators, links to the searchable databases of ERIC Digests (brief reports on educational issues), information on using the Internet in the classroom, and links to other Internet sites. Under both American and world history, AskERIC offers descriptive and adaptable lesson plans for grades 1–12.

### The Avalon Project: Documents in Law, History, and Government
http://www.yale.edu/lawweb/avalon/avalon.htm

History teachers frequently use documents to enrich lesson plans and illustrate key ideas. The Avalon Project of the Yale Law School provides connections to a wealth of documents from pre-eighteenth century through the twentieth century. An alphabetic author and title list for all documents in the collection and a search engine within the project make this a user-friendly Web site that is accessible for all grade levels.

### Awesome Library—K–12 Education Directory
http://www.neat-schoolhouse.org/awesome.html

Awesome Library "for teachers, students, and parents" gives users links to all teaching fields. Under the social studies link, you can click into history and lesson plans or make connections to more specialized history-related fields such as current events, ecology, holidays, and multicultural resources.

### Biographical Dictionary
http://www.s9.com/biography

Biographical Dictionary offers biographies of more than 25,000 men and women "who have shaped our world from ancient times to the present." Users can search the list by names, birth or death years, professions, literary and artistic works, and other keywords, making these men and women easily accessible for students and teachers.

### Biography.Com
http://www.biography.com

This Web site is the gateway to the popular Arts and Entertainment television series "Biography." The Biography.com Store currently stocks more than 1500 videos that have run on the cable network. For teachers who use videos to supplement class presentations, this site will be quite valuable.

## CLNET History Resources
http://latino.sscnet.ucla.edu/research/history.html

This Web site from UCLA provides a gateway (with annotations) to more than thirty sites on Chicano/a and Latino/a history. The diverse resources list links the user to topics such as historical documents, "Hispanics in the American Revolution," the Chicano movement in history, and the Mexican American civil rights movement in the United States.

## Core Documents of U.S. Democracy
http://www.access.gpo.gov/su_docs/dpos/coredocs.html

This Web site from the Government Printing Office delivers more than the title suggests. Beyond such "core documents" as the Declaration of Independence, the Constitution and Bill of Rights, and Supreme Court decisions, users get a statistical abstract of the United States, a weekly compilation of presidential documents, and more. This site will be useful for history teachers who bring current events into their classrooms.

## Dolly and Buster's K–4 Main Page
http://www.concentric.net/~Bigdog89/

For teachers at lower grade levels, Dolly and Buster is a good place to start looking for ideas for the classroom. Users will find everything from lesson plans and classroom activities to teacher tips, information on specific topics, and a teacher e-mail idea exchange. Each site provides more links "to an almost infinite amount of educational resources." The front page also includes a "classroom jump page" as a starting point for K–4 students using the Web, promising "safe, educational, fun links."

## Encyclopedia of Women's History
http://www.teleport.com/~megaines/women.html

This Web site, "written by and for the K–12 community," publishes biographies of historical and contemporary women written by elementary and secondary students. There is a useful alphabetized index of entries and links to "further research" and to other collections on women.

## FREE: Federal Resources for Educational Excellence
http://www.ed.gov/free/index.html

FREE is the result of a "partnership" of teachers and federal agencies to develop Internet-based learning modules and learning communities. The agencies include the CIA, FBI, National Park Service, Library of Congress (American Memory), NARA (Digital Classroom), White House, and others. A "site map" provides connections to various topic areas, including the social studies. Topics are arranged alphabetically with the sponsoring agency identified. There are no annotations, but the descriptive titles give good direction for users.

### The History Channel
http://www.historychannel.com

This Web site provides an easy gateway into the video materials that play on the cable network, The History Channel. "The History Store" is the place to order videos, but this is more than just a commercial site. "Traveler" introduces historic sites and "Great Speeches" provides clips of "the words that changed the world," spoken by such diverse characters from Franklin D. Roosevelt, Malcolm X, and Martin Luther King Jr. to Babe Ruth and Casey Stengel. Classroom materials are available on-line to accompany videos, including vocabulary terms, discussion questions, and extended activities.

### History Departments Around the World
http://chnm.gmu.edu/history/depts

Maintained by George Mason University, this site provides an index of links to all history departments around the world that have an on-line presence. An in-site search engine allows a search for departments in or outside the United States, or a searcher can browse the entire list.

### History Happens
http://www.ushistory.com

History Happens is a commercial site that advertises and sells music video materials for the classroom. Self-described as mirroring the old ABC television series "School House Rocks," History Happens says its primary audience is teachers and parents of children ages eight to fifteen.

### The History Net: Where History Lives on the Web
http://www.thehistorynet.com

When you first look at the History Net, with its clickable list of historical times and topics along the edge, you might think it is just another history Web site. In fact, its major role is to provide links to published articles on the times and topics, using journals such as *Civil War Times, Military History, Vietnam, British Heritage, Wild West,* and *American History.* For an interesting sidebar, the History Net also provides a link to materials on "alternate history," that is, the history that might have been if events had run differently.

### The History Place
http://www.historyplace.com/index.html

The History Place provides a variety of links that will be useful to history teachers, especially at the secondary level. At this point, the site emphasizes American history, but there are some strong sections on Hitler and the Holocaust, with an annotated bibliography on Hitler's Germany. Other European topics are listed "in progress." Users will find time lines (e.g., the Civil War through quotations), photographs, and "points of view," which are reviews and reflections from established writers and historians. The site also offers an annotated list of "Great History Videos."

### History on Public Television
http://www.current.org/hi1.html

Drawing from *Current,* a biweekly newspaper on public television and radio in the United States, this site provides a guide to history programming on PBS, access to stories from back issues of *Current,* and links to various media sites. Teachers will find useful materials to supplement classroom videos that aired originally on PBS.

### H-Net Teaching
http://www.h-net.msu.edu/teaching

H-Net Teaching provides a gateway to an extensive number of sites on teaching maintained by the H-Net system (Humanities and Social Science OnLine) out of Michigan State University. Each of these sites includes edited, threaded discussions on topics of interest to list subscribers and archives, complete with search mechanisms, on previous discussions. H-Net Teaching includes the following:

*H-AfrTeach*—Teaching African history and studies
*H-High-School*—Teaching high school history and social studies (an indispensable site for secondary history teachers)
*H-Mmedia*—High-tech teaching, multimedia, CD-ROM
*H-Survey*—Teaching United States history survey courses (a "must-see" site for college American survey teachers)

*H-Teach*—Teaching history at all levels, with enlightening discussions on a wide range of important topics for history teachers (my personal favorite of the H-Net sites)
*H-W-Civ*—Teaching Western Civilization courses (a companion to H-Survey)

### IBM K–12 Education
http://www.solutions.ibm.com/k12

This site, designed and maintained by IBM, does much more than promote the products designed and sold by "Big Blue." Users will find links to various social studies topics such as American history, baseball, holidays, inventions, maps and mapping, Native Americans, and multicultural education, as well as teacher resources.

### Inter Active Teacher
http://interactiveteacher.com

This site provides an on-line forum with articles and multimedia presentations related to teaching in general. Overall, it has minimal value for history teachers except for a fine list of links to museums around the world that can become the source for virtual field trips for students.

### Internet Archive of Texts and Documents
http://history.hanover.edu/texts.html

This internet archive from Hanover College delivers a variety of primary texts and documents on United States and European history, all from the public domain. The site promises additions for Latin America, Africa, the Middle East, and Asia. Some of the documents come through the Hanover Historical Texts Project; others arrive via links to other repositories.

### Internet for Educators: History and Social Studies Resources
http://www.speakeasy.org/educators/history.html

This site provides a large database of links for K–12 teachers in history, with a clickable chart that allows easy moves into other disciplines, some of which have value in the history classroom, such as arts resources and diversity resources. The list of sites now available in history is small but useful.

### InforMNs—Internet for Minnesota Schools
http://informns.k12.mn.us

Here is another site designed with the needs of teachers in a state—here Minnesota—as the primary focus. But as with the Learning Space (Washington) and SCORE (California) sites (described above), InforMNs delivers information and links useful to a much wider audience. The site also allows quick jumps to search engines, metasearch engines, subject directories, and topical directories through a link to TIES (Technology and Information Educational Services).

### Internet Modern History Sourcebook: History and Music
http://www.fordham.edu/halsall/mod/modmusic.html

As this site notes, it does not provide a history of music. Instead, this section of the Internet Modern History Sourcebook links the user to musical texts and sounds (lyrics and/or music) that illustrate selected topics and times in modern history. Some songs get "streamed" over the Internet through Real Audio. Times run from the Reformation into Modern Europe, while topics include such themes as nineteenth-century nationalism and imperialism. The United States gets some play, but most materials apply to European history.

### K–12 History on the Internet Resource Guide
http://www.xs4all.nl/~swanson/history

This K–12 site, run by two teachers from the Netherlands, provides a series of valuable links for history teachers. Clicking on "general information sources," users enter into a section called "charting the unknown," where a variety of navigational tools and information resources introduce connections to history-related sites around the world.

### The Library in the Sky
http://www.nwrel.org/sky/index.html

Run by the Northwest Regional Educational Laboratory in Portland Oregon, the Library in the Sky offers more than 6,300 links to educational resources for teachers, librarians, students, and parents, in every field of study. History and the social studies get enough attention to make this a useful site for the K–12 community.

### Multimedia/Hypermedia
http://eng.hss.cmu.edu/multimedia

This site offers a sizable collection of media and hypertext materials run through the English server at Carnegie Mellon University and other servers across the Internet. Users will find a good selection of multimedia materials, including ASCII art, audio, public-domain clip art, hypermedia, maps, soundtracks, and videos (using QuickTime technology).

### National Center for History in the Schools
http://www.sscnet.ucla.edu/nchs

The National Center for History in the Schools, located at UCLA, publishes on-line the National Standards for United States History, K–4 and 5–12, the National Standards for World History, and the Revised Standards for History. In addition, "Bring History Alive" introduces source books for U.S. and world history, grades 5–12, with more than 1,200 activities arranged by grade level and keyed to the revised standards.

### Northwest Ohio Computer Association
http://www.nwoca.ohio.gov/www/default.html

The NWOCA home page links users to search engines and subject areas, including history and the social studies. Included here are links to government, news and media, and educational sites. With some topics, world history for example, NWOCA highlights "featured topics" and describes lesson plans from teachers and classroom projects from students.

### ParkNet—National Park Service
http://www.nps.gov

The National Park Service, through ParkNet, delivers one of the best Web sites run and maintained by a U.S. government agency. "Links to the Past" sends users to "Tools for Teaching" (archeology, historic landscapes, structures, and more) and "Teaching with Historic Places" (which gets a full description below). "Visit Your Parks" opens links for all NPS properties. Some of these—Olympic National Park in Washington state, for example—have expanded Web sites that provide attractive resources for teachers, such as lesson plans to pick up and use with ease.

### Presidential Letters—U.S. Postal Service
http://www.usps.gov/letters/volume2/pres-main.html

Organized by the U.S. Postal Service, this site provides—what else—a series of letters that show the "hopes, dreams, [and] passions" of America's executive leaders. With letters from fifteen different presidents from Washington to Reagan, the purpose is "to humanize the men we have chosen to lead our nation." These letters will provide nice supplements for lectures, class projects, and research assignments, especially for secondary-level courses.

### Project Gutenberg
http://www.promo.net/pg

One of the best-known early WWW sites, Project Gutenberg provides a wealth of "fine literature digitally re-published" to bring hundreds of classic works in world history and literature into the classroom as electronic texts at the click of a mouse. An in-site search engine allow users to find e-texts by checking alphabetical lists of authors and titles, which can be downloaded via FTP or the Web.

### Smithsonian Institution Social Studies Lesson Plans
http://educate.si.edu/resources/lessons/lessons.html

The Smithsonian Institution is a storehouse for artifacts in American and world history. This site allows users to tap into the assets of the Smithsonian to find lesson plans in several disciplines, including social studies. This is a developing site that promises to enrich our teaching across the span and scope of history. For an example of the melding of objects and stories, one plan now available focuses on the Bering Sea Eskimo people. Others offer in-depth looks at historical Africa and Japan.

### Social Studies Resources
http://www.kent.wednet.edu/curriculum/soc_studies/soc_studies.html

This Web site from the Kent School District in Washington state provides a variety of lesson plans in all disciplines, including social studies, where teachers can make connections in history, state history, family history, and more. The lesson plans are broken into grade levels—K–3, 4–6, junior high, and high school—which makes them easy to identify and introduce at any level. The resources area, with outline lessons, project ideas, and minilessons, includes separate sections for every grade level K–12.

### Social Studies School Service
http://catalog.socialstudies.com

This commercial site advertises the wares of the Social Studies School Service in Culver City, California. Here users can bypass printed catalogs to locate and order CD-ROMs, laser discs, maps and globes, videos, simulations, and reproducibles, as well as books. Different mechanisms allow searches by grade level; by reading level; or by author, title, and subject.

### Teachers Helping Teachers
http://www.pacificnet.net/~mandel/index.html

Teachers Helping Teachers opened in 1995 under the direction of Scott Mandel, a middle school English and history teacher in Pacoima, California, who updates the site each week during the school year. Now with more than one million hits—testimony to its value for teachers—the site provides lesson plans (all submitted by teachers) for K–12 grade levels. Many of these plans are easily adaptable to a variety of teaching situations. Other useful sections include a teacher chat room and links to educational resources on the Web that have been alphabetized by subject.

### Teaching with Historic Places
http://www.cr.nps.gov/nr/twhp/home.html

This site, run through the National Park Service, focuses on the teaching opportunities presented by properties on the National Register of Historic Places. The purpose is to "enliven" the teaching of history by moving students beyond textbooks to help them "connect history to their own lives." The NPS provides lesson plans, education kits, and workshops to facilitate the integration of historic places into the curriculum.

### Teachnet.Com
http://www.teachnet.com

Opening with the "brainstorm of the day," actually several ideas introduced in one paragraph each, this attractive site packages a mix of materials and ideas that teachers will enjoy and use. Some of the more useful links are "lesson ideas," "teacher-2-teacher," and "how-to" ideas that include everything from classroom decor to classroom management.

### THOMAS
http://thomas.loc.gov/#thomas

Thomas bills itself as "legislative information on the Internet." It is certainly that and much more. Run through the Library of Congress, Thomas follows the work of the United States Senate and House of Representatives, providing summaries, status reports, and full texts of legislation in Congress. The site also provides directories for members of Congress, making it a critical tool for teachers who use current events in their classrooms.

### UCLA's Social Sciences Division
http://www.sscnet.ucla.edu

The UCLA Social Sciences Web site, a fine starting point for social studies links, contains connections to social science departments, institutes, and resources at UCLA. By working through several layers in some program descriptions, notably the American Indian Studies Center, users will get to a series of useful links to other WWW resources.

### United States Department of Education
http://www.ed.gov

This is the official home page of the U.S. Department of Education. It is a good place to learn about federal educational initiatives, and it contains links to related sites, e.g., FREE (described above). Those who are interested also can find a variety of policy documents on-line at this site.

### Web66: A K12 World Wide Web Project
http://web66.coled.umn.edu

For most teachers, the greatest value of Web66 is its ability to link users to most American elementary and secondary schools with a WWW presence, encouraging all kinds of exchanges between teachers across cities, states, and country. Web66 also provides access to Mustang, a "Web cruising vehicle" to help teachers "cruise" rather than "surf" the Web. And the site provides links to many WWW resources in history and the social studies that make it particularly suited to the needs of history teachers.

### Words and Deeds in American History
http://lcweb2.loc.gov/ammem/mcchtml/corhome.html

Here is one more site from the Library of Congress. Actually an offshoot of American Memory (described above), Words and Deeds gives a condensed collection of manuscript materials (with some ninety "representative documents") that can enrich the teaching and study of history. The Library of Congress has provided a detailed description to accompany each document and links to other resources in the library's collection that connect to the documents.

# 13

## Using the World Wide Web for Primary Source Research in Secondary History Classes

*Wilson J. Warren*

One of the most common complaints about secondary school history instruction is that it lacks a critical research focus. It seems that few junior high or high school history teachers do much beside teach the textbook. I often ask my social studies methods students to think about the secondary-level science classes they took in comparison to their history classes. Students can recall dissecting frogs, mixing chemicals, and testing hypotheses in their biology and chemistry classes. But in history students cannot remember looking at historical documents. In fact, based on what they did in secondary school history classes, many have no idea what a primary source is, let alone know how to pose a historical question.[1]

This lack of a critical research focus also contributes substantially to another common complaint about secondary history instruction—its dullness. As sociologist James W. Loewen says in the opening sentence of his widely acclaimed *Lies My Teacher Told Me: Everything Your American History Textbook Got Wrong*, "[h]igh school students hate history." Students typically think of history as not only the most boring but also the most irrelevant subject they take in school. This perception is again directly related to the pedagogical emphasis of most secondary-level history instructors: textbook reading combined with teacher's rehearsal and regurgitation of factual material. Students are not exposed to the interpretive dimensions of the discipline when this type of pedagogy dominates. They also miss out on the potential for interest created by examining the "mysteries" posed by actual historical documents.[2]

Of course, until very recently nearly all secondary history teachers could have honestly protested about limited access to primary sources. Most secondary school libraries contain next to nothing that might be useful for this purpose. Providing students with primary source materials would have entailed photocopying items from a nearby research library or considerable logistical creativity and use of class time in transporting students to larger public libraries, local history museums, or county courthouses. But with the explosion of materials available on the World Wide Web and increasingly widespread Internet access in schools, teachers can less legitimately complain about lack of availability of primary source materials.[3]

As historians, we tend to feel that the advantages of primary source research need no explanation, but it is useful to identify the benefits for secondary students. Without an exhaustive list of these benefits, several can be stated succinctly. Students need to develop the historian's critical thinking perspectives, or "habits of mind," that can be acquired only through the systematic analysis of historical materials. As David Kobrin has outlined in his valuable text, *Beyond the Textbook: Teaching History Using Documents and Primary Sources*, students involved in historical research can learn how "to pose pertinent questions, define problems, analyze relevant information, support their conclusions, and understand their own values." While developing these skills and a more critical perspective, primary research exercises also help students learn to question authority, particularly the typical reliance created by the repetitious use of textbooks and direct instruction by teachers. By helping students pursue primary source analysis and their own construction of history, teachers can also motivate students to become more active in their learning. In the process of engaging in primary source research, many students become enthusiastic about history rather than being bored by it.[4]

Still, convincing the typical secondary-level history teacher to adopt a more inquiry-based approach to the subject can be a challenge. In this respect, my junior and senior social studies methods students are usually as skeptical as the typical secondary school veteran teacher. Their skepticism typically stems from questions about the nature of adolescents' intellectual development—that is, can most kids really adopt the historian's "habits of mind"?—and the ability of adolescents to engage in serious historical inquiry. These are valid concerns. Researchers have found that typical adolescents believe they can understand history without using a process of inquiry and that authorities should not be questioned. After all, many secondary-level students, especially during the middle school grades, are only starting to develop formal operational thinking skills; they are still immersed in what Lawrence Kohlberg identifies as a "conventional stage of moral development."[5]

Instead of simply accepting students' natural limitations, however, secondary teachers need to direct their intellectual development. Studies suggest that students can follow teachers who model good historical practices. Ronald Evans, for instance, has argued that teachers who have clear conceptions of the nature of the discipline can not only make appropriate curriculum decisions, but also successfully shape their students' understanding of history. Other researchers have found that secondary-level students need active, hands-on instructional activities in order to develop their abilities to think more abstractly and ideologically across the entire spectrum of the social sciences.[6]

The most effective (and attention-grabbing) way to engage students in hands-on primary source exercises is by provoking interest, particularly in the affective learning domain. That is, adolescents will be most interested in exercises that challenge their values and beliefs. Kieran Egan has noted that teachers who use historical materials that involve "abstract binary opposites" create dramatic tension that is compelling to students. Egan argues that this can be done without reducing historical issues to simplistic black and white explanations. Interesting details that emerge from strange, awe-inspiring, or unexpected historical episodes are the most effective fodder for historical inquiry activities.[7] For example, history teachers might encourage students to examine slave owners' justifications of how slaves were treated better than industrial workers in the North. Students might even be asked to role play this position.

Another typical concern of my methods students and secondary history teachers is the time required for such investigatory exercises. While it is obviously true that having students engage in primary source examinations takes time away from other activities, the time required does not need to be excessive. Indeed, brief exercises, requiring two or three fifty-minute periods, are probably much more effective for secondary students than longer exercises. As described below, the types of primary source exercises I model for my methods students are designed to take no more than a couple of days of instructional time.

Convinced of the importance of such activities for secondary students, I have my social studies methods students examine the World Wide Web for the purpose of finding sites that could be used for secondary-level primary source research exercises. I usually start my instruction on this topic by modeling two types of Web site use. One is the "prepackaged" primary source exercises that one can adopt for classroom use without much alteration or explanation. The other encourages students to consider sites that might lend themselves to the construction of their own historical inquiry exercises. (The Appendix includes a list of both types of primary source Web sites that could be useful for secondary history classes.)[8]

Some of the best prepackaged exercises can be found on the National Archives teaching materials site.[9] Currently, the site contains nearly twenty sets of documents on topics ranging from the Constitution, the *Amistad* case, black soldiers in the Civil War, the development of barbed wire, women's suffrage, the Zimmermann telegram, the poster art of World War II, Jackie Robinson, to Watergate. Each document site contains reproducible copies of primary documents from the National Archives' holdings. The introductory material for each theme is also linked to the National History Standards and National Standards for Civics and Government. Other related curricular connections are suggested as well. The main National Archives teaching Web site also has reproducible document worksheets that can be adapted for use with other primary source documents a teacher might want to use.[10]

The site on the development of barbed wire lends itself nicely to an integrated thematic approach to industrialization and frontier settlement in the late nineteenth century. I have my methods students consider this site because secondary students are likely to be curious about how barbed wire, a material they would consider mundane, is worthy of serious historical investigation. Secondary students might be intrigued: Just *how* did the development of barbed wire link the frontier's development to industrialization? When my methods students examine the site, I ask them to consider how they might have a class of eleventh-grade U.S. history students use the site after finishing units on the westward movement and the growth of urban-industrial America. Although complete in virtually all other respects, the National Archives sites typically do not provide teachers with suggestions about context. I suggest to my students that they examine the site with this research question in mind: How did the introduction of barbed wire shape the settlement of the West *and* necessitate an urban-industrial society?

The following procedural steps are all provided in the teaching activities of the site. After a nicely focused, yet concise historical background reading, the site provides links to a precise reproduction of Joseph Glidden's 1874 patent application and the accompanying drawing of the barbed wire itself. If computers with Web access are available for the entire class, students working in pairs (as suggested in the teaching activities) could then examine the documents and answer the document analysis questions provided in the site. The teacher should replicate these questions on a study guide for each student. Or, as the site's instructions also suggest, the instructor might make transparencies of both artifacts and project them through an overhead for the entire class.

For document analysis, the site suggests three related steps. The first is free association and brainstorming about images associated with barbed wire. Students then examine the drawing and text of the patent application to answer the following questions: For whom was the drawing intended? Why was it created? What is the inventor actually seeking to patent? What are the strengths of the invention? How well does the written description depict the physical design and intended use? What aspects of the description need enhancement? Finally, after these questions have been answered, students are asked to ponder more complex historical connections to previously learned material: What skills were necessary for the inventor to design these improvements? What skills were required to manufacture, market, and sell the product? What are some connections to professions and technical skills of the era?

Although an instructor might reasonably choose to end the activity at this point, the site provides several ideas for related activities (though pursuing any of them would add to the amount of instructional time needed). In "Writing and Defining a Position," instructors are asked to divide students into four groups, which then write about how the development of barbed wire affected various groups (cowboys or herders, farmers, Native Americans, and wire manufacturers). In "Comparing Written and Visual Descriptions," students are asked to write a description of how they might improve an object they commonly use in class (like a pencil sharpener). Once students have also redesigned this object and compared it to their description, they could then discuss why the patent office requires both visual and written descriptions of inventions.

In "Relating Personal Experiences," students could discuss their personal encounters with barbed wire and speculate about why people today are interested enough in the material to collect it. "Creative Interpretations" suggests that students listen to Cole Porter's "Don't Fence Me In" and read the lyrics. They would then translate the images suggested by the song to some other written medium. The "Further Research Activity" offers the possibility of structuring a similar exercise around another invention that shaped the West, such as the plow or the firearm.

Once the students complete the document analysis and discuss their findings, I feel it is crucial to once again return to the original historical question: How did the introduction of barbed wire shape the settlement of the West *and* necessitate an urban-industrial society? Students should be asked to write a coherent essay response to this question that draws upon their document analysis. A culminating discussion based on their responses may also prove worthwhile.

Although the number of sites offering "prepackaged" exercises using primary documents is steadily increasing, history instructors interested in constructing their own exercises also have a wide array of sites to choose from. Because I stress the use of quantitative information with my methods students, partly since I have used it frequently in my own research and partly because secondary students need more opportunities to manipulate numerical data outside math classes, I have found that the United States Historical Census Data Browser lends itself nicely to quantitative research exercises.

Created by the Inter-university Consortium for Political and Social Research (ICPSR), the site provides access to state and county level data for each of the censuses from 1790 to 1960.[11]

Although not as complete as the published census, the "virtual" census still provides a wealth of data and is certainly more user-friendly, especially for youngsters, than the bound census volumes. Instead of having to handle heavy, dusty, and intimidating tomes, students can learn very quickly how to click on various categories to compile the data they need. While many secondary-level students will initially be intimidated by an exercise focusing on the use of numbers, the potential attraction is not unlike that raised by the National Archives' teaching unit on the introduction of barbed wire. Students are likely to be mystified by how numbers convey important historical insights. It is incumbent upon the creative and adventuresome secondary history teacher to "sell" the use of census data to clear up this mystery.

I introduced my methods students to the virtual census by asking them to envision teaching a unit for an eighth- or eleventh-grade U.S. history class on Gilded Age industrialization. After discussing this era for the nation as a whole, the class would study how industrialization impacted their own area. Given Indiana State University's location in Vigo County, I ask them to examine this issue for our county. To understand Vigo County's economic development during the late nineteenth century, my methods (and their future high school students) must examine change over time. Thus the research question I pose to them: How did Vigo County change as a result of industrialization from the late nineteenth century through the mid-twentieth century?—A question that is particularly relevant since Vigo County has a long industrial heritage.

To begin, I provide each student with a blank chart on which to record census data. Students use the virtual census site to look up county-level data on a variety of variables for the years 1870, 1930, and 1950, including total population, total number of foreign-born, total number of whites, total number of blacks, total number of manufacturing plants, and total number who worked in manufacturing. As in the published census volumes for these years, the census categories that record these variables change somewhat over time, particularly those involving manufacturing employment. I ask my students to combine categories to come up with the most meaningful and consistent answers over time. For instance, while the 1870 and 1930 census categories provide straightforward calculations for the number of people who worked in manufacturing, the 1950 census provides a much more detailed (and convoluted) breakdown by occupation. Students would need to think about the types of jobs involved in manufacturing before realizing that male and female craftsmen and operatives were the four most relevant census categories for that year. For secondary-level students, teachers would certainly need to prompt and direct discussion about such interpretive issues.

After students gathered the raw data on the chart, the next step involved converting, where relevant, the absolute numbers to relative numbers (percentages) for the purpose of comparing the data over time. This type of statistical calculation draws upon skills already learned by middle school students. Still, at the secondary level, history teachers need to explain why percentages are the most useful way of comparing, say, the number of foreign-born to the total population or changes in the number of manufacturing workers to total employment in Vigo County over time. In the manufacturing category, students might also calculate the proportion of workers per manufacturing plant for each year.

Once the percentages are added to the chart, students could then tackle the research question: How did Vigo County change from the late nineteenth century through the mid-twentieth century? I encourage my methods students to start by listing visible trends before composing a more structured essay. To be sure, a teacher should note that these categories are not the only relevant measures of change over time. But even among my methods students, there was a wide discrepancy between those who analyzed the information carefully and systematically and those who simply drew a few rather obvious conclusions. For instance, while the county's total population increased in each year, some pointed out that the rate of change slowed considerably over time. Others noted that the total number of manufacturing plants declined drastically over time while the total and relative number of manufacturing workers increased steadily (which was most evident in their calculations of the proportion of workers per plant).

Because my methods students already had considerable U.S. history background, they could explain this change by references to the trend toward industrial consolidation. At the secondary level, given students' much more limited historical backgrounds, a teacher might urge them to speculate why this trend is evident. In this way, the exercise would help students learn to construct meaningful historical hypotheses that could be "tested" as they learned more history.

Whether secondary history teachers use prepackaged primary source exercises or construct their own, the World Wide Web should prove invaluable for injecting needed authenticity into secondary history classrooms. After some experimentation and careful attention to structuring the assignments, secondary history teachers should realize that many Web sites are quite accessible to their students. In turn, students who tend to be fascinated by Web sites already, will be drawn into historical inquiry exercises in a way that may transfer to greater enthusiasm for the discipline in general.

## Notes

1. Larry Cuban, "History of Teaching in Social Studies," in *Handbook of Research on Social Studies Teaching and Learning: A Project of the National Council for the Social Studies*, ed. James P. Shaver (New York: Macmillan Publishing Company, 1991), 197–209.

2. James W. Loewen, *Lies My Teacher Told Me: Everything Your American History Textbook Got Wrong* (New York: The New Press, 1995), 1.

3. For a generally negative assessment of the Internet's value to historians, see Andrew McMichael, "The Historian, the Internet, and the Web: A Reassessment," *Perspectives* (American Historical Association Newsletter), 36 (February 1998): 29–32. The U.S. Department of Education's *The Condition of Education 1998* reports that, between the fall of 1994 and 1997, Internet access in public schools increased from 35 to 78 percent. More important, by the fall of 1997, 27 percent of instructional rooms had Internet access.

4. David Kobrin, *Beyond the Textbook: Teaching History Using Documents and Primary Sources* (Portsmouth, NH: Heinemann, 1996); O.L. Davis Jr. and Elizabeth Yeager, "Classroom Teachers' Thinking about Historical Texts: An Exploratory Study," *Theory and Research in Social Education* 24 (1996): 146–66; Marcy Singer Gabella, "Beyond the Looking Glass: Bringing Students into the Conversation of Historical Inquiry," *Theory and Research in Social Education* 22 (1994): 340–363; Steven A. Stahl, Cynthia R. Hynd, Bruce K. Britton, Mary M. McNish, and Dennis Bosquet, "What Happens When Students Read Multiple Source Documents in History?" *Reading Research Quarterly* 31 (October/November/December 1996): 430–456. Stahl et al. are cautious about the utility of primary source analysis for history students, but they do suggest that if teachers structure these exercises carefully students can think like historians. Also useful in providing suggestions for a more creative and hands-on (applied) secondary history teaching focus are James A. Percoco, *A Passion for the Past: Creative Teaching of U.S. History* (Portsmouth, NH: Heinemann, 1998); and Bruce A. Van Sledright, "Arbitrating Competing Claims in the Classroom Culture Wars," *OAH Newsletter* 27 (February 1999): 7–8.

5. Quoted in Gabella, "Beyond the Looking Glass."

6. See, for instance, several of the essays in *Handbook of Research on Social Studies Teaching and Learning: A Project of the National Council for the Social Studies*, ed. James P. Shaver (New York: Macmillan Publishing Company, 1991), especially James A. Mackey, "Adolescents' Social, Cognitive, and Moral Development and Secondary School Social Studies," 134–143; Mark C. Schug and William B. Walstad, "Teaching and Learning Economics," 411–419; and Murry R. Nelson and Robert J. Stahl, "Teaching Anthropology, Sociology, and Psychology," 420–426. Also see Andrew S. Hughes, "Toward a More Thoughtful Professional Education for Social Studies Teachers: Can Problem-Based Learning Contribute?" *Theory and Research in Social Education* 25 (1997): 431–445.

7. Kieran Egan, "Layers of Historical Understanding," *Theory and Research in Social Education* 17 (1989): 280–294.

8. Kathleen M. Noonan, "Untangling the Web: The Use of the World Wide Web as a Pedagogical Tool in History Courses," *The History Teacher* 31 (February 1998): 205–219. Noonan's essay targets the use of the Web with college students. But her essay's three main emphases (providing material normally not available, supplement-

ing course themes, and developing critical skills for evaluating Internet sources) apply equally well to secondary-level students.

9. http://www.nara.gov/education/teaching/

10. Lee Ann Potter, "National Archives Expands Digital Classroom," *Perspectives* (American Historical Association Newsletter) 37 (February 1999): 3–4, includes a concise yet thoughtful evaluation of the primary source activities found in the National Archives' web site.

11. http://fisher.lib.Virginia.edu/census/. For a detailed description of a census database project designed for the college U.S. history survey level, see Trudi Johanna Abel, "Students as Historians: Lessons from an 'Interactive' Census Database Project," *Perspectives* (American Historical Association Newsletter) 35 (March 1997): 1, 10–14. The United States Census Data Browser site also allows for more complicated cross-tabulations for more sophisticated searches.

## Appendix

### *Primary Source Web Sites*

1. History Texts/Documents, *http://history.hanover.edu/texts.html*
2. The History Place, *http://www.historyplace.com/*
3. Library of Congress, *http://www.loc.gov/*
4. National Archives, *http://www.nara.gov/education/teaching/*
5. United States Historical Census Data Browser, *http:// fisher.lib.Virginia.edu/census/*
6. New Deal Network, *http://newdeal.feri.org/*
7. Internet Modern History Sourcebook, *http://www.fordham.edu/ halsall/mod/modsbook.html*
8. Japanese American Exhibit and Access Project, *http:// www.lib.washington.edu/exhibits/harmony/*
9. Cybrary of the Holocaust, *http://remember.org*
10. University of Oklahoma Law Center History Documents, *http:// www.law.ou.edu/hist/*
11. University of Kansas WWW-VL, *http://history.cc.ukans.edu/ history/WWW_history_main.html*
12. The Labyrinth: Resources for Medieval Studies, *http:// georgetown.edu/labyrinth/*
13. American Memory Project, *http://rs6.loc.gov/amhome.html*
14. AFL-CIO, *http://www.aflcio.org/*
15. The Great Chicago Fire and the Web of Memory, *http:// www.chicagohs.org/fire/*
16. History of Elections, *http://www.multiEd.com/elections*
17. Hagley Museum and Library, *http://www.hagley.lib.de.us*

# 14

# Facilitating "Incursions into the Novel" Now and in the Future

## The Use of Computers in Middle School Social Studies

*A. Keith Dils*

## Introduction

In *Democracy and Education*, John Dewey argues that learning is a personal "incursion into the novel."[1] This paper investigates present and future benefits, as well as problems, associated with using technology in a middle school classroom to facilitate incursions into novel concepts of history and social studies. The sections that follow detail a technology-aided initiative devised to demonstrate three main aspects of facilitating such an incursion: (1) how the computer diversifies the curriculum by enabling the teacher to reach various learning styles of middle school students; (2) how the application of constructivist computer activities can effectively address experiential learning styles; and (3) how traditional teacher-centered approaches—augmented with the use of Microsoft PowerPoint presentations—can effectively reach verbal, kinesthetic, and visual learning styles. The discussion ends with a cautionary note regarding uses of technology that do *not* contribute to the learning objectives of the classroom.

## Student Use of Technology with Constructivist Learning Principles

Constructivist learning principles—supported by the writings and theories of Dewey, Piaget, and von Glasersfeld—afford history and social studies educators one way to facilitate "incursions into the novel" via a diversified curriculum.[2] When using this approach, educators can effectively reach students with experiential learning preferences, because constructivist approaches do not rely solely on the direct transfer of knowledge from the teacher to the student (as in teacher-centered approaches). More wisely, constructivist approaches take into account that "learners do not passively absorb knowledge, but rather construct it from their own experiences."[3] Accordingly, teachers who use constructivist approaches act as coaches who provide students with appropriate learning experiences that lead to "incursions into the novel."[4] These teachers also act as knowledgeable guides who can empower students to reflect on those experiences as they relate to the goals of education.[5]

## Constructivist Learning: An Example of a Technology-Aided Project

To be sure, a main goal of public education is to teach students to be responsible, active citizens.[6] However, because active citizenship is beyond the direct experience of most eighth graders and because the experience provided by an isolated classroom does little to expand that experience, constructivist history and social studies teachers can engage students by providing multimedia forays into the world outside the classroom. Instead of attempting to browbeat students into accepting the value of democratic participation, I undertook a technology-aided project that challenged students to increase voter turnout in their town.

Students were provided with a desktop computer, video camera, and a handheld audiotape recorder. The students then wrote, produced, and acted in a public service announcement that was placed on the air by a local radio station throughout election day. The goal of the project was that students construct their own knowledge of the benefits of voting. The public service announcement suggested that citizens should voice their complaints and influence policy not by verbally complaining, but by voting. After the service announcement had played in the community, students utilized the computer to run comparisons between the voter turnout of past years and the current year's turnout. While the increase in voter turnout from 60 to 61 percent could not be necessarily tied to the student's project, they were then encouraged to hypothesize about the effect of their project on voter attitudes. By considering the results and implications of their constructions, students recognized the potential impact of their efforts on the democratic process.

Other students in the class used a video camera to create a public service announcement for television. However, due to the lack of editing equipment, the quality was poor. That project did not continue beyond the classroom. The "incursion into the novel" for those students ended on the teacher's desk.

## Future Technology-Aided Project

John Dewey also states that it is crucial for students to reflect on the "relation between what we try to do and what happens in consequence."[7] Those students who created high-quality radio spots had many positive consequences to consider. Unfortunately, the students who lacked the proper video-editing equipment did not experience as many positive consequences. If both sets of students had the technology to produce high-quality work, then the reflection on both learning experiences would have been profound. With additional software and computer memory, both classroom experiences would help to provide a lifetime of positive reflection on the relation between what the students tried to do and the resultant positive outcomes.

In the near future, I will have a computer with editing software and the appropriate memory to capture and edit video as well as audio. As the price of this technology drops, it will be purchased inexpensively by school districts and will greatly enhance the students' understanding that participation in a democracy can effectuate positive consequences. Even though eighth-grade students cannot participate by voting, they *can* influence others to vote. Such influence may very well reinforce the effectiveness of democratic participation. Nonetheless, this is not the only goal of history and social studies.

### Constructivist Learning: The Creation of a Classroom Multimedia Presidential Trivia Game

Another main goal of public education in history and social studies is the development of research and critical-thinking skills applied to "real world" problems. These skills have been developed, at times, in the public schools before the introduction of computers. But computers have increased the speed and ease of research. The Internet appears to be the quickest and potentially most useful research tool for middle schools, but there is some evidence that much Internet research is of dubious quality.[8] Students need, therefore, not only to be skillful researchers, but also to be critical in evaluating what they have researched. Learning experiences involving research must be designed so that the computer's speed is used to facilitate both research and the verification of the accuracy of that research.

One way to use a constructivist approach in fostering such skills involves having students construct an accurate and entertaining computer presentation depicting a presidential trivia game. After conducting library research on U.S. presidential facts, I gave the students one class period to complete Internet research at our school's computer lab. The students gathered information and worked in pairs to construct PowerPoint presentations showing the results of their research. The presentations were saved on a floppy disk and taken back to the classroom to be presented to the class.

The classroom learning experience component included three different modes. Whereas one pair of students gave their PowerPoint presentation on a big screen television, two teams of students sat at computer terminals hooked to the Internet and to CD-ROM encyclopedias in order to check the accuracy of the presentation. The rest of the students sat at their seats and used their textbooks to check the accuracy of the presentations. This type of critical analysis not only focused student attention on the historical information, but also enabled the class to observe the possible inaccuracies of research and to verify the authenticity of information gathered from various Internet sites.

**Future Internet Presidential Trivia Web Site**

The researched information about U.S. presidents can be applied to the "real world" by having students construct an educational Internet Web page. Most schools in the near future will have a home page that can house a collection of all the research done by students throughout the year (including traditional student papers demonstrating more extensive historical investigations). A presidential trivia game could entice World Wide Web "surfers" to explore the rest of the home page. Students would have experience the intrinsic pleasure of discovery in response to the "real" problem of attracting readers to our history/social studies research Web site.

**Constructivist Learning: Authentic Computer and
Noncomputer Learning Stations**

Constructivism and reflective inquiry learning principles challenge teachers to provide excursions that convert abstract concepts into concrete understandings. This is done by allowing students to analyze "real" situations. Many Internet and some CD-ROM activities are available to generate this type of analysis.[9] Still, there is a problem: getting thirty or more students onto a limited number of terminals during one class period is a herculean challenge in many schools. The use of stations provides a possible answer.

For example, when covering the Bill of Rights, students were actively engaged by rotating through both authentic computer as well as authentic noncomputer activities. One computer activity entailed showing a video clip on the use of a fire hose against demonstrators during the Civil Rights movement. Students then participated in a small group discussion concerning which amendment was involved and whether the video clip depicted the abuse of rights. After several minutes of discussion and analysis, students recorded their observations and then moved to a noncomputer station displaying, for instance, the school's disciplinary referral form stating, "Johnny will serve detention for praying before a test." Once again, students held a small group discussion concerning which amendment was concerned and whether the hypothetical student's rights were being abused. The students continued this process until they reached all the computer and noncomputer stations.

## Future Authentic Computer Experiences

Within the near future, students at our middle school will be able to engage in station work that includes videoconferencing with citizens from other parts of the country and the world. Students at a station will be able to communicate visually and verbally with citizens in Australia. This would provide a valuable addition to a debate, for example, on mandatory voting, since Australia is a country where voting is mandatory. For now, stations may be the only way to get all students involved in this type of classroom activity. A decrease in the cost of technology hopefully will reduce the need for stations as students' access to personal laptop computers increases. No matter how students utilize computers with constructivist strategies, they are but one part of a diversified curriculum, which also includes the traditional teacher-led lecture/discussion format.

## Teacher-Centered Instruction: The Use of Computers to Enhance Lecture and Discussion Formats

Computers in the classroom also help to diversify the middle school curriculum by enhancing the traditional teacher-led incursions. Essential knowledge provides what the writers of a Yale Report of 1828 called the "furniture of the mind," or the mental structures that abstract ideas may inhabit.[10] The traditional teacher-centered approach may be the best learning experience for introducing students to such essential knowledge. The computer can be a tremendous tool for helping teachers to accomplish this. In fact, some evidence indicates that the visual appeal of computer presentations enhances motivation and achievement.[11] Although the traditional teacher-centered approaches of lecture/discussion are effective for students who are verbal learners, the computer can augment presentations to more effectively reach students with other learning styles.

## Teacher-Centered Instruction: An Example of Computer-Assisted Teacher Presentations Facilitating Kinesthetic and Visual Learning

The use of presentation software (e.g., Microsoft PowerPoint or Apple HyperStudio) can enhance lectures covering the recent history of the Republican and Democratic parties. For example, a series of Likert-type survey questions was designed to help kinesthetic learners assess their stance on issues as they related to Democratic and Republican platforms. This Likert-type scale was then constructed and projected via PowerPoint so that students could read and respond to questions about the death penalty, abortion, and military spending. Responses were then correlated to a line on the chalk board with the words "liberal" on the left, "moderate" in the middle, and "conservative" on the right. After calculating their responses, kinesthetic learners then experienced a kind of human scatter plot, or representations of data on a scale, by walking up to their place on the liberal-conservative continuum.

Presentation software can also assist visual learners during lecture/ discussion. In teaching the Bill of Rights, I have challenged my students to develop mnemonic devices that I then converted into a visual equivalent and projected to the class via PowerPoint. For example, the students suggested that the First Amendment's ideals of freedom of expression be associated with the pop singer Madonna's number one hit song "Express Yourself" and that the freedoms of religion, assembly, press, petition, and speech be associated with the anagram R-A-P-P-S (a further association with Madonna's "rapping"—a form of singing she is known to use). A PowerPoint projection of Madonna "rapping" helped put the First Amendment into the long-term memory of my eighth graders. Students also created another mnemonic device that made remembering the Second Amendment's right to bear arms almost effortless—"two bare arms." In order to reach the visual learners, I showed a PowerPoint image depicting a man reaching into a pile of guns with two bare arms.

Video clips provide another means to reach visual learners. A vicarious experience of watching a clip of Jimmy Stewart's filibuster in *Mr. Smith Goes to Washington* enabled eighth-grade students, in an otherwise isolated classroom, to take a trip to the Senate floor. After a class debate about the removal of President Nixon from office at the end of the Watergate scandal, a video clip of Nixon resigning connected, in a powerful way, what was said in class to what actually happened. Finally, rather than merely talk about what it would be like to experience Martin Luther King's power as leader during the Civil Rights movement, the showing of his "I Have a Dream" speech, at a critical time in the lecture, brought to life that moment in history. Inserting a three-minute clip of a video at a crucial time in a lecture/ discussion can help fulfill what Dewey has termed a "quest for something that is not at hand."[12]

**Future Use of Computers to Enhance Lecture and Discussion Formats**

In the future, teachers may be able to insert in a lecture or discussion virtual excursions for students via computerized information provided by digital icons, indexes, and symbols. This use of technology is very different from its current application. As Kimberley M. Osberg notes:

> Virtual reality goes at least one level above multimedia in terms of perceptual richness and locus of control. The primary difference is in intent; multimedia is a representation, whereas virtual reality is a simulation, intended to fool the senses into believing that the participant is perceiving their "physical" body to be in another place. And yet, it is the reintegration of the body in the search for knowledge that provides such a compelling tour de force to the technology. . . . This last point is particularly powerful in education. By bringing our bodies back into the search for meaning, we can at long last become fully, not just intellectually, integrated.[13]

Even though this technology is still emerging, one can imagine the possibilities of its future educational applications.

**Conclusion: A Cautionary Note Concerning the Reliance upon Technology**

The value of using the computer in a middle school history or social studies classroom derives from its utility in diversifying the curriculum and, therefore, addressing the various learning styles of middle school students. Experiential learning styles can be effectively exploited by applying constructivist learning principles activities such as having students use technology to increase voter turnout, construct presidential trivia Web sites, and engage in authentic station work. In addition, augmenting traditional teacher-centered approaches with the PowerPoint presentations can effectively accommodate verbal, kinesthetic, and visual learning styles. However, as with any learning activity, if it is not used properly, then it will not help educators reach their educational objectives.

I observed a classroom engaging in a virtual debate conducted over the Internet with another school. At the time of the debate, the majority of schools with this technology were suburban schools attended by students of similar socioeconomic backgrounds. Because the schools had similar students, no materially different perspectives were added to the dialogue. Such use raises an important question. Rather than use technology to scan the globe for what can become a "safer," more detached virtual interaction, why not develop the students' interpersonal communication skills and critical-thinking skills by forgoing the use of technology and having students look each other in the eye and experience the risky, spontaneous face-to-face exchange of ideas? Whether teachers use computers in support of constructivist learning experiences or traditional teacher-centered learning experiences, it should be done in a way that increases the attainment of educational objectives—not merely for the sake of using technology. With either learning approach, the thoughtful application of computers in a middle school classroom can be an excellent way to provide the conditions for students to enjoy "incursions into the novel."

## Notes

1. John Dewey, *Democracy and Education* (New York: Macmillan, 1916), 158.
2. John Dewey, *How We Think* (1910; reprint, Lexington, MA: Heath, 1982); Jean Piaget, *To Understand Is to Invent* (New York: Viking Press, 1972); Ernst von Glasersfeld, "A Constructivist Approach to Teaching," in *Constructivism in Education*, ed. L. Steffe and J. Gale (Hillsdale, NJ: Lawrence Erlbaum, 1995), 3–16.
3. P.T. Ashton, "Editorial," *Journal of Teacher Education*, 43, no. 5 (1992): 322, quoted in James M. Jennings, "Comparative Analysis, HyperCard and the Future of Social Studies Education," ERIC Documents ED381439 (1997): 3.
4. Barbara A. Boyer and Penelope Semrau, "A Constructivist Approach to Social Studies: Integrating Technology," *Social Studies and the Young Learner* (January/February 1995): 14–16.
5. James M. Jennings, "Comparative Analysis, HyperCard and the Future of Social Studies Education," ERIC Documents ED381439 (1997): 3.
6. National Council for the Social Studies. *Expect Excellence: Curriculum Standards for Social Studies*. Electronic Publication on NCSS Online (January 1996).
7. Dewey, *Democracy*, 144–145.
8. Kevin M. Oliver, Gene L. Wilkinson, and Lisa T. Bennett, "Evaluating the Quality of Internet Information Sources," ERIC Documents ED412927 (1997).
9. For example, *Virtual Senator* is a real-time role-playing game where one is cast in the part of a United States senator, found on the Web at http://tqd.advanced.org/2900/cgi-bin /sim.htm; Microsoft Encarta 1999 CD-ROM Encyclopedia contains several video clips and other hands-on activities.
10. Excerpts from the Yale Report of 1828 are published in *American Higher Education: A Documentary History*, ed. Richard Hofstadter and Wilson Smith, 2 vols. (Chicago: University of Chicago Press, 1961), 275–291.
11. Adel Sultan and Marshall Jones, "The Effects of Computer Visual Appeal on Learners' Motivation," ERIC Documents ED391488 (1995); Bill Heidenreich, "The Effects of HyperStudio on the Achievement of Seventh Grade Social Studies Students," ERIC Documents ED412895 (1992): 58.
12. Dewey, *Democracy*, 148.
13. Kimberley M. Osberg, "Constructivism in Practice: The Case for Meaning-Making in the Virtual World," http://www. hitl.washington. edu /publications/r-97–47/.

## Bibliography

Ashton, P.T. "Editorial." *Journal of Teacher Education*, 43, no. 5 (1992): 322. Quoted in James M. Jennings, "Comparative Analysis, HyperCard and the Future of Social Studies Education." ERIC Documents ED381439 (1997): 3.

Boyer, Barbara A., and Penelope Semrau. "A Constructivist Approach to Social Studies: Integrating Technology." *Social Studies and the Young Learner* (January/February 1995): 14–16.

Dewey, John. *Democracy and Education*. New York: Macmillan, 1916.

———. *How We Think*. 1910. Reprint, Lexington, MA: Heath, 1982.

Heidenreich, Bill. "The Effects of HyperStudio on the Achievement of Seventh Grade Social Studies Student." ERIC Documents ED41289 (1992): 58.

Hofstadter, Richard, and Wilson Smith, eds. *American Higher Education: A Documentary History*. 2 vols. Chicago: University of Chicago Press, 1961, 275–291.

Jennings, James M. "Comparative Analysis, HyperCard and the Future of Social Studies Education." ERIC Documents ED381439 (1997): 3.

National Council for the Social Studies. *Expect Excellence: Curriculum Standards for Social Studies*. Electronic Publication on NCSS Online (January 1996).

Oliver, Kevin M., Gene L. Wilkinson, and Lisa T. Bennett. "Evaluating the Quality of Internet Information Sources." ERIC Documents ED412927 (1997).

Osberg, Kimberley M. "Constructivism in Practice: The Case for Meaning-Making in the Virtual World." http://www.hitl.washington. edu /publications/r-97–47/

Piaget, Jean. *To Understand Is to Invent*. New York: Viking Press, 1972.

Sultan, Adel, and Marshall Jones. "The Effects of Computer Visual Appeal on Learners' Motivation." ERIC Documents ED391488 (1995).

von Glasersfeld, Ernst. *A Constructivist Approach to Teaching*. In *Constructivism in Education*, ed. L. Steffe and J. Gale. Hillsdale, NJ: Lawrence Erlbaum, 1995, 3–16.

# 15

# Social Studies Simulations in Upper Elementary Classrooms

## R. Bruce Lewis

### Background of the Problem

As America's educational systems move into the twenty-first century, teachers and administrators are encountering increasing pressure from parents, students, business, and government to make effective use of emerging computer technologies. A few years ago, teachers and parents demanded that students should have access to a fairly recent set of encyclopedias; now they want students to have access to CD-ROM encyclopedias and on-line research materials.

This demand reflects the dramatic reductions in cost that have brought powerful computers and sophisticated software within the reach of most students and their families. The twenty-first-century classroom and its resources will be vastly different from the classroom of the 1950s, and teachers must adjust to the influences of new electronic technologies and our growing knowledge-based society.[1] Previously, education was teacher- and textbook-centered. Electronic technology has almost made textbooks obsolete, as Brian Plane argues elsewhere in this volume, especially from the viewpoint of updating references in modern history and geography books.[2] With electronic encyclopedias available that are constantly updated, the year-end encyclopedia annual supplement is an item of the past. For example, a set of encyclopedias with a publication date of 1987 would now have twelve or so annual supplements, if purchased each year. Obviously, not many children researching a report on the planet Saturn are likely to look through twelve additional volumes to see what new material has become available. The CD-ROM encyclopedia or an on-line reference source is much more likely to contain current discoveries and analyses.[3]

Our present rate of knowledge explosion calls for teachers to investigate ways to keep themselves and their students current.[4] Most schools have recognized the growing shift in telecommunications within their midst and have adopted system-wide responsible use policies that students and guardians are required to sign. For example, the West Warwick School Department in Rhode Island has its responsible use policy on-line.[5]

## Statement of the Problem

When teachers do not provide today's students with a classroom approach that models the integration of varied skills and disciplines, they are neglecting the future.[6] As Wicklein and Schell have demonstrated in their case studies of integrated mathematics, science, and technology instruction, a multidisciplinary approach helps students understand how subjects fit together and build upon each other.[7] In this vein, America's future lies with embracing the Technology Age, and this must begin in the classroom.

Unfortunately, educators do not seem to be using the available technology to promote critical thinking skills. The author's research evaluated the growth in critical thinking skills that may result from the incorporation of Minnesota Educational Computing Consortium (MECC) social studies simulation software into the upper elementary curriculum as compared to more traditional classroom approaches.[8] Through an interdisciplinary approach that incorporated MECC's *The Yukon Trail* simulation software, the critical thinking skills of analysis, evaluation, and synthesis were strengthened.[9] Activities were modeled for use in social studies, mathematics, science, geography, literature, and language arts classes. This approach increased the students' ability to assess the importance of information in a hypothesis, to judge the reliability of information on the basis of its source, to judge whether a statement follows from the premises, and, finally, to identify assumptions.[10]

As many studies have shown, computerized simulations such as MECC's software can also increase motivation and promote authentic learning in the classroom.[11] Farris and Cooper state forcefully that the appropriate use and integration of educational technology is "fundamental" to successful social studies instruction.[12] This changing role for teachers means additional and different preparation of student teachers and a modification of attitudes toward student learning.

## Simulations

Simulations are simplified models of activities that call upon the student to assume roles and make decisions according to the constraints imposed by the game or program.[13] In the mid-1950s computerized simulations were introduced into business training programs.[14] Flight simulation programs were one of the first examples of simulation games sold when microcomputers became popularly available in the early 1980s. These early flight simulators also provided a glimpse of the educational potential of interactive role-playing games. Research showed that groups who played the games performed significantly better than a no-game group in the subsequent test flights.[15]

The Minnesota Educational Computing Consortium was one of the pioneers in social studies simulations with *The Oregon Trail*. Other titles have followed with the same basic premise of participants making decisions, enduring hardships, and performing tasks similar to those faced by the adventurers the particular game seeks to portray. As the children go through the simulation, they not only learn about the history, geography, and culture described in that particular software program, but also improve in reading comprehension, logic, and problem solving.[16]

Chapin and Messick discuss social studies simulations as learning activities that present an artificial problem or event that tries to duplicate reality, but without any risk to the participants.[17] Simulations have a gamelike quality that students enjoy, often motivating them to work at a higher level. One advantage of *The Yukon Trail* simulation is that it can help students understand such abstract concepts as supply and demand and inflation.[18] Students also learn to weigh multiple perspectives and the future impact of decisions made today. A quality simulation cannot be mastered in one sitting, but rather requires some reasonable amount of time to be proficient and master the scenario's complexities. Jonassen has observed that effective simulations require well-structured activities, such as those outlined in the author's research.[19]

Using simulations prior to the actual instruction alerts students to what is transpiring in the instructional process.[20] Computer-Aided Instruction (CAI), such as *The Yukon Trail*, is not intended to replace teachers, but to supplement the teacher's role, especially in instructional tasks that require intensive record-keeping. In circumstances where students cannot keep pace with their class and require a great deal of individual attention and special tutoring, teachers can give these students a CAI software program that keeps them working on appropriate tasks that they can manage while the teacher devotes attention to others. CAI will enable the teacher to have more time for motivational tasks, handling discipline, and providing individual instruction to other specific student needs.[21] Wicklein and Schell indicated that one of their case studies reported improved student motivation and a reduction in discipline problems as a result of the cooperative efforts of the students involved in the integrated curriculum approach.[22] Another case study reported that the students themselves were able to see the direct applications of the course they were taking.

Small-group collaborative projects organized around a computer-based social studies simulation can avoid problems experienced with more traditional collaborative learning exercises, particularly the lack of a detailed record of team activities and individual contributions for grading purposes.[23] Cooperative activities build socially acceptable behaviors, including open communications involving honesty and trust, cooperation, conflict management,[24] friendliness, assertiveness,[25] self-esteem, and coping ability.[26] These social skills seem to have tremendous impact on academic success, since peer relations and interaction skills forecast overall school achievement. A sense of perspective, the ability to see the other person's point of view, is also negatively related to later delinquency.[27] As students work through *The Yukon Trail* program and listen to the advice and opinions of the various characters, they must make decisions related to their interpretation and understanding of that character's perspective.[28]

## Critical Thinking

Critical thinking is a complex concept, but an understanding of critical thought enables students to take the basic tools of critical thinking that they learn in one subject and extend them, with proper adjustments, to all the other subjects that they study. Once students learn these generalizable critical thinking skills, they need not be taught a subject simply as a body of facts to memorize; history, for example, can be taught as historical reasoning. Curriculum can be designed so that students learn to think historically, and mathematics can emphasize mathematical reasoning. Students can be taught so that they learn how to bring the basic tools of disciplined reasoning into every academic subject.[29]

Teaching for critical thinking enables students to explicate, understand, and critique their own deepest prejudices, biases, and misconceptions. Genuine fair-mindedness is achieved by developing critical thinking skills in dialog with others where students gain empathic practice in entering into points of view that they are fearful of or hostile toward.[30] Unfortunately, most assessments are based on lower-order learning and thinking. The chief culprits have been the multiple-choice, machine-graded assessments focused on surface knowledge. Higher-order thinking and critical thinking abilities are increasingly crucial to success in every domain of personal and professional life.

Students should be able to demonstrate the ability to "distinguish clearly between purposes, inferences, assumptions, and consequences; discuss reasonably the merits of different versions of a problem or question; decide the most reasonable statement of an author's point of view; and recognize bias, narrowness, and contradictions in the point of view of an excerpt." They should also be able to "distinguish evidence from conclusions based on that evidence; give evidence to back up their positions in an essay; recognize conclusions that go beyond the evidence; distinguish central from peripheral concepts; identify crucial implications of a passage; evaluate an author's inferences; and draw reasonable inferences from positions stated."[31]

## Using Technology to Develop Critical Thinking

Jonassen identifies databases, spreadsheets, semantic networks, content expert systems, computer-mediated communications, multimedia, and hypermedia as "mindtools," selected application programs for engaging and enhancing thinking in students.[32] He believes that students learn from thinking in meaningful ways and that they can then use computer applications to represent what they know. He argues that the most appropriate use of computers is as a cognitive tool for accessing information and interpreting and organizing personal knowledge. The computer application programs that Jonassen identifies as "mindtools" can be used to represent knowledge in a variety of subject areas; they are "generalizable" and engage learners in critical thinking.[33]

Critical thinking skills such as evaluating and analyzing can be engaged through the process of information retrieval, particularly through research on the Internet. The Internet is a worldwide network of interconnected computers from universities, military bases, government agencies, corporations, and organizations, and millions of microcomputers in businesses and homes. Through the World Wide Web (WWW), students can easily correspond electronically with others around the world. Telecommunications can be used to send and receive electronic mail, "chat" with other computer users around the world, look up information in databases, explore computer bulletin boards, or download files (transfer them from another computer to your computer) via modems that are used to modulate and demodulate computer information, so that it can be sent over a standard phone line.[34]

But the power of the WWW lies beyond mere access to and retrieval of information. The Web has the potential to not only change how and when we access information resources but also impact the way we process and communicate knowledge and information, both in written and oral form.[35] Critical thinking skills such as assessing and identifying assumptions can be engaged via e-mail, while computer conferencing using listservs, bulletin boards, and newsgroups can integrate the analysis and evaluation of the issues being discussed. Computer conferencing can engross participants in elaborating on ideas, analyzing opinions and perspectives, and then synthesizing various positions.[36]

MECC simulation software (*Africa Trail*, *MayaQuest*, *Oregon Trail*, *Oregon Trail II*, and *The Yukon Trail*) can be used in a variety of ways relating to the skills appropriate to different fields. For example, in language arts, *The Yukon Trail*'s computerized journal can be used for writing exercises and reflections about research and readings done by the students.[37] During *The Yukon Trail* simulation, one of the characters the students encountered at Dawson City was Jack London, the author. To expand this element, some of the classes were asked to select oral readings from London's *The Call of the Wild*. In the future, students could be asked to read a complementary or contrasting account, such as Velma Wallis's *Two Old Women: An Alaska Legend of Betrayal, Courage and Survival*, that is applicable to the Yukon Trail experience.[38]

In geography, teachers made use of the map skills developed in the software program and through the selected readings from *The Call of the Wild* and poems by Robert W. Service. The map skills were reinforced through application to tracking (through live Internet coverage) the annual Iditarod Sled Dog Race.[39] In conjunction with simulation software, such exercises provide powerful education tools. Mapping skills, strategy formulation, record-keeping, and deductive reasoning are all developed by game-type problem-solving programs and simulations such as *The Yukon Trail*.[40]

For science, students reviewed weather conditions for Seattle, Washington (where the journey to the gold fields begins), Skagway and Dawson, Alaska (two cities in the region around the gold fields), and the Northwest and Yukon Territories of Canada. Students can also monitor the weather via the Internet sites for the Iditarod race. Students were also asked to investigate relevant minerals (relative value of gold, silver, iron ore, etc.), mining techniques and methods (1897 compared with 1998), and materials and clothing production (1897 compared with 1998).[41]

In math, teachers explored supply and demand economics and inflation. The mathematics for calculating and assessing percentage changes (as supplies dwindle, prices increase) were also treated. Distances between significant sites were determined, and the distance traveled each day in the Iditarod race could be charted.[42]

In *Elementary and Middle School Social Studies: A Whole Language Approach,* Farris and Cooper suggest that social studies teachers use the K-W-L strategy to integrate materials and to connect with students' existing knowledge.[43] This is a three-step approach in which students take an active role in understanding social studies materials by discussing what they already know (K) and what they want (W) to know about a subject. In the case of the MECC simulation, students were asked what they already knew about the Yukon gold strike, then what they might want to know, and finally, after the simulation exercises, they were asked to explain what they had learned (L).[44]

Farris and Cooper also indicate that cooperative learning is an effective instructional approach that allows for peer interaction in a noncompetitive environment.[45] *The Yukon Trail* software program lends itself to cooperative learning, as most activities are best accomplished in pairs or small teams; therefore, each of the treatment classes was divided into smaller groups of four based on the availability of computers.[46] For the author's research, groups of four students worked together on the computerized simulation, with one serving as the facilitator, one as the recorder, one as the researcher, and one as the reporter for the group.[47]

Additional ideas and information about using technology in the classroom were made available at the researcher's Web site on the Internet and through several discussion groups.[48] Also, Abenaki Associates made twenty-two lesson plans for using the Internet available on-line.[49] Groups that are available in the areas of educational technology and social studies education include Educational Technology/EDTECH,[50] H-NET's Discussion List for the Association for History and Computing/H-AHC,[51] and the National Council for the Social Studies/NCSS-L.[52]

Since those characters in *The Yukon Trail* software program who have both a first and last name are, supposedly, real people, teachers had the students use print sources and the Web to research a particular character. The students then gave oral reports in their language arts classes about their chosen character.[53] Some of the groups also provided printouts, posters, and other types of visual presentations. Due to a lack of computer and software availability, multimedia presentations were not attempted.[54] Sealey discusses the latest enhancements to multimedia authoring packages, including Wagner's *HyperStudio* and Pierian Spring's *Digital Chisel 3*.[55] He identifies these tools as having a small learning curve and the power to motivate students to design exciting interactive projects. These products have the ability to combine text, sound, and still and animated graphics into customized interactive presentations.

A recent posting to the discussion list "Middle level education/early adolescence (10–14)" revealed that "in 1996, Internet access was available in about half (53 percent) of the schools in which seventy-one percent or more students were eligible for free or reduced-price lunch programs and in fifty-eight percent of schools in which thirty-one to seventy percent of students were eligible. In comparison, seventy-two percent of schools with eleven to thirty percent of students eligible for the free or reduced-price lunch program had Internet access, and seventy-eight percent of those with less than eleven percent of students with free or reduced-price lunch eligibility were connected to the Internet."[56] The school involved in Lewis's research had a text-only connection to a local university in only one of the third-grade classrooms. These research activities were conducted in fourth-grade class-rooms that did not as yet have the necessary technology available for graphical Internet connections. However, an informal assessment by the researcher showed that approximately half of the students had graphical Internet connections on their home computers.[57]

## Summary

Numerous studies, such as those by Desberg and Fisher, have demonstrated the usefulness of simulations in enhancing later student performance. Other studies have addressed the issue of using technologies, such as databases, spreadsheets, semantic networks, content expert systems, computer-mediated communications, multimedia, and hypermedia, as "mindtools" for enhancing thinking in students.[58] However, few studies have addressed the specific concern of the possible impact of social studies simulations upon critical thinking. The author's study addressed that particular shortcoming.[59]

## Methodology

To evaluate the growth in critical thinking resulting from the incorporation of MECC's simulation software into the upper elementary curriculum compared with more traditional classroom approaches with no intervention, the researcher created and provided to the teachers of the classes weekly lesson plans for integrating *The Yukon Trail* software program, related materials, and the Internet into the regular curriculum. The lesson plans were specifically designed to build critical thinking skills in fourth-grade students. The success of this interdisciplinary and multimedia approach in developing and enhancing the student's critical thinking skills of analysis, evaluation, and synthesis was measured by the Cornell Critical Thinking Test.[60]

## Participants

Twelve self-contained elementary classes were selected from the Madison County, Alabama, Public School system. Intact classes were selected so that both the control group and the treatment group were as nearly comparable as possible, particularly with regards to gender, race, and socioeconomic backgrounds; however, it was anticipated that the statistical procedure of analysis of covariance (ANCOVA) would be necessary to equate the treatment and control groups for initial differences on the pretest.[61] Six elementary classes were selected for the treatment group, while the remaining six served as the control group. Each of the students in the selected groups was administered the Cornell Critical Thinking Test as a pretest and a posttest.[62] The treatment group incorporated MECC's *The Yukon Trail* simulation software into all areas of the curriculum, assisted by the researcher, while the control group continued with regular classroom approaches with no intervention from the researcher.[63]

## Collection of Data

The author determined that four to five elementary classes as a treatment group would be sufficient for testing the hypothesis,[64] but Vickey Sullivan, Technology Training Specialist for Madison County Schools, was able to arrange for six classes to participate. Groups of this size provide a representative sample and produce generalizable results according to educational researchers.[65] The purposes of the study were explained to school authorities and assurances given that no students would be identified individually. The participants in this study were pretested in spring 1998 in their respective classrooms by their respective teachers, with the aid of the researcher.[66]

## Instrument

The researcher used the Cornell Critical Thinking Test, Level X, developed by Robert H. Ennis and Jason Millman, as a pretest and a posttest. The test, in four sections, assesses the importance of information on a hypothesis, assesses the ability to judge the reliability of information on the basis of its source, assesses the ability to judge whether a statement follows from the premises, and, finally, focuses on the identification of assumptions.[67] Mark Davison and Karen Anderson, researchers at the University of Minnesota's Center for Applied Research and Educational Improvement, acknowledge that the Cornell Critical Thinking Test has "a solid theoretical basis" and "sound technical characteristics."[68]

## Statistical Treatment of the Data

The fourth-grade classes in this study were administered the Cornell Critical Thinking Test, as a pretest and a posttest; however, the actual number of students varied due to normal absences and transfers. The statistical method used to test the hypothesis in this study was the Analysis of Covariance (ANCOVA) at the .05 probability level, with the dependent variable being the critical thinking score as measured by the posttest completed by the participants. This ANCOVA was used to equate the treatment and control groups for initial differences. It was hypothesized that there would be an increase in performance on the posttest due to the dependent variable (the treatment). The ANCOVA was used to determine if a significant difference existed between the treatment group and the control group on the posttest scores, as a sign of the effectiveness of the treatment.[69]

## Analysis of the Data

This study focused on the dependent variable of critical thinking skills, as measured by the Cornell Critical Thinking Test, Level X, completed as a pretest and a posttest by the participants in spring 1998. As indicated by Crowl, this study was quasiexperimental since, in educational settings, it was deemed appropriate to the research to use intact classroom groups. The specific school was selected by Vickey Sullivan, Technology Training Specialist for Madison County Schools, based upon her assessment of the available technology within the school and the system. The school's principal, Eleanor Smithers, and each of her fourth-grade teachers agreed to participate in the mid-March to mid-May research and treatment.[70]

The researcher was aware that, because intact classrooms were used and the study was quasiexperimental, the treatment and control groups might not be similar at the beginning. Therefore, a two-sample t-test was run on the pretest scores. As expected, the number of participants varied with 133 students taking the pretest in the treatment group and 121 students taking the pretest in the control group, with the results shown in the table.

**Participants, Means, and Standard Deviations**

| Madison County School System, Alabama | Cornell Critical Thinking Test Statistics | |
| --- | --- | --- |
| | Treatment group | Control group |
| Pretest participants   254* students | 133 students<br>30.79 mean<br>8.73 SD | 121 (63 58)<br>33.97 mean<br>8.23 SD |
| Posttest participants   252* students | 136 students<br>33.89 mean<br>8.57 SD | 116 (64 52)<br>34.90 mean<br>7.32 SD |

*Not all of the pretest participants were available for the posttest and certain others took the posttest who had not taken the pretest.

Additionally, the two-sample t-test revealed that the control group scored statistically significantly higher at the .05 level than the treatment group [t (251) = 2.99; $p$ = .0031]. Therefore, an analysis of covariance (ANCOVA) was used to control for these initial differences between the control group and the treatment group.

An ANCOVA on posttest scores, with pretest scores as covariate, according to Dugard and Todman, "usually provides a more appropriate and informative analysis" than an analysis of variance (ANOVA).[71] The ANCOVA also "provides a more powerful test of the hypothesis" than the ANOVA approach. While the ANCOVA computation is complex, the increased power of modern computers has eliminated the extra computational effort as an issue of concern for the researcher.[72]

In the ANCOVA, the adjusted posttest scores were analyzed to compare the treatment and control groups.[73] The analysis yielded an F ratio of 141.30 for the treatment and 6805.59 (dfs = 248) for the pretest. The ANCOVA was set to yield a 95% confidence level,[74] but in fact the result was a $p$ value that was less than .001. The treatment group's performance on the Cornell Critical Thinking Test was statistically significantly different at the .001 level, revealing that the treatment group performed much better than the control group.[75] Consequently, the null hypothesis was rejected.[76]

**Discussions of Findings**

The null hypothesis stated that there would be no statistically significant difference, at the .05 probability level, in the critical thinking skills, as measured by the Cornell Critical Thinking Test, between the treatment and control groups. An Analysis of Covariance (ANCOVA) was used to analyze the posttest scores, with pretest scores as covariate, and determined that the differences were statistically significant at the selected probability level of .05.[77] These results are in keeping with the researcher's review of the relevant scholarly literature.[78]

The researcher conducted a preservice training session for the treatment teachers and provided follow-up staff development on a weekly basis. Each of the treatment classes had at least one Macintosh PowerPC computer for student use, on which the author installed *The Yukon Trail* software donated for this project by MECC. An introductory lesson was provided by the researcher to each class, introducing the simulation program to the teachers and students, and setting forth the basic ideas and purposes for this research project. Particular attention was paid to building the critical thinking skills of analysis, evaluation, and synthesis that would be necessary for success as the student teams worked through *The Yukon Trail* simulation. Some teachers expressed limited familiarity with the technology and, therefore, were specifically targeted by the researcher for extra attention and training. No indication was given as to the extent of previous use and familiarity with interdisciplinary approaches with social studies or technology.[79]

Further, weekly lesson plans for integrating *The Yukon Trail* software program and related materials were created by the researcher and provided to the teachers of the treatment classes. Several pieces of particularly relevant literature from Robert W. Service and Jack London were made available by the researcher and read orally to the classes by their teachers. Although graphically based access to the Internet was not available in the classrooms, an informal survey of the fourth-grade students indicated that about half of them had Internet access available at home; therefore, some limited Internet research topics were also included in the weekly lesson plans and integrated into the regular curriculum. Many of these students indicated that indeed they had visited the author's Web site for the Fourth-Grade Technology Project.[80] The researcher's weekly lesson plans were specifically designed to build critical thinking skills in the fourth-grade students. This integration of the technology, combined with an interdisciplinary approach, increased the critical thinking skills of analysis, evaluation, and synthesis as measured by the Cornell Critical Thinking Test and verified by the analysis of the data via the ANCOVA.[81]

Growth in critical thinking skills was anticipated from the incorporation of MECC's simulation software into the upper elementary curriculum as compared to more traditional classroom approaches. Through this interdisciplinary approach with the use of MECC's *The Yukon Trail* simulation software, the critical thinking skills of analysis, evaluation, and synthesis were strengthened, as had been suggested by Farris and Cooper. *The Yukon Trail* software program lent itself well to cooperative learning,[82] and each of the treatment classes was divided into groups of four, with each team having an equal opportunity, on a rotating schedule, to interact with the computers available in the individual classrooms.[83] Farris and Cooper state forcefully that the appropriate use and integration of educational technology is "fundamental" to successful social studies instruction, and the weekly lesson plans provided to the treatment groups by the researcher took advantage of the available technology, both in the school classrooms and at home.[84]

As the student teams moved through *The Yukon Trail* simulation, the team's reporter was called upon to explain what decisions the team was making and to provide a critical justification for those decisions. This provided an opportunity for the teachers to monitor each team's progress and to provide feedback as to the quality of the decisions being made along the journey in the simulation. Several times during the course of this research, the teachers reminded the students of the need to make wise decisions and rehearsed with them the critical thinking terms and definitions provided by the researcher in the weekly lesson plans. The emphasis throughout the project was upon making wise decisions, not upon finding gold at Dawson City, Yukon Territory. Consequently, the teams were never in competition over the amount of gold discovered, but rather over making wise decisions that would produce success in actually making it to the goldfields of Dawson in plenty of time before winter.[85]

The integration of technology and the interdisciplinary approach with *The Yukon Trail* materials resulted in a modified role for the treatment group's teachers. This new role was modeled by the researcher in the weekly activities suggested in the lesson plans and by interaction between the researcher and the teachers. The six teachers of the treatment groups volunteered their time and made additional and different preparations for their lesson planning than was normally expected of regular classroom teachers. As a result, many of them were able to view student learning with a new approach and a modification of attitudes.[86]

The selected schools were located in suburban Madison County, Alabama. The Madison County School System educates almost 20,000 K–12 students, with 52 percent boys and 48 percent girls, 12.75 percent minorities, and 21.87 percent on the USDA's National School Lunch Program/National School Breakfast Program (free and reduced-price). The treatment school consisted of 914 students in grades K–6 with 16.85 percent minorities, and 27.79 percent on the free and reduced-price program. The control schools consisted of 1,327 students (678 and 649, respectively) in grades K–8 and K–5, respectively, with 10.02 percent minorities (6.64 percent and 13.56 percent, respectively) and 22.31 percent on the free and reduced-price program (20.80 percent and 23.88 percent, respectively). These figures illustrate that the three schools were equivalent to each other and to the county as a whole; therefore, these results are generalizable for all of the county's fourth-grade students.[87]

All six self-contained fourth-grade classrooms were chosen from the treatment school based upon the guidance of Vickey Sullivan, technology training specialist for Madison County Schools, and the agreement of Eleanor Smithers, principal, and her fourth-grade teaching staff. Two schools were selected for the control group due to the availability of self-contained fourth-grade classrooms, with three teachers from each school agreeing to participate in the administration of the pretest and posttest of the Cornell Critical Thinking Test.[88]

## Summary of Findings

The simple purpose for this study was to investigate whether growth in critical thinking skills would result from the incorporation of MECC's simulation software into the upper elementary curriculum as compared to more traditional classroom approaches. An interdisciplinary approach with the use of MECC's *The Yukon Trail* simulation software was conducted over a ten-week period, from mid-March to mid-May. The results of the Cornell Critical Thinking Test show that the critical thinking skills of analysis, evaluation, and synthesis were strengthened.[89]

Lesson plan activities developed by the researcher were used in social studies, mathematics, science, geography, literature, and language arts lessons that integrated various aspects of *The Yukon Trail* simulation software, pertinent and authentic literature from the Yukon Trail experience by Jack London and Robert W. Service, and the Internet. Activities were planned for the classroom and as outside reading and research. Based upon informal conversations among the researcher, teachers, students, and parents, it appears these lesson plans were utilized as intended for the project. For example, during one of the briefing sessions conducted by the researcher with each of the six treatment classes, the students indicated familiarity with particular poems and short stories, map activities, math activities, and critical thinking terminology that had been a part of previous lesson plans provided to the teachers by the researcher. This approach with the treatment group increased the students' ability to assess the importance of information on a hypothesis, to judge the reliability of information on the basis of its source, to judge whether a statement follows from the premises, and, finally, focus on the identification of assumptions.[90]

### Findings/Conclusions

Examination of the data indicates that the following conclusions may be warranted: Growth in critical thinking skills results from the incorporation of MECC's *The Yukon Trail* simulation software into the upper elementary curriculum through an interdisciplinary approach as opposed to more traditional classroom approaches. This interdisciplinary approach with the use of *The Yukon Trail* simulation software improved the critical thinking skills of analysis, evaluation, and synthesis. The Cornell Critical Thinking Test assessed four areas of the students' critical thinking ability: the ability to assess the importance of information on a hypothesis; the ability to judge the reliability of information on the basis of its source; the ability to judge whether a statement follows from the premises, and, finally, the ability to identify assumptions. These skills were specifically targeted in the weekly lesson plans and in the preparation and pursuit of success on *The Yukon Trail* simulation. The lesson plans developed by the author highlighted attention to the process of the critical thinking, as well as the integration of the social studies simulation into all of the fourth-grade curricular areas.[91]

**Implications of Findings**

A two-sample t-test performed on the pretest scores indicated a statistically significant difference between the treatment and control groups, with the control group enjoying the edge by about 3.17 points on the average. However, after the treatment, a corresponding two-sample t-test on the posttest scores indicated that the treatment and control groups were no longer statistically significantly different. The ANCOVA verified that indeed the treatment was of statistically significant positive benefit to the treatment group. While the control group did improve slightly, 0.93 points on the average, this improvement was largely due to the normal maturation of fourth-grade students.[92]

Although it was beyond the scope of the current research and inappropriate to follow individual students in detail, it can be noted that while 147 different students participated in the fourth-grade Technology Project, only 119 (81percent) could be positively tracked as having taken the pretest, participated in all ten weeks of the treatment, and then taken the posttest. This is due to normal absences on either the pretest or posttest dates, to students moving in or out of the local school area, and/or to poor or improper demographic information on the answer sheets. Of those 119 students who can be tracked, seventy-nine (66.4 percent) showed improvement on their critical thinking scores. Whereas the control group experienced nominal growth of less than a point on the overall average, the treatment group showed a gain of 3.10 points on the overall average. Those 119 students who can be tracked showed an impressive gain of 4.16 points on the overall average. The ANCOVA verifies that the treatment group showed a statistically significant positive difference due to the treatment received as a result of this research project.[93]

Considering the analysis presented, social studies simulation software and prudent use of the Internet integrated into the elementary school curriculum can prove beneficial to the growth of students' critical thinking skills. This approach requires modification of current methods of preservice teacher training by providing instruction in the development of critical thinking skills in preservice teachers and through the modeling of these skills by education professors. Accomplishing this task calls upon all college and university instructors and professors to give activities and provide tests that go beyond mere rote memory into higher order thinking skills, such as the critical thinking skills of analysis, evaluation, and synthesis. The Cornell Critical Thinking Test is available in an edition, Level Z, for up to and including freshmen and sophomores in college and adults.

Additionally, continuous training for in-service teachers, not only in the use of the technology, but also in the inclination toward lesson preparation and delivery, must be provided. The integration of materials from one subject area across all disciplines requires additional thought and preparation, but can pay huge benefits in building the critical thinking skills of students. Very few of the teachers that this researcher talked with during the course of this project were actually using the available technology in a meaningful way with students. Most were using a reading program, or a math drill program, but few were utilizing the technology to its full potential. Definitely, the need for more training is apparent, but even more needed is the provision of teachers with their own computers so that they can practice on their own what they received training for in the technology training centers and during in-service workshops. If a teacher touches a computer only during formal training, that training will be lost almost as soon as the teacher walks out the door. Each of us recognizes that students learn by doing, but so also do their teachers, particularly with the newer technologies.[94]

The results of this study provide technology coordinators with confidence and information that continued training programs for teachers and administrators are a necessity. Through the use of social studies simulation software, integrated into the regular curriculum, administrators and faculty can enhance student academic performance, particularly with regard to critical thinking skills.[95]

## Notes

1. C. Dickens, "Course Syllabus: EDCI 573 Audio Visual Education" (cited 14 February 1998); available from http://posiedon.tnstate.edu/www/Courses/EDCI573Sp98.html

2. P.J. Farris and S.M. Cooper, *Elementary and Middle School Social Studies: A Whole Language Approach*, 2nd ed. (Madison, WI: Brown Benchmark, 1997).

3. R.B. Lewis, "Developing Critical Thinking Through an Interdisciplinary Approach with Social Studies Simulation and Technology in 4th-grade Classrooms" (Ph.D. diss., Tennessee State University, 1998).

4. Farris and Cooper, *Elementary and Middle School Social Studies*; P. Desberg and F. Fisher, *Teaching with Technology,* 2nd ed., (CD-ROM). Available: Allyn and Bacon (1998 January 15); M. Smith, e-mail to author, 1997.

5. West Warwick School Department, "Students-Information-Telecommunications and Networked Services,*"* (Rhode Island, 1997–[cited 15 February 1998]); available from http://horgan.ww.k12.ri.us/www/Central%20Office/int.pol.html

6. Farris and Cooper, *Elementary and Middle School Social Studies.*

7. R.C. Wicklein and J. Schell, "Case Studies of Multidisciplinary Approaches to Integrating Mathematics, Science and Technology Education," *Journal of Technology Education* 6 (1995): 2.

8. Lewis, "Developing Critical Thinking."

9. Farris and Cooper, *Elementary and Middle School Social Studies.*

10. R.H. Ennis and J. Millman, "Cornell Critical Thinking Test, Level X," (1997 [cited 23 February 1998]); available from http://ericae.net/tc2/tc006077.html; Lewis, "Developing Critical Thinking."

11. P.W. Agnew, A.S. Kellerman, and J.M. Meyer, *Multimedia in the Classroom* (Boston: Allyn and Bacon, 1996); J.R. Chapin and R.G. Messick, *Elementary Social Studies: A Practical Guide*, 2nd ed. (White Plains, NY: Longman, 1992).

12. Farris and Cooper, *Elementary and Middle School Social Studies.*

13. J.U. Michaelis, *Social Studies for Children: A Guide to Basic Instruction*, 10th ed. (Boston: Allyn and Bacon, 1992).

14. C.D. Maddux, D.L. Johnson, and J.W. Willis, *Educational Computing: Learning with Tomorrow's Technologies*, 2nd ed. (Boston: Allyn and Bacon, 1997).

15. Desberg and Fisher, *Teaching with Technology*, 2nd ed.

16. Ibid.

17. Chapin and Messick, *Elementary Social Studies.*

18. Farris and Cooper, *Elementary and Middle School Social Studies.*

19. D.H. Jonassen, *Computers in the Classroom: Mindtools for Critical Thinking* (Englewood Cliffs, NJ: Prentice-Hall, 1996); Lewis, "Developing Critical Thinking."

20. A.A. Gokhale, "Effectiveness of Computer Simulation for Enhancing Higher Order Thinking," *Journal of Industrial Teacher Education* 33 (1996): 36–46.

21. Desberg and Fisher, *Teaching with Technology*, 2nd ed.

22. Wicklein and Schell, "Case Studies of Multidisciplinary Approaches."

23. WCHASE, "Students Dislike Computerized Math Classes," in *H-Net List for Multimedia and New Technologies in Humanities Teaching* (1997 [cited 14 February 1997]); available from H-MMEDIA@H-NET.MSU.EDU; Maddux, Johnson, and Willis, *Educational Computing.*

24. S. Berman, "Educating for Social Responsibility," *Educational Leadership* 48 (1990): 75–80.

25. J.W. Maag, "Promoting Social Skills Training in Classrooms: Issues for School Counselors," *The School Counselor* 42 (1994): 100–103.

26. McWhirter et al., "High-and-Low Risk Characteristics of Youth: The Five Cs of Competency," *Elementary School Guidance and Counseling* 28 (1997): 188–196.

27. Berman, "Educating for Social Responsibility."

28. *The Yukon Trail*, 1994, MECC, Minnesota.

29. Chapin and Messick, *Elementary Social Studies;* Dr. Richard Paul, interview by R. Paul, *Think Magazine* (cited 22 November 1997); available from http://www.sonoma.edu/cthink/K12/k12library/questions.nclk

30. Chapin and Messick, *Elementary Social Studies;* R. Paul, "A Brief History of the Idea of Critical Thinking" (cited 22 November 1997); available from http://www.sonoma.edu/cthink/K12/k12library/cthistory.nclk

31. Paul, "A Brief History"; Chapin and Messick, *Elementary Social Studies;* Farris and Cooper, *Elementary and Middle School Social Studies*; R.F. Biehler and J. Snowman, *Psychology Applied to Teaching*, 7th ed. (Boston: Houghton Mifflin, 1993).

32. Jonassen, *Computers in the Classroom.*

33. Chapin and Messick, *Elementary Social Studies.*

34. Desberg and Fisher, *Teaching with Technology*, 2nd ed.

35. JRATHBURN, e-mail to author, 14 February 1998.

36. Jonassen, *Computers in the Classroom;* JRATHBURN.

37. Chapin and Messick, *Elementary Social Studies.*

38. Farris and Cooper, *Elementary and Middle School Social Studies*; Lewis, "Developing Critical Thinking."

39. The official Web site of the Iditarod race may be found at http://www.iditarod.com and the Iditarod SuperSite at http://www.dogsled.com

40. Biehler and Snowman, *Psychology Applied to Teaching*; Chapin and Messick, *Elementary Social Studies*.

41. *The Yukon Trail;* Lewis, "Developing Critical Thinking."

42. *The Yukon Trail.*

43. Farris and Cooper, *Elementary and Middle School Social Studies*.

44. Lewis, "Developing Critical Thinking."

45. Farris and Cooper, *Elementary and Middle School Social Studies*.

46. *The Yukon Trail.*

47. Lewis, "Developing Critical Thinking."

48. http://home.acneas.net/rblewis/4thgrade.htm

49. Abenaki Associates, "Sample Internet Lesson Plans and Learning Projects" (1996– [cited 13 February 1998]); available from http://schoolnet2.carleton.ca/english/ext/aboriginal/lessons/index.html

50. Available via subscription request to LISTSERV@MSU.EDU

51. Available via subscription request to LISTSERV@H-NET.MSU.EDU

52. Available via subscription request to LISTPROCZ@ECNET.NET; R.B. Lewis, "Discussion Groups in Educational Technology and Social Studies Education: Availability, Guidelines for Use, and Threads," (Tennessee State University, 1997).

53. *The Yukon Trail.*

54. Lewis, "Developing Critical Thinking."

55. M. Sealey, "Multimedia Authoring 1997," *Technology Learning* 18 (1997) : 12–17.

56. Kirk Winters, "Middle Level Education/Early Adolescence (10–14)," (1997– [cited 6 October 1997]); available from MIDDLE-L@POSTOFFICE.CSO.UIUC.EDU

57. Lewis, "Developing Critical Thinking."

58. Jonassen *Computers in the Classroom*.

59. Lewis, "Developing Critical Thinking."

60. Ibid.

61. T.K. Crowl, *Fundamentals of Educational Research*, 2nd ed. (Madison, WI: Brown Benchmark, 1996); L.R. Gay, *Educational Research: Competencies for Analysis and Application*, 2d ed. (Columbus: Charles E. Merrill, 1981).

62. R.H. Ennis (RHENNIS@uiuc.edu), e-mail to author, 27 February 1998.

63. Lewis, "Developing Critical Thought."

64. Ennis, e-mail to author.

65. Crowl, *Fundamentals of Educational Research*; Gay, *Educational Research*.

66. Lewis, "Developing Critical Thinking."

67. Ennis and Millman, "Cornell Critical Thinking Test."

68. M.L. Davison and K. Anderson, "Performance Assessments of Critical Thinking: The Reflective Judgment Approach" (1998 [cited 23 February 1998]); available from http://carei.coled.umn.edu/ResearchPractice/v2n1/performa.htm

69. Lewis, "Developing Critical Thinking."

70. Ibid.

71. P. Dugard and J. Todman, "Analysis of Pretest-Posttest Control Group Designs in Educational Research," *Educational Psychology* 15 (1998 [cited 16 May 1998]): 181–199; available from http://www.ebscohost.com/cgi-bin/epwtop/key=x07POhD

72. Ibid.

73. Crowl, *Fundamentals of Educational Research*; Gay, *Educational Research*.

74. Gay, *Educational Research.*
75. Lewis, "Developing Critical Thinking."
76. Dugard and Todman, "Analysis of Pretest-Posttest Control Group."
77. Gay, *Educational Research.*
78. Lewis, "Developing Critical Thinking."
79. Ibid.
80. See http://fly.HiWaay.net/~rblewis
81. Lewis, "Developing Critical Thinking."
82. Chapin and Messick, *Elementary Social Studies.*
83. *The Yukon Trail.*
84. Farris and Cooper, *Elementary and Middle School Social Studies.*
85. Lewis, "Developing Critical Thinking."
86. Ibid.
87. Crowl, *Fundamentals of Educational Research.*
88. Lewis, "Developing Critical Thinking."
89. Farris and Cooper, *Elementary and Middle School Social Studies*; Chapin and Messick, *Elementary Social Studies*; Lewis, "Developing Critical Thinking."
90. Ennis and Millman, "Cornell Critical Thinking Test."
91. Lewis, "Developing Critical Thinking."
92. Ibid.
93. Ibid.
94. Ibid.
95. Ibid.

# 16

# On-line Teacher Education

## An Analysis of Student Teachers' Use of Computer-Mediated Communication

### *Cheryl L. Mason*

Thomas Jefferson introduced his Bill for the More General Diffusion of Knowledge to the Virginia legislature in 1779. This legislation declared that the state had the responsibility to inspire an educated and literate citizenry. "If a nation expects to be ignorant and free, in a state of civilization, it expects what never was and will never will be," Jefferson said.[1]

Jefferson's plan called for the development and support of public schools to educate America's citizens. The notion of public schools assumes that our nation will take all steps necessary to develop and sustain the most effective education system for all citizens. For generations, Americans have attempted to heed Jefferson's clarion call to provide their children with the education they deserve.

Two centuries later, the desire of Jefferson, a forefather of public education, is not yet fulfilled. In 1983, *A Nation at Risk* rang a fire bell in the night. The frightening proclamation: American schools were drowning in a "rising tide of mediocrity." American schools were not providing their students with the education they needed or deserved. Countless proposals for educational reform followed the publication of this report. School reform initiatives focused on new resources such as textbooks, curriculum packages, testing, and television.[2]

But the proposals fell short. They ignored improving the education of teachers. John Goodlad argued that little attention has been paid to teacher education reform because the school reform movement and the teacher education reform movement have not been connected.[3] Teacher education reform has been labeled the "unstudied problem."[4]

To address this essential ingredient of school reform, the National Commission on Teaching and America's Future developed a strategy for school reform centered on the classroom teacher. Emphasizing the essential role the teacher plays in school reform, the Commission's blueprint for change is based on three basic tenets:[5]

1. What teachers know and can do is the most important influence on what students learn.
2. Recruiting, preparing, and retaining good teachers is the central strategy for improving our schools.
3. School reform cannot succeed unless it focuses on creating the conditions in which teachers can teach, and teach well.

Recognizing these principles will help our nation meet the overall goal of this initiative: to provide all "students what should be their educational birthright: access to competent, caring, and qualified teachers."[6] This is the education that Thomas Jefferson envisioned in 1779. To effectively pursue this goal, colleges of education must challenge their traditional teacher education programs and "reinvent" them.

The National Commission recommended that teacher education programs structure their programs around standards. Specific standards to focus on include, but are not limited to, preparation for collaboration with colleagues and parents, technological skills for supporting student learning and professional learning in the Information Age, and strong emphasis on reflection and inquiry as means to continually evaluate and improve teaching.[7]

The following study was designed to examine these three specific standards through the voices and actions of a six-member social studies middle-school preservice teacher cohort during their student teaching experiences. An electronic network provided the opportunities for the participants to collaborate and develop reflective teaching skills.

This chapter begins an exploration of applications of computer mediated communication (CMC) to teacher education programs. CMC was facilitated by desktop videoconferencing and Web-based groupware. Desktop videoconferencing sessions were held weekly using CU-SeeMe software, while Web-based groupware messages were posted voluntarily with NetForum software.

**Review of Literature**

*Teacher Education*

In 1904, John Dewey declared that the ultimate intent of teacher education programs should be to prepare teachers to reflect upon the relationship between theory and practice. He cautioned against a technocratic approach to teacher preparation and encouraged reflection upon the theoretical issues and their practical implications.[8] Dewey defined reflection as "the active, persistent, and careful consideration of any belief or supposed form of knowledge in light of the grounds that support it and further conclusions to which it tends."[9] The application of his definition to colleges of education redefines the role of the university in teacher preparation.

If we accordingly conceive of the education of teachers not simply as the training of individual classroom performers, but as the development of a class of intellectuals vital to a free society, we can see more clearly the role of educational scholarship and theoretical analysis in the process. Building on this belief, Kenneth Zeichner calls for the development of a reflective teacher.[10] The reflective teacher analyzes classroom situations and develops as a professional in his or her decision making. To meet this urgent need, Goodlad recommends the development and nurturing of cohort groups for teacher education students.[11]

A cohort group is a cluster of preservice teachers who stay together throughout the duration of their preservice teaching experience. Knowles, Cole, and Presswood have identified three key benefits of cohort collaboration during the preservice teaching experience: serving as sounding boards and mirrors on emerging practices, helping to make sense of classroom participation, and creating a safety net as new methods are tried.[12] Cohort groups that are structured to provide intellectual guidance and support hold the potential of developing teachers who are active agents in the learning of others, rather than being passive learners.[13]

To best prepare social studies educators for today's children, Beverly Armento declares that social studies teacher education programs have a responsibility to "build ongoing and stimulating collaborative linkages among social studies educators."[14] Intellectual cohort groups may serve as a step in the right direction for teacher education reform.

Nonetheless, the time that a preservice teacher is placed in the field is often a period of disequilibrium and isolation.[15] There is a well-documented gap between university-based methods courses and the ability to teach.[16] A number of researchers have discussed the inadequacies of the traditional student teaching models.[17] Kirkbusch's study reveals that social studies teachers during their field experience emphasize the transmission of factual knowledge rather than critical thinking skills.[18] The weak links between social studies content and pedagogical skills are evident, as the student teachers in his study did not incorporate social issues or multiple perspectives on topics into their teaching.

The weak links act as barriers that restrict the preservice teacher from engaging in the kind of discourse among professors, teachers, and students that is vital to the development of reflective, inquiry-oriented teachers.[19] Time and geographical obstacles often restrict the group members' interactions once they are in the field. Developments in telecommunications offer the potential of reducing the impact of these barriers. Telecommunications allows individuals to communicate with others in geographically disparate locations.

**Computer-Mediated Communication (CMC)**

Telecommunications is revolutionizing the way we teach and learn. New technologies have found their way into many of our schools. Schrum maintains that telecommunications holds the potential of restructuring preservice and staff development. CMC can be used to optimize preservice education by "enhancing meaningful preservice experiences and giving teachers knowledge and confidence about using these tools in their classrooms."[20] However, Brooks and Kopp report that integration of technology into teacher education programs lags behind other fields of education.[21] The use of CMC in teacher education programs is relatively new.[22] A majority of these studies focus on the effects of e-mail on the preservice teacher/university supervisor relationship.[23] Researchers have discovered that CMC is used primarily as a conduit for social and emotional support, rather than reflective inquiry.[24] A review of the literature reveals that the most widely used mode of CMC being used in teacher education programs is e-mail.

Casey has found that the major benefits of using e-mail during the student teaching experience are increased reflectivity; feeling of rapport and support from university supervisors; access to supervisors and university personnel; team support; and self-esteem due to mastering technology and receiving positive support through e-mail messages.[25]

Thomas, Clift, and Sugimoto's research, however, reveals that student teachers in the field found e-mail discussions a "cool, impersonal medium."[26] The student teachers in this study missed the social presence found in face-to-face interactions and the rapid response they received from either face-to-face or telephone conversations. According to the media richness model, new technologies such as videoconferencing may enhance electronic communication. The media richness model implies that communication media differ in their ability to facilitate understanding and reduce ambiguity.[27]

Face-to-face is considered the richest way to communicate.[28] It allows timely mutual feedback and the simultaneous communication of nonverbal gestures. Desktop videoconferencing is less powerful than face-to-face communications, but has greater information than the telephone. It supports both verbal and nonverbal language, feedback is rapid, and natural language is used.[29] David Fetterman agrees that these benefits are highly desirable: "Electronic communication is a little more personal and a lot more effective when you hear the nuances of tone and see nonverbal language such as gestures and expressions, cues you normally depend on in face-to-face interactions."[30]

Videoconferencing systems, however, are often restricted to those who can afford elaborate expensive software and infrastructure. The complexity and high cost of videoconferencing systems cause many educators to view them as futuristic. The advent of desktop videoconferencing is changing this perception. Desktop videoconferencing now permits faculty, students, and practitioners to participate in on-line dialogue, enhanced by audio and video.[31] With relatively inexpensive software and hardware, they can do this from an Internet-connected computer in their office, classroom, or home.

## Method

The research questions that guided this study were

1. What were the patterns of CMC among the cohort members?
2. To what extent did CMC facilitate reflective discourse among the cohort members?
3. What were the patterns of CMC between the members of the cohort and their supervisor?
4. To what extent did the student teachers use the different forms of CMC?

## Participants

Participants were selected purposefully because they met two criteria: an established preservice social studies teaching cohort and placement in schools that were over thirty minutes from a central location. Six preservice teachers and their university supervisor were selected as the participants for this study. These students were enrolled in a course that met daily for seven weeks until the full-time field placement commenced. The students were assigned to three different schools. Pseudonyms are assigned to provide anonymity for each informant and school. The schools are referred to as Tuxford Middle School, Farnham Middle School, and Woodburn Middle School. The course instructor and university supervisor is referred to as Betsy. The preservice teachers are referred to as Daminga, Melissa, Charles, Laura, Eleanor, and Pam, five women and one man. A middle school language arts university professor who taught these students a previous semester joined one of the

CU-SeeMe sessions and posted a number of NetForum entries. She is re-ferred to as Caroline. A clinical instructor from the university observed three of the student teachers. She is referred to as Anita. Anita voluntarily did not participate in any of the CMC. Initial participant and school descriptions are presented below:

"Daminga" is an African-American female. As a preservice teacher, she was placed in eighth-grade social studies and language arts at Woodburn Middle School. She described her prior computer experiences as "challenging, stressful, and helpful." "Melissa" is an African-Ameri-can female. As a preservice teacher, her placement was seventh-grade social studies and language arts also at Woodburn Middle School. She described her prior computer experiences as "fun, easy to learn, and learn by doing." "Charles" is a white male. As a preservice teacher, he was assigned sixth-grade social studies and language arts at Tuxford Middle School. He described his prior computer experiences as "game-oriented and communication-oriented." "Eleanor" is a white female. As a preservice teacher, her placement was sixth-grade social studies and lan-guage arts at Woodburn Middle School. She described her prior com-puter experiences as "frustrating, exciting, and stimulating." "Laura" is a white female. As a preservice teacher, she was assigned sixth-grade social studies and language arts at Farnham Middle School. She described her prior computer experiences as "creative, hard, and challenging." "Pam" is an African-American female. As a preservice teacher, she was also placed at Woodburn Middle School in eighth-grade social studies and language arts. She described her prior computer experiences as "con-fused, disaster, and getting lost." "Caroline" is a white female. She was the instructor for the participants' methods course. She is the former assistant principal of Woodburn Middle School and is currently a doctoral student in the Department of Curriculum and Instruction. She describes her prior computer experiences as "frustrating, foreign, necessary."

The following chart provides information on each of the schools and the computer used by the participants:

| School | School Population | Type of Computer and Internet Connection | Distance from University | Computer Location |
|---|---|---|---|---|
| Woodburn Middle School | Grades 6–8 Rural | Macintosh 5200 connected to a local-area-network (LAN) | Approximately thirty miles | Media center |

| Tuxford Middle School | Grades 6–8 Suburb | IBM Think-Pad with a dial-up connection through a modem | Approximately fifteen miles | Computer lab |
| Farnham Middle School | Grades 6–8 Rural | IBM, running Windows 3.2 with a dial-up connection to the Internet through a modem | Approximately twenty miles | Media center |

## Role of Researcher

### Technical Consultant

I acted as the participants' technology consultant both prior to and after their student teaching experience. My preparation for the on-line dialogues included visiting the participants' methods class three weeks into the course and presenting a two-hour telecommunications workshop. This hands-on workshop took place in one of the university computer labs. CU-SeeMe and NetForum software were demonstrated and time was allowed for individual exploration of each program. I wrote a step-by-step users' guide for each of the software programs and distributed them during the workshop. These directions were also placed on-line, and the URL was distributed to the participants.

Prior to the commencement of the student teaching experience, I visited each of the three middle schools where the students were to be located. There, I secured the use of the computer and network resources by the preservice teachers and installed the required software and hardware on each school's computers. During my initial visit, I installed the hardware and software and demonstrated it to the technology coordinators. I provided the coordinators with copies of the users' guides for the software that had been created for the student teachers and encouraged the technology coordinators to use the new equipment with the teachers and students in the school.

My role as technical consultant continued throughout the semester. Occasionally, when the student teachers had questions or problems with their telecommunications equipment, they would send an e-mail or make a phone call. The participants were given the phone number of the campus computer lab from which I participated in the on-line seminars. Each one of them called at some point to ask a question about their equipment or the network. The student teachers also turned to me for technical assistance when they were designing instructional materials or methods for classroom instruction.

## *Participant Observer*

Originally, I had not planned to actively participate in the on-line dialogues. Rather, my role was only that of an observer, intending to monitor the on-line interactions "through a one-way mirror."[32] The preservice teachers, however, called for this status to change during the first CU-SeeMe session. As the informants logged into the server for the first time, they all saw each other, but did not see my picture. They questioned where my video was. I reminded them that my role was as observer and that they were to interact with one another. The informants responded with a clear message: "NO LURKERS ALLOWED!" A lurker is one who participates in a video-conference, but does not send a video. They followed this posting with the rationale that I should join their on-line community to add to the conversation and be more readily available for technical support if needed. Hence, my role evolved to that of participant observer. As a participant observer, my video was included in the on-line seminar and I regularly posted messages in response to the preservice teachers' questions or to prompt reflectivity among the cohort.

## Data Analysis

The constant comparative method was used to analyze the data collected from the various sources. Strauss and Corbin refer to this method as "a general methodology for developing theory that is grounded in data systematically gathered and analyzed."[33] The data collection and data processing occurred simultaneously, in a pulsating fashion.[34]

A running list of emerging themes was kept in my reflexive journal. As the research evolved, new patterns were added to the list and revisions made. With the completion of data collection, the list of patterns was clustered, yielding five main themes:

1. Peer collaboration for professional development.
2. Computers as a mode of communication.
3. Conflicts between theory versus practice.
4. Personal development and personal issues.
5. Instructional methods and materials.

## Ethical Electronic Qualitative Research

Qualitative researchers are expected to adhere to ethical frameworks that protect participants from harm. Electronic qualitative researchers, however, must be in tune with emerging ethical issues. Just as telecommunications has altered the ways that we communicate with one another, telecommunications is changing the way we may conduct research. As data may now be collected virtually, a new dimension to data collection has emerged. This means electronic messages, such as e-mail, digital video, and postings on a Web page, may be collected and analyzed as data. The implications of conducting research in cyberspace must be seriously considered, as Lynne Schrum emphasizes: "Moving into an electronic community is even more invasive than joining a face-to-face organization or taking notes at a meeting. Participant rights and copyright issues must be considered at the moment a researcher decides to become an electronic ethnographer."[35]

Schrum has developed procedures to inform ethical electronic research. This study was designed in conformity with these guidelines. Among the "Ethical Electronic Research Guidelines," the following items most influenced this study:[37]

- Researcher must consider the respondents and participants as owners of the materials that are created; the respondent should have the ability to modify or correct statements for content, spelling, substance, or language.
- Researchers should strive to create a climate of trust, collaboration, and equality with electronic community members, within an environment that is nonevaluative and safe.
- Researchers should treat electronic mail as private correspondence that is not to be forwarded, shared, or used as research data unless express permission is given.

## Findings

The study investigated how computer-mediated communication (CMC) can be used to enrich the preservice period of professional development. I was interested in the extent to which the telecommunications software, CU-SeeMe and NetForum, would provide the student teachers with opportunities for reflective discourse. Of particular concern were how the telecommunications software was used and which of the two telecommunications software programs (CU-SeeMe and NetForum) was most effectively used.

### Inferences

In the following discussion, I describe how four inferences emerged from the data and place them within the context of the professional literature.

*Inference 1.* As a result of the participants' active participation in an on-line learning community, opportunities for peer collaboration and reflection were enhanced.

*Inference 2.* CMC allowed the participants to engage in self-directed and self-initiated professional dialogue.

*Inference 3.* The participants translated the use of technology from the personal context to the classroom context.

*Inference 4.* Desktop videoconferencing as a mode of communication provided more immediate and satisfactory feedback for the participants than the Web-based groupware.

*Inference 1. As a result of the participants' active participation in an on-line learning community, opportunities for peer collaboration and reflection were enhanced.*

Allen Griffin has concluded that the "development of the student's capacity for independent reflection is the school's special contribution to the democratic way of life."[38] Social studies educators have long embraced reflective inquiry as the overarching goal of the social studies curriculum. Reflective inquiry, defined by Dewey, is "active, persistent, and careful consideration of any belief or supposed form of knowledge in the light of the grounds that support it and the further conclusions to which it tends."[39] Teacher education programs that model reflective inquiry provide preservice teachers with the opportunity to develop images of what classroom inquiry is, as well as what it is like to experience such inquiry from the perspective of the learner.[40]

The weekly CU-SeeMe sessions and the constant availability of the NetForum provided the opportunities for peer collaboration and reflection. The student teachers in this study were each placed at least thirty minutes from the university campus. The CU-SeeMe sessions allowed the participants to regularly interact from their field placement, requiring no travel time. NetForum was available on the Internet at any time of the day, from any networked computer. The accessibility of NetForum provided opportunities for interaction atypical of the professional semester.

Charles's reflections on the on-line sessions illustrate the benefits of using CMC to connect a cohort of student teachers:

> There are so many things we have to do during these weeks of student teaching . . . it can be overwhelming sometimes. It was really nice to be able to just walk over to the Media Center in my school to talk to everyone instead of having to drive back to campus. We were able to talk to everyone more than if we had to wait for a class on campus.

Compared to the tool of collegial journals, CMC is more effective because it allows for more immediate feedback to encourage reflection through self-evaluation and collaboration.[41] The drawback of using collegial journals is the lapse of time in receiving feedback.[42] Prompt response to journal entries is especially difficult if student teachers have to physically exchange journals with their peers in different schools. The synchronous CMC supported by CU-SeeMe was found to encourage reflection among colleagues, while providing spontaneous feedback. The data suggest that its timeliness makes CMC a more effective tool for reflection than collegial journals.

The participants' CMC was consistent with Frances Fuller's work on reflection and the development of beginning teachers.[43] Fuller's research has examined the developmental concerns–based stages of novice teachers with personal aspects of classroom instruction. Fuller argues that teacher educators should acknowledge the developmental conceptualization of student teachers' concerns to best meet their needs as students and as professionals.

Fuller has identified three stages of concerns: survival, teaching, and student.[44] Her research shows that beginning teachers move from the personal stage to management provided they have ample time for reflection and appropriate support and scaffolding from their learning community. Reflection is the key component of the process that promotes their progression through the developmental stages.[45]

For this study, an analysis of the participants' discourse revealed their development from personal to management as they engaged in conversations about classroom methods and materials. The participants' development corroborates the professional literature, in that there is data to support the three stages for each of the participants. It is important to note that the CMC provided the context for this type of reflection and peer support to take place.

It is obvious that the quantity of opportunities for reflection was increased since students had continuous access to NetForum. The participants were able to post comments to the NetForum Web page at any time of the day, from any Internet-connected computer. The participants were also able to meet on-line from the convenience of their field placement. Because travel time to the university was not a factor, the on-line sessions were held at convenient times before, during, or after the school day.

The quality of reflections in this study was also enhanced by CMC. However, the case for quality is more difficult to make since this is not a comparative case study. The synchronous nature of the CU-SeeMe software contributed to the participants' reflective discourse. Thomas, Clift, and Sugimoto report e-mail to be a significant communication tool for student teachers and university supervisors. Yet they also report the asynchronous nature of e-mail supports a very low social presence and media richness.

Thomas, Clift, and Sugimoto define low social presence and media richness as the absence of face-to-face communication and automatic feedback.[46] In this study, on the other hand, there was a high social presence since the CU-SeeMe software supported synchronous communication. Eleanor reflects on the spontaneity of CU-SeeMe: "It was just really nice to be able to count on everyone being there when you logged on. I liked being able to tell them about what had happened that day and hearing what they had to say about it right then—and not have to wait until later for them to respond [as with NetForum]."

The student teachers were motivated to discuss their classroom experiences because they could depend on peer responses. Also, the student teachers were on-line together, which contributed to the collaborative nature of their discourse.

*Inference 2. CMC allowed the participants to engage in self-directed and self-initiated professional dialogue.*

Three reasons that the technology context promoted self-directed dialogue are the participants' shared language, the inherent nature of the technology, and the limited role of the supervisor.

The participants displayed a high level of openness with one another. Whether discussing personal or professional issues, honesty and trust were always implicit in their communications. The trust they felt for one another is one characteristic of shared language among community members.[47]

The student teachers' conversations about future plans highlight this shared language. Topics of conversation related to post–student teaching included whether or not they really wanted to be a classroom teacher, other careers they may pursue besides teaching, how to apply for teaching jobs in local school systems, and how to interview for a teaching position. As some of the student teachers had interviews with school systems, they shared their experiences with one another. Each of the cohort members expressed at some time a hint of uncertainty about the choice they had made to become a teacher. They shared these doubts very comfortably with one another. Pam summed up her feelings about this in her post-interview: "I worked so hard to get this far, my mom would think I was crazy if I hinted at not being a teacher . . . but they [cohort] all understand."

These patterns of discourse support what the literature reports about a shared language among community members. Rogoff describes learning through the lens of the social constructivist as a "transformation of participation."[48] According to this model, growth occurs from the participation in the socially relevant activity of a group. Burbles argues that the foremost initiative of teacher education programs should be to involve students in the discourse of the profession.[49] Participation in professional dialogue leads to membership in a community of learners. Gee defines the dialogue shared within a community of learners as "a socially accepted association among ways of using language, of thinking, feeling, believing, valuing, and of acting that can be used to identify oneself as a member of a socially meaningful group or social network."[50]

The shared discourse among the cohort made possible by the CMC helps to combat the "lone-wolf" paradigm. Huberman observes that our schools force each teacher to operate in isolation, as a "lone wolf."[51] This paradigm does not support community building or community language. Rather, educators work in professional isolation. Huberman claims that the architectural and social structure of public schools contributes to the absence of collegiality.

The intervention of CMC in this study made it possible for the participants to engage in professional dialogue with a community of learners from their various field placements. The inherent nature of CMC motivates individuals to take more responsibility for their learning. The quality of the reflective discourse among the participants in this study was enhanced by the technology. Daminga comments:

> The CU-SeeMe sessions are different than regular seminars in a classroom. For example, we usually start off just venting about what has been happening the past week. Someone usually had a situation to tell us about or someone had a question to ask. It wasn't like we walked into a classroom and waited for a teacher to ask a question. As soon as two people were logged on—we were talking.

Daminga's reflections on CMC are consistent with the literature in that CMC encourages collaboration and participation by all on-line users. CMC fosters the building of strong communities, but also encourages collective problem in a democratic manner, void of hierarchies.[52]

The university supervisor's role was limited in this study. Her limited experience with technology and limited access to technology may have contributed to her diminished participation. Despite repeated encouragement to play a more effective role in the CMC, the supervisor's role in this study was much like the role of the electronic supervisor in the literature. Thomas, Clift, and Sugimoto's research, linking student teachers via e-mail, reveals that the majority of the electronic messages focus on course requirements.[53] Blanton, Trathen, and Moorman similarly report the need for the supervisor to structure the on-line dialogue to encourage pedagogical dialogue.[54] They designed their study to engage their student teachers in professional dialogue in which the supervisors who participated entered electronic messages related to the social constructivist perspective. That is, they entered thoughtful questions and probed students to engage in the dialogue of professional teachers.

It is interesting to note even though the supervisor's dialogue centered primarily on course requirements, the student teachers' dialogue primarily focused on classroom instruction and student concerns. This is a key point because in essence what happened is the on-line learning community served the function of a typical supervisor. That is, the CMC facilitated the student teachers' progression through Fuller's developmental stages. [55]

One possible explanation for the supervisor's limited role in this study may be that the student teachers felt more control and assumed more responsibility for their learning. Schrum's research findings support the shift of learner responsibility from supervisor to student teachers: "the world of electronic communication assumes and demands that people take initiative for their own learning and growth."[56] The supervisor commented on the student teachers' initiative and enthusiasm during an interview: "They have just taken off with the CU-SeeMe! By the time I get to the Media Center, they are already gathered around the computer, connected with one of the other schools. Sometimes, I just watch and listen to them—they almost teach themselves!"

The student teachers, however, were not deterred by the supervisor's lack of participation in the CMC. Rather, they engaged in self-directed communication. The contribution of CMC to the learning environment of student teachers is significant, as it facilitated their professional growth. But it is not clear whether their self-directed learning is a result of the supervisor's lack of participation or the inherent nature of CMC.

*Inference 3. The participants translated the use of technology from the personal context to the classroom context.*

As a result of translating the use of technology, they acquired perceptions of themselves as technology users.

The literature reports that individuals communicating on-line use technology for two main purposes. The first purpose is that technology is a repository, simply storing information to be exchanged.[57] The second purpose is that technology actually encourages a paradigm shift so that it becomes the environment for learning.[58] The findings from this study support the notion that technology prompted a paradigm shift in the way the participants viewed technology as a tool.

"YES! I would consider myself techno-literate!" exclaimed Daminga during the on-line focus group session. Techno-literate is the term the participants coined to express their newfound technological confidence. Prior to this study, none of the participants had used CU-SeeMe, and only one had used NetForum. Their telecommunications experience was limited to sending text-only e-mails and occasional Web surfing.

All of the student teachers included evidence of technology integration in their professional teaching portfolios. However, three of the six participants in this study made a self-described shift from technology novices to techno-literates. This shift encouraged the student teachers to integrate technology into their own classrooms. In her initial interview, Laura described her previous computer experiences as "creative, hard, and challenging." To the same question in her post interview, she responded, "exciting, fun, and frustrating." Laura's self-described shift to techno-literacy may be explained by her experiences in an on-line learning community. She reflected on the role technology played in her professional semester:

> The passport activity I did with my students was one of the best. I am really proud of that—because the kids really liked it and seemed to learn from it; and because it was one of the most creative activities I did all semester . . . the idea just came to me one morning during one of our CU-SeeMe sessions. I was waiting for everyone to log on and was trying to come up with a way that I could use CU-SeeMe or at least the digital camera in my class.

Eleanor described her computer experiences at the beginning of the professional semester as "frustrating, exciting, and stimulating." To the same question at the end of the semester, she answered "cooperative, frustrating, and empowering." Eleanor explained why she chose these last three words:

> Cooperative because that's how we used it this semester—to talk to each other and to work together. Plus, I've learned to just ask for help when I have technology problems. Frustrating because it doesn't always work. Sometimes the network wasn't working or someone's camera wasn't plugged in right. Empowering because sometimes I would stop and realize that I was actually talking over a computer line—and that I could connect my students with people all over the world from the Media Center. Amazing!

Casey identifies similar shifts in attitude toward technology among student teachers.[59] She reports an increased use of the computer for classroom instruction and professional development by student teachers who used e-mail during their field experience. Schrum's research concludes that this phenomenon is due to the presentation of theory and application within the context of technology use.[60] In other words, once individuals have the opportunity to use new technologies in a personal context, the technology integrates seamlessly into the learning environment.

*Inference 4. Desktop videoconferencing as a mode of communication pro-vided more immediate and satisfactory feedback for the participants than the Web-based groupware.*

As suggested by the media richness model,[61] tools for CMC differ in their ability to facilitate communication. Some tools have great ability and are considered to have more media richness, while some are low in media richness and have less ability to facilitate communication. Two modes of CMC were included in this study. The CU-SeeMe software represented the richest mode of CMC as it allowed for the synchronous exchange of video, text, and audio. The NetForum software represented the lowest mode of media richness in that it supported the asynchronous exchange of text.

The desktop videoconferencing software, CU-SeeMe, was the most often used medium for CMC. Each of the student teachers used the CU-SeeMe at least once a week for the duration of their field experience. Despite the limitations of using this software, CU-SeeMe was the most effective form of CMC. The fact that desktop videoconferencing is synchronous proved to be significant to the participants. They found it the best use of their time to engage in on-line dialogue because of the prompt feedback they received.

The unique aspect of the data presented in this study is the importance of spontaneous feedback. The literature supports the participants' desire for timely CMC. Posner reports the significance of timeliness to encourage re-flective inquiry and to keep up with the immediacy of classroom teaching.[62] Schrum and Berenfeld highlight the significance of spontaneous feedback in their discussion of student teachers during the Gulf War: "When fighting broke out in one part of the world, the students and their advisors discussed how to handle it in the classroom, what to teach, and how to answer questions from their students. They did not receive relevant print materials for almost a month, which would have hardly helped in the urgency of the moment."[63]

The transmittal of real-time video was not as important to the participants as the real-time exchange of audio and text. The NetForum did not provide the same spontaneous feedback. Although the NetForum could be accessed at any time of the day, from any computer, the majority of the participants felt they benefited the most from the desktop videoconferences. Laura was the only participant who felt that the NetForum was most helpful for her.

> I just always got so frustrated from trying to connect in to CU-SeeMe early in the mornings and having it not work sometimes. It was much easier for me to just pull up the [Net]Forum Web page, look to see what was new, and put in my questions or thoughts. . . . The Web page was good at first, then

everyone got too busy to post things, so I even stopped checking it as much because there were too many days when there weren't new things.

Laura's reflections on the different modes of CMC remind us that the social and personal environment of on-line communication is significant to its effectiveness. Harasim asserts that we cannot focus only on the technical aspects of CMC, but also on the environmental aspects: "Lessons gained over the past two decades of experience in network communication highlight the importance of designing the environment. Networlds are the intersection of social and technical systems; design involves both technical and social considerations."[64]

## Conclusions

Communication among cohort members and university personnel was facilitated by the CMC, especially the desktop videoconferencing software. Weekly CU-SeeMe sessions provided opportunities for the participants to interact with one another and with their university supervisor. These sessions were effective because they increased the quality and quantity of the participants' opportunities for peer collaboration and reflection.

The student teachers exhibited high levels of trust and openness in their communication. Their collegial discourse provided the scaffolding for reflective inquiry. As a result of their participation in the CMC, the participants assumed more responsibility for their learning during the CU-SeeMe sessions.

The student teachers also developed a new confidence to integrate technology into their classrooms. They translated the effective use of technology in the personal context to the classroom context. Each of the students developed and taught technology-infused lessons during their field experience.

It appears that the findings of this study are consistent with Casey's research.[65] The student teachers in her study were linked via e-mail. Casey found the major benefits of using e-mail during the student teaching experience to be increased reflectivity, feelings of rapport and support from the university supervisor, and increased team support. She also found that the student leaders' self-esteem increased due to mastering technology and receiving positive support through e-mail messages.

The characteristics of the CMC software in this dissertation study, however, distinguish the results from others in the field. CU-SeeMe allowed synchronous dialogue and the exchange of video. NetForum organized the postings into threads of conversation. These software features contributed to increased reflectivity among the participants. Although not conclusive, the data suggest that the spontaneity of the CU-SeeMe sessions ensured prompt feedback and encouraged spontaneous reflection. Desktop videoconferencing among student teachers is a relatively unexplored phenomenon. As new technologies emerge, teacher education programs should continue to explore ways to enhance teacher education through the use of instructional technology.

## Recommendations

This case study linked a cohort of middle school social studies student teachers via the Internet to explore the nature of their discourse during on-line weekly seminars. Their voices and stories have provided a rich description of the attempt of one teacher education program to apply new technologies to the student teaching experience. These student teachers used technology to enrich their professional experience.

The data, however, provide more than an interesting glimpse into student teachers' use of CMC. New insights into the infusion of instructional technologies into teacher education have emerged. From an analysis of the data, and through reflection on my own experiences, I have developed recommendations for future applications and research.

First, teacher education programs should continue to pioneer the integration of newly refined and developed technologies. As new technologies emerge, they should be explored for applications to the professional development of teachers. Second, the structure of student teachers' on-line discourse should be compared to student teachers' face-to-face discourse. Further research should be conducted to investigate the differences between on-line reflective seminars and traditional campus-based reflective seminars. Third, research should investigate which student teachers have the greatest success in using the different modes of CMC. Individuals' learning styles should be correlated with their communication styles to ensure the best match of CMC for each individual. Fourth, teacher educators should not attempt to work independently toward the seamless integration of CMC into their programs, since, alone, they cannot take full advantage of emerging technologies. Rather, the teacher education community should work collaboratively with the computer science, instructional technology, and business communities.

## Notes

1. A.C. Ornstein and D.U. Levine, *An Introduction to the Foundations of Education* (Boston: Houghton Mifflin, 1984), 155.

2. J.I. Goodlad, *Teachers for Our Nation's Schools* (San Francisco: Jossey Bass, 1991).

3. Ibid.

4. S. Sarason, D. Davidson, and B. Blatt, *The Preparation of Teachers: An Unstudied Problem in Education* (New York: Wiley and Sons, 1962).

5. National Commission on Teaching and America's Future, *What Matters Most: Teaching for America's Future* (New York: National Commission on Teaching and America's Future, 1996), 6.

6. Ibid., vi.

7. Ibid., 76.

8. J. Dewey, "The Relation of Theory to Practice in Education," in *The Relation of Theory to Practice in the Education of Teachers, Third Yearbook, Part I* (Bloomington, IL: Public School Publishing, 1904), 9–30.

9. Dewey, J., *How We Think* (Chicago: Henry Regenry, 1933), 9.

10. K.M. Zeichner, "Alternative Paradigms of Teacher Education," *Journal of Teacher Education* 34, no. 3 (1983): 3–9; K.M. Zeichner, "Myths and Realities: Field-based Experiences in Teacher Education," *Journal of Teacher Education* 31, no. x (1980): 31–35.

11. Goodlad, *Teachers for Our Nation's Schools*.

12. J.G. Knowles, A.L. Cole, and C.S. Presswood, *Through Preservice Teachers' Eyes* (New York: Macmillan, 1994).

13. Goodlad, *Teachers for Our Nation's Schools*.

14. B.J. Armento, "The Professional Development of Social Studies Educators," quoted in *Handbook of Research on Teacher Education*, 2nd ed., ed. J. Sikula, T. Buttery, and E. Guyton (New York: Macmillan, 1996), 497.

15. F.F. Fuller, "Concerns of Teachers: A Developmental Conceptualization," *American Educational Research Journal* 6, no. 2 (1969): 207–226; J.I. Goodlad, *A Place Called School* (New York: McGraw Hill, 1984); J. Scott and J. Smith, *The Collaborative School* (Oregon: ERIC Clearinghouse on Educational Management, 1990).

16. J.E. Lanier and J.W. Little, "Research on Teacher Education," in *Handbook of Research on Teaching*, 3rd ed., ed. M.C. Wittrock (New York: Macmillan, 1986), 526–569.

17. S. Feiman-Nemser and M. Buchmann, "When Is Student Teaching Teacher Education," *Teaching and Teacher Education* 3 (1987): 255–273; B. Schlagal, W. Trathen, and W. Blanton, "Structuring Telecommunications to Create Instructional Conversations about Student Teaching," *Journal of Teacher Education* 47, no. 3 (1996): 175–181; Goodlad, *Teachers for Our Nation's Schools*; Zeichner, "Myths and Realities."

18. K.W. Kirkbusch, "A Civic Education and Preservice Education," *Theory and Research in Social Education* 15, no. 3 (1987): 173–188.

19. W.E. Blanton, M.S. Thompson, and S.O. Zimmerman, "Applications of Technologies to Student Teaching," *Electric Journal of Virtual Culture* (1994).

20. L. Schrum, "Teacher Education Goes On-line," *Educational Leadership* 11 (1991): 42.

21. Donald M. Brooks and Thomas W. Kopp, "Technology in Teacher Education," *Journal of Teacher Education* 40, no. 4, (1989), 2–8.

22. K.K. Merseth, "Supporting Beginning Teachers with Computer Networks," *Journal of Teacher Education* 42 (1991): 140–147.

23. Ibid., 140–147.

24. Schlagal, Trathen, and Blanton, "Structuring Telecommunications."

25. J.M. Casey, "Teachernet: Global Connections to Improve Preservice, Inservice Teaching World-Wide," paper presented to the National Education Computing Conference, Seattle, WA, 1997.

26. L. Thomas, R.T. Clift, and T. Sugimoto, "Telecommunications, Student Teaching, and Methods Instruction," *Journal of Teacher Education* 47 (1996): 165–174.

27. R.L. Daft and R.H. Lengel, "A Proposed Integration among Organizational Requirements, Media Richness, and Structural Design," *Management Science* 32 (1986): 191–233; L.K. Trevino, R.L. Daft, and R.H. Lengel, "Understanding Managers' Media Choices: A Symbolic Interactionist Perspective" in *Organization and Communication Technology,* ed. J. Fulk and C. Steinfeld (Newbury Park, CA: Sage, 1990), 71–94.

28. Daft and Lengel, "A Proposed Integration."

29. Ibid.

30. D.M. Fetterman, "Videoconferencing Online: Enhancing Communication over the Internet," *Educational Researcher* 25, no. 4 (1996): 23.

31. Ibid., 23–27.

32. R.C. Bogdan and S.K. Biklen, *Qualitative Research for Education*, 2nd ed. (Boston: Allyn and Bacon, 1992).

33. A. Strauss and J. Corbin, *Basics of Qualitative Research: Grounded Theory Procedures and Techniques* (Newbury Park, CA: Sage, 1994), 273.

34. Bogdan and Biklen, *Qualitative Research.*

35. L. Schrum, "Framing the Debate: Ethical Research in the Information Age," *Qualitative Inquiry* 1, no. 3 (1995): 317.

36. Ibid.

37. "Ethical Electronic Research Guidelines" (1997).

38. A.F. Griffin, *A Philosophical Approach to the Subject Matter Preparation of Teachers of History* (Washington, DC: National Council for the Social Studies, 1992), 20.

39. Dewey, *How We Think*, 9.

40. S. Adler, "Reflective Practice and Teacher Education," quoted in *Reflective Practice in the Social Studies,* ed. E.W. Ross (Washington, DC: National Council for the Social Studies, 1994), 57.

41. Reiman and Thies-Sprinthall, (1993); E. Kusnic and M.L. Finley, "Student Self-evaluation: An Introduction and Rationale," *New Directions for Teaching and Learning: Student Self-Evaluation: Fostering Reflective Learning* 56 (1993): 5–14.

42. N.G. Holmes, "Collegial Journals as Portrayals of Self-efficacy and Professional Development for Experienced Secondary Teachers" (Ph.D. diss., North Carolina State University, 1997).

43. Fuller, "Concerns of Teachers."

44. Ibid.

45. F.F. Fuller and O.H. Brown, "Becoming a Teacher," in *Teacher Education: The Seventy-fourth Yearbook of the National Society for the Study of Education,* ed. K. Ryan (Chicago: University of Chicago Press, 1975), 25–52.

46. Thomas, Clift, and Sugimoto. "Telecommunications."

47. B. Rogoff, "Developing Understanding of the Idea of Communities of Learners," *Mind, Culture and Activity* 1 (1994): 209–229.

48. Ibid.

49. N.C. Burbles, *Dialogue in Teaching: Theory and Practice* (New York: Teachers College Press, 1993).

50. J.P. Gee, *Social Linguistics and Literacies: Ideology in Discourse* (New York: Falmer Press, 1990), 143.

51. M. Huberman, "Professional Careers and Professional Development: Some Intersections" in *Professional Development in Education: New Paradigms and Practices,* ed. T.R. Guskey and M.B. Huberman (New York: Teachers College Press, 1995), 193–224.

52. J.B. Harris, "An Internet-based Graduate Telecomputing Course: Practicing What We Preach" in *Technology and Teacher Education Annual,* ed. D. Carey, R. Carey, D.A. Willis, and J. Willis, eds. (1993), 641–645; S. Zuboff, *In the Age of the Smart-Machine* (New York: Basic Books, 1989).

53. Thomas, Clift, and Sugimoto, "Telecommunications."

54. Bob Schlagal, Woodrow Trathen, and William Blanton, "Structuring Telecommunications to Create Instructional Conversations about Student Teaching," *Journal of Teacher Education,* 47, no. 3, (1996), 175–183.

55. Fuller, "Concerns of Teachers."

56. L. Schrum, "Social Interaction Through Online Writing," in *Computer Conferencing: The Last Word,* ed. R. Mason (Victoria, BC: Beach Holme, 1993), 193.

57. R.L. Boston, "Remote Delivery of Instruction via the PC and Modem: What Have We Learned?" *The American Journal of Distance Education* 6, no. 3 (1992): 45–57.

58. C.J. Dede, "Emerging Technologies: Impacts on Distance Learning," *Annals of the American Academy of Political and Social Science* 514 (1991): 146–158.

59. Casey, "Teachernet."

60. L. Schrum, *"Information Age Innovations: Online Teacher Enhancement,"* paper presented to the Association for the Advancement of Computing in Education, Technology and Teacher Education Annual Meeting, 1992.

61. Daft and Lengel, "A Proposed Integration"; Trevino, Daft, and Lengel, "Understanding Managers' Media Choices."

62. G.J. Posner, *Field Experience: A Guide to Reflective Teaching* (White Plains, NY: Longman, 1993).

63. L. Schrum and B. Berenfeld, *Teaching and Learning in the Information Age: A Guide to Educational Telecommunications* (Boston: Allyn and Bacon, 1997), 89.

64. Linda Harasim, "Collaborating in Cyberspace: Using Computer Conferences as a Group Learning Environment," *Interactive Learning Environments,* 3, no. 2, 119–130.

65. Casey, "Teachernet."

# 17

## The Changing Face
## of History Education

### The *I, Witness to History* Program at
### Larksfield Place Retirement Community

*Terryl M. Asla and Rita S. Pearce*

### Introduction

> *Every time an old person dies, it is as if a library*
> *had burned down.*
> —Alex Haley[1]

History educators ask, "How can we use technology to bring history to life for young students?" The authors, Terryl Asla and Rita Pearce, working in a retirement community setting, ask, "how can we use technology to reempower the oldest members of our society, so that they once more feel they are useful, productive, valued members of society?" One solution to both questions: help older adults preserve their life stories in all their wonderful diversity and then disseminate them in an organized fashion on the Internet for use by history students. This is the goal of the *I, Witness to History* program (http://larksfieldplace.org/iwitness.htm) that was established in 1996 at Larksfield Place Retirement Community, Wichita, Kansas, with the assistance of faculty from Wichita State University and Emporia State University.

The steadily growing amount of material located on the *I, Witness to History* Web site includes oral histories, interviews, life histories, and life stories. This archive of primary historical information is a potentially valuable resource for historians interested in inspiring history students—not to mention psychologists, sociologists, anthropologists, communicators, genealogists, gerontologists, and those who simply enjoy learning about our shared past. In reading these accounts, one frequently comes across small details that bring a moment in history truly alive, details like the floured pie pan in "The Dust Storm" that you had to be there to notice:

Using a pie pan to flour the steak, the potatoes mashed, gravy made, the usual Sunday dinner was in progress. As usual, the wind was blowing, the air was thick, the conversation around the table friendly, but lacked enthusiasm. The lighted chandelier above the table swayed as the wind hit the house with gusts. Suddenly the lights went out, no, there was a light there, what happened? The room was dark, the air thicker than usual, what was happening? We got up from the table, went to the kitchen, the pie pan that held the flour was now a dusty brown color, we looked out the window and could not see the neighbor's house. Yes, it was a dust storm, the worst one yet, it was that BLACK SUNDAY in Western Kansas in the spring of 1935.[2]

The pieces on the *I, Witness to History* Web site are as diverse as those who created them. What they all have in common is that their creators could say, "This is the way it was. I know. I was there. I was a witness to history."

The goal of this report is to introduce the *I, Witness to History* program to educators unfamiliar with it, in order that they may determine how it might be used in their classes to help bring history to life. To facilitate this, we will discuss the ways in which both the storyteller and the storylistener benefit from this sharing process; review the development of the program; and describe the current methodology used to "preserve, publish, and promote" the residents' accounts; and, finally, provide a model for ways history educators might utilize the resources of *I, Witness to History* in their classrooms.

### Storytellers and Storylisteners in a Global Village

> *We are only at the beginning of understanding the power of storytelling and storylistening in co-authoring each other's lives and experiencing the best that human love and aging have to offer.*
> —Kenyon et al.[3]

In Chapter Thirteen of this book, author Wilson J. Warren makes the case that the systematic analysis of primary historical materials can excite students about history while developing much needed critical thinking skills and perspectives, such as posing pertinent questions, defining problems, analyzing relevant information, and supporting conclusions. In the process, Warren argues, students come to better understand their own values.[5] While a definitive history has yet to be written concerning the changing forms of older adult storytelling and the changing uses to which the stories are commonly put, storytelling has traditionally been, and still remains, a common social practice in old age. They are "no longer the sacred and technological archives of the tribe," he noted, but are still used to offer counsel on being and doing well.[4]

For Kenyon and others, such tales appear to take on added significance in a postmodern world in which the dogma of traditional authority institutions (including historians) is challenged by the vast, uncontrollable, and mostly unevaluated bodies of knowledge offered by the Internet and other information systems.[5] If the Internet has facilitated the growth of the postmodernist movement, they argue, it has also provided older people with an opportunity to revive the role of elders as storytellers—only now for generations of storylisteners living in a global village. These new stories contribute important and practical insights into how to find hope and meaning in the face of change, loss, and disillusionment. In short, the stories may offer an antidote, as they have in the past, to the rapid advance of technical knowledge, with its impersonal character and its short half-life. "These narratives become crucial. They are the very structures of coherence, continuity, identity, and emotionality."[6]

Pursuing this concept of defining personal identity further, Sharon Kaufman, in *The Ageless Self*, finds that older people do not see aging as a significant part of their identity. Rather, they feel they are who they have always been, only older.[7] We believe this is one of the major lessons—*perhaps, the major lesson*—the storyteller can share with the storylistener, either directly or indirectly. "I may be older," the storyteller is saying, "but I am still creative and productive. I am just like you on the inside—just older on the outside."

If they are giving a great gift, the storytellers receive a great gift in return. For Larksfield Place residents in their eighties and nineties, publishing their accounts on the Internet is another way of sharing and reaffirming their values of family, work, honor, and religion. We have repeatedly observed marked improvements in residents' sense of self-worth when they received feedback from someone who had read, or listened to, their accounts. This conforms to gerontologist Anthony Traxler's observation that many elders have a strong desire to leave a legacy after death. Wanting to fulfill the elder function by sharing their years of experience, they tend toward self-reflection and reminiscence, a kind of life review.[8] In addition, there is strong scientific evidence that socialization and productivity extend older people's lives. The 1999 study, "Population Based Study of Social and Productive Activities as Predictors of Survival Among Elderly Americans," concludes that such activities lower the risk of all causes of mortality as much as do fitness exercises.[9]

Unfortunately, there are often not enough opportunities for older persons to make meaningful use of their time. In our well-intentioned efforts to meet the needs of older people, individuals, the retirement industry, and society in general often are guilty of what Palmore calls "benign ageism."[10] As benign bigots, we patronize older people on the assumption that they are all incapable of doing for themselves. We try to do too much for them. Such well-intentioned helpfulness, research shows, can reduce older adults' independence and may cause distress.[11] *Whether the caregivers are family members, history students, or the staff of a retirement community, they undermine the dignity, independence, and self-worth of the older person when they cross the thin line between helping and doing.* In light of this problem, a sincere effort has been made to assure that the *I, Witness to History* program provides

1. a positive sense of function in society after retirement,
2. opportunities for societal input,
3. treatment as competent adults, both cognitively and affectively, and
4. education on how to access resources.[12]

### The Birth and Early Growth of *I, Witness to History*

> *This seems an exquisite moment for communicating ideas from generation to generation because, in the great swings of social change, society is now at a turning point; and the meaning attached to age, in popular usage and in scientific theory, has shifted in the last century and may well be utterly transformed in the next.*
> —M. W. Riley et al.[13]

In 1996, Larksfield Place became one of the first not-for-profit retirement communities to establish a Web presence. At that time, a graphics computer was a major purchase. In order to justify the expense, the decision was made to house it temporarily in an empty one-bedroom apartment and make it a Resource Center for residents. The first program that the newly appointed director, Terryl Asla, established was *I, Witness to History.* (The inspiration for the name was a PBS program, *I, Claudius.*) It was believed that placing residents' stories on the new corporate Web site would attract visitors, while preserving life stories that might otherwise be lost. The results were gratifying, and visitors did come to the site. More important for the future of the embryo project, it attracted several Larksfield Place residents who supported the concept. They quickly discovered they were not only wanted, but truly needed; no operational monies were allocated for hiring staff to help grow the new program or for purchasing new equipment and furnishings. One resident recounts coming into the new Resource Center during those early days and finding files stored in the apartment's unused oven and refrigerator because there was no filing cabinet.

Thanks to their support, the Resource Center moved to a newly renovated area of the Larksfield Place Commons in June 1998. The new facility featured state-of-the-art computers, high-resolution scanners that reproduced treasured photos, and photo-quality printers for publishing residents' works in full color—all paid for with donations. One very welcome gift was a $10,000-a-year pledge that permitted hiring two Wichita State University graduate students to help with the growing workload.

The two students joined an active advisory steering committee that had been formed the year before when it became clear that the program required additional formal structure and professional organization in order to become a serious historical archive. The committee, chaired by resident Faye McCoy, included resident Sylvia Muse; Susan Huxman, Ph.D., WSU professor of Communications; Nancy Knapp, Ph.D., director of the ESU Art Therapy program; and Mike Kelly, M.L.S., Director of Special Collections for the WSU Ablah Library. The committee helped Asla establish formal guidelines and policies, and held training courses in the fall of 1997 for individuals engaged in collecting oral histories. One of the graduate students, Rita Pearce, eventually assumed responsibility for the oral history portion of the program. In 1999, after receiving her Master's in Communications, she became a Larksfield Place staff member and the program's manager. At the present time, the Resource Center/*I, Witness to History* team consists of the director and manager, a half-time administrative assistant, whose salary is paid for by the Senior Work Experience Program, and about fourteen resident volunteers.

## Program Methodologies: Preservation, Publication, and Promotion

> *When Larksfield decided to open the Resource Center, miracles began to happen.* I, Witness to History *showed us that our life stories were important.*
> —Larksfield Place resident and LifeWork author

The various activities on which the *I, Witness to History* team work may be broken down into three. For ease of recall, they are known as The Three P's: Preservation, Publication, and Promotion.

## Preservation

Today, *I, Witness to History* is a comprehensive program that gives residents the opportunity to preserve their life stories as oral histories and/or as written documents published in hard copy and/or on the Internet. The first step in the process is to obtain written authorization giving *I, Witness to History* permission to reproduce the material in print and electronically. This authorization, and examples of other documents discussed here, may be found on the *I, Witness to History* Web site.

All residents are encouraged to give a formal oral history. Although some choose to write their life stories instead, most agree to be interviewed, and many of those have found that the final transcript makes an excellent place from which to begin a written LifeWork. Regardless of their decision, their wishes are always respected. After obtaining the resident's written authorization and a completed biographical worksheet, the interviewer normally conducts and records a chronological interview of the resident's entire life. If there are historically noteworthy episodes, follow-up interviews and tapings may be scheduled. Residents and their families are then provided with copies of the tapes.

Accounts may also be transcribed. These transcriptions exist in two versions. The first is a literal transcription that includes the nonfluencies: uh, er, um, and ah; throat clearing; and other emotional responses. This version is intended only for use by researchers and must be requested in writing. A second, edited version of the transcript is then created without these interjections and given to the resident for review. (Initially, interviewees were provided with the unedited version. This led to extreme negative reactions and comments like "I sound stupid!") Once the interviewee approves the revised transcript, it is usually archived on the *I, Witness to History* Web site. Copies of the tape and edited transcription may also be archived in the Special Collection at the Wichita State University Ablah Library if they have significant local historical value. Since May 1999, these items have also been archived at the Kansas State Historical Library in Topeka.

Most Larksfield Place residents who do an oral history go on to write at least one additional piece. The accounts on the *I, Witness to History* Web site include autobiographies, biographies, life histories, and life stories. Autobiographies and biographies are well-established literary forms. Nineteenth-century anthropologists used the term "life history" when referring to both first-person accounts and other people's biographical accounts of the same life.[14] Sociologists use "life history" in much the same manner, referring to life stories told by the individual and supplemented with data from other sources.[15] The life story it follows is but one part of life history, the part that is told to another.[16] Regardless of their form, all the pieces found on the *I, Witness to History* Web site are also called *LifeWorks*. We use the term as a descriptive reminder that the process, rather than the completed product, is of primary importance. That process involves a formal organization of one's life and an extended period of thoughtful self-review.

To encourage one another in their literary efforts, residents founded their own support group in February 1999. Calling themselves *Questors*, they now meet monthly to read their latest efforts and offer one another encouragement. The group has grown steadily and the active members now number twenty-one. *While the* Questors *support group is fairly new, its popularity suggests that the socialization it provides may be one of the key factors in determining resident satisfaction and participation.*

**Publication**

Publication of the LifeWork is the critical next step. Those interested in the technical specifications and professional guidelines will find them on the *I, Witness to History* Web site. We will limit our comments here to the publication process as it relates to resident participation. By publication, we mean creating a finished work intended for public dissemination, both on the Internet and in hard copy. The latter is very important because people still judge books by their covers—especially older authors of LifeWorks. The printed versions of their LifeWorks, we believe, often mean more to these residents—are more familiar and "real"—than the electronic versions on the *I, Witness to History* Web site or on CD-ROM.

Good production values cannot be overemphasized. Residents may say that writing a LifeWork was rewarding. But when they see the finished piece in print, or on the monitor screen, typeset and in full color, the word we hear most often is "miraculous." Most residents do not possess the design or computer skills needed to publish their own works, so *I, Witness to History* staff members and resident volunteers assist them to whatever extent necessary. To assure the maximum sense of ownership, the author is strongly encouraged to participate in the decision-making process throughout the publication cycle. *Experience has shown that the author's wishes in publication matters should always take precedence, unless there are pressing legal or practical considerations. In such cases, these issues should be discussed and changes mutually agreed upon before proceeding.*

**Promotion**

Hard copies of the finished LifeWork are proudly presented to family and friends and may be checked out of the Resource Center. Newly completed LifeWorks are also highlighted on the *I, Witness to History* Web site, and in the monthly *Larksfield Place News* and its companion E-newsletter that may be accessed from the Larksfield Place homepage, http://larksfieldplace.org. At the monthly *Questors* meeting, new authors are presented with special pens, capped with a pewter book, to acknowledge their accomplishments.

In 1998, team members began to introduce the *I, Witness to History* concept to other not-for-profit retirement communities at the conventions of our state and national associations. That year, the Kansas Association of Homes and Services for the Aging (KAHSA) invited us to present at its state convention and, in 1999, honored *I, Witness to History* with its *Innovation of the Year Award*. A presentation at the 1998 national convention of the American Association of Homes and Services for the Aging (AAHSA) in Los Angeles led to a cover story in the February 1999 issue of its newsmagazine, *Currents*, and an invitation to present again at its 1999 convention to be held in Chicago. Despite this interest on the association level, the administrators of individual retirement communities have been slow to accept the idea of either resource centers or *I, Witness to History*. However, adults over fifty are one of the fastest growing segments of Internet users,[17] and demands for such services from incoming residents could change the situation rather quickly.

Following the 1998 AAHSA conference, we also began to contact historians. By this point, the steering committee felt there were enough primary historical resources on the Web site to justify serious consideration from national organizations and educators. In April, the director made a presentation at the 1999 American Association for History and Computing (AAHC) conference at Temple University in Philadelphia. This, in turn, led to an invitation to be part of a panel presentation, "History.edu Meets History.com" at the Sixth International Conference for Computers in the History Classroom, held at Skidmore College in Saratoga Springs. That presentation became the basis for this report.

The early enthusiasm and openness historians have shown for the *I, Witness to History* program have been very heartening. We suspect that retirement community administrators are reluctant to initiate similar programs, partly because they and their staffs have even less expertise in history than they have in computers and resource centers. It logically follows that if history educators approached retirement communities and offered to help set up *I, Witness to History* programs, this might help reduce administrators' concerns and expedite diffusion. With this idea in mind, let us examine some ways that history educators might utilize this program in their classes.

### Possible *I, Witness to History* Projects for History Classes

> *America's elderly population is now growing at a moderate*
> *pace. But not too far into the future, the growth will become*
> *rapid. So rapid, in fact, that by the middle of the next century,*
> *it might be completely inaccurate to think of ourselves as a*
> *nation of the young: there could be more persons who are*
> *elderly (65 or over) than young (14 or younger)!*
> —Economics and Statistics Administration,
> U.S. Department of Commerce[18]

There may never have been a better time for young people to interface with their elders than now, as we face the pending dramatic change in our society brought on by the aging of the Baby Boom generation. Students could

1. develop support materials for LifeWorks on the *I, Witness to History* Web site,
2. interface directly with the residents who have done LifeWorks via e-mail and/or video or audio conferencing, and
3. help residents at local retirement communities do LifeWorks of their own and arrange for them to be linked, or added, to the *I, Witness to History* Web site.

### Developing Support Materials

A good example of a cooperative endeavor is "The Brown Diaries Educational Project." In the spring of 1999, a Larksfield Place resident approached the *I, Witness to History* staff with a remarkable collection of small leather-bound diaries written by her late husband's grandfather, the Rev. I.G. Brown, between the years 1853 and 1885. She wanted the diaries preserved and shared as a memorial to her late husband.

Pat Michaelis, director of Library and Archives for the Kansas State Historical Society, examined the diaries and found them to be remarkably well preserved, lucid, and full of small historic details. Because the Rev. Brown spent his entire career "marrying and burying" parishioners, the little books contain a good deal of genealogical information. In addition, the Rev. Brown had spent the Civil War years ministering at a church not far from Gettysburg. His personal thoughts and feelings regarding the War Between the States provide uniquely human insights regarding the events taking place around him. Later, the Rev. Brown and his family migrated to Kansas, where he founded two mission churches. The details of daily life in pioneer Kansas during the 1880s are equally revealing.

*I, Witness to History* team members helped facilitate the donation of the diaries to the Historical Society. We also approached Dennis Trinkle, Ph.D., executive director of the AAHC and professor of history at DePauw University, for help placing selected diaries and support materials on the Internet and diffusing the information among history educators. With Dr. Trinkle's help and the assistance of AAHC journal editor and Pacific University history professor, Jeffrey Barlow, Ph.D., the project began work in the late summer of 1999. If all goes according to plan, *I, Witness to History* staff and volunteers will scan in the diaries and place the images on the *I, Witness to History* Web site. Pacific University history students will work on historiography. DePauw University graduate research assistants will help transcribe the diaries, the first step toward creating a searchable database. This is a good example of a cooperative project between historians and *I, Witness to History*, a project that significantly adds to the body of knowledge while bringing satisfaction and a sense of accomplishment to an older individual.

### Intergenerational Sharing

Many Larksfield Place residents who have their LifeWorks on the *I, Witness to History* Web site are willing to answer students' questions regarding their experiences. For example, during the 2000 spring semester, DePauw students enrolled in Twentieth Century European History will review one Larksfield Place resident's LifeWork recounting his experiences as a POW in a German *stalag* during World War II. Then, they will have an opportunity to discuss what they read with the resident himself, either by e-mail or conference call. In addition to his personal account, the Web site also includes support materials such as a transcription of the war diary he kept before his B-17 was shot down on his tenth mission, photos taken by his German jailers, drawings by fellow POWs, and a U.S. military intelligence report on the living conditions at Stalag Luft I, where he was imprisoned until he was repatriated.

### Gathering Original *I, Witness to History* Accounts

The most ambitious project would be for students to help residents of local retirement communities create their own LifeWorks and link them, or have them added, to the *I, Witness to History* Web site. While such a project would be beneficial to older persons in any setting, there are several good reasons to approach residents of one of this country's some 2,100[19] retirement communities. We have found that individuals who move to a local retirement community often are decision makers and leaders who possess a great deal of valuable knowledge regarding local history. Those in the Independent Living apartments and homes are generally active, intellectually alert, and more apt to be able to participate in a project like this than, say, the frailer residents of nursing homes or assisted living facilities. Indeed, retirement community residents have often already started their own computer classes. Finally, retirement community residents usually are comfortable financially. We can testify that this definitely makes it easier to secure gifts and funding for such an ambitious project in the beginning. After the program is well established, it may then be extended to the greater community. (We have just completed our first outreach class at one of the local churches.)

Regardless of the chosen location, the teacher and administrator are encouraged to make certain that the program places equal emphasis on the intellectual growth and satisfaction of both the student/storylistener and the older person/storyteller. We believe this would be best accomplished by having the older person create a LifeWork, either of their full life history or an incident. (History classes working with *I, Witness to History* residents could select one that is already on the Web site.) The student should read the LifeWork, noting any topics, issues, values, historical discrepancies, or vocabulary that require further explanation for today's readers. Then the student and older person interface and discuss these issues, e.g., "What did you mean when you said farmers in Kansas 'listed' their fields during the Dust Bowl years to keep the topsoil from blowing away?" Following this, the student creates a support document clarifying the unclear points. This can be linked to the appropriate parts of the LifeWork as the older person and the student work together to place the story on the Internet and connect it to the *I, Witness to History* Web site.

The authors prefer this approach to the more traditional one of having the student interview the older person and write a biographical sketch. The increased involvement in the creative process and intellectual exchange is valuable to the older person and should help assure accuracy. One of the unique abilities of older people is that they can, in the words of Kenyon, Ruth, and Mader, "re-story" their life experiences.[20] This ability to help the reader understand how it was to live in past times is sometimes missing when younger people interview older adults and write about what they have learned.

A case in point is the LifeWork, "Childhood in the 1920s in South-Central Kansas." The then eighty-five-year-old female resident described her youth with affection while objectively comparing it to life in the 1990s for the benefit of younger readers. This same resident described another account written by a young student after interviewing the resident's cousin, who was the same age as she and grew up on the next farm over. According to her, the two accounts are quite different in tone. The young interviewer, only able to see the cousin's life from the perspective of her own contemporary values, found childhood in the 1920s to be dirty and depressing, bereft of both modern conveniences and entertainment. *The lesson to be learned from this is that, when helping an older person with a LifeWork, it is critical that the student historian not inject personal views other than to ask for elaboration on points that might otherwise be unclear to today's readers.*

Finally, there are four primary areas of emphasis involved when conducting oral histories and assisting in autobiographical writing in a retirement community: history, psychology, communication, and gerontology.

## The Historical Emphasis

First, remember that the stories are historical because the perspective of the everyday person reflects actual experience during a potentially significant time frame. Although objective (verifiable) points may be made, the information is subjective—the stories reflect the individual's version or perspective of what happened at a given time. Therefore, it is possible to extract varying viewpoints from different storytellers regarding the same set of circumstances. Some stories seem to avoid mention of anything that appears to be historically significant. In that case, the student may ask questions, but if the resident shows discomfort or reluctance to stay with, or expound upon, those questions, then the resident must be allowed to go on with the story in the way that he or she wants to tell it. Historians, who expect to delve into the employment or emphasize certain points in the stories,[21] may be faced with an interviewee who does not want to further detail a happening. *Sensitivity to the interviewee's reactions and responses is imperative in a retirement setting.* The resident is not required to tell this life story or episodic event. The resident who decides to do so must be allowed to star in the creation and the telling of the story. *Residents tell their stories if a rapport has been established and so they feel at ease with the interviewer and with relating their past experiences.*

## The Psychological Emphasis

Second, the telling of the story is psychological because of the therapeutic effect that storytelling may have on the storyteller. Some older persons may need to ponder on themselves and their life courses to confirm their identity and to maintain integrity and well-being.[22] Tornstam implies that during the maturation process in old age, gero-transcendence occurs. In this state, the aging self is more occupied with philosophical pondering on life and restorying time and reality. Time blurs in relation to the borders of the past, present, and future. Reality is approached with a sense of affinity with both past generations and the unknown.[23] *The importance for the history student here is to note that, psychologically, the storyteller may experience a therapeutic effect in which identity, integrity, and well-being play a part, but time and reality may be viewed differently as aging occurs.*

## The Communication Emphasis

Third, the stories in retirement communities are also communication-based, because of the interaction that takes place and in the perceptual framing and salience of points made in both oral and written forms of stories. Framing allows the narrator to present a situation as he or she wants it to be known. Storytellers use good reasons or justification for action as the mode for communication and storymaking.[24] As storytelling animals, people use good reasons or justification for action as the mode for communication and storymaking.[25] In computer terms, each person's outside story (what happened to the storyteller) is the hardware of the system. The inside story (what the person makes of what happened) is the software. The inside-out story is [the LifeWork] that he or she shares with others, who, in turn, make their own interpretation, outside of what its text might mean.[26]

Villaume, Brown, and Darling write that many stereotypes exist about how older adults communicate, including certain tendencies toward withdrawal, repetitiveness, domination, loudness, and the narration of lengthy stories. If hearing loss has occurred, individuals may refrain from initiating conversations or asking for clarification. They may experience a loss of confidence that results in anxiety, depression, or social isolation. Many compensate for what they cannot hear well by using lip-reading, eye contact, or inferencing strategies, such as paralanguage or nonverbal cues, which lead them to surmise what has been said.[27] In working with older individuals, hearing loss is a concern. Early dementia may involve other communication adaptations. *If we are to consider the residents' best interests, students of history must realize that the interviewees have specific internal reasons for communicating in a certain way.*

## The Gerontological Emphasis

Finally, storytelling in a retirement community is gerontological. Individuals age in three different ways: biologically, psychologically, and socially. Chronological age does not encompass the other aspects of aging, so it is impossible to blanket-categorize gerontologically. It is more appropriate to examine older individuals and their characteristics individually.[28] Ritchie points out that gerontologists speak of the life review processes of older people, while oral historians refer to conducting autobiographical accounts from childhood to the present. *Ritchie advises the oral historian who conducts even a subject-oriented or episodic event to consider expanding the scope to document as much as possible.*[28] The broader nature of this questioning establishes links that the interviewer or interviewee may not have considered in the more narrowly focused session. *Students of history should be aware that accessing the overall life experience may yield considerably more information than a more limited focus.*

## Conclusion

Herzog and Markus sum up the matter admirably when they ask, "How do people maintain active involvement and a sense of well-being across the life span? Why is it that despite the loss and decline apparently associated with aging, many older people experience themselves as feeling exceptionally good, often better than when they were younger?" The answer, they suggest, is an adaptive aging process that emphasizes flexibility, planning, and anticipation.[29] The latter—setting new goals, constructing new future plans, and developing new roles—is encouraged by the *I, Witness to History* program with its emphasis on challenging oneself to grow intellectually and making the commitment to undertake new projects. We firmly believe that preserving as many older persons' LifeWorks as humanly possible is a noble, valuable, and achievable goal.

## Notes

1. E. Polster, *Every Person's Life Is Worth a Novel* (New York: Norton, 1987).
2. Eula May Nunemacher resourcecenter@larksfieldplace.org, in *I, Witness to History*, http://larksfieldplace.org/iwitness/nunnemacher/duststorm.htm, July 5, 1999.
3. G.M. Kenyon, H. Ruth, and W. Mader, "Elements of a Narrative Gerontology," in *Handbook of Theories on Aging*, ed. V.L. Bengston and K.W. Schaie (New York: Springer, 1999), 40–58.
4. Quoted in A.M. Wyatt-Brown, "Literary Gerontology Comes of Age," in *Handbook of the Humanities and Aging*, ed. T.R. Cole, D.D. Van Tassel, and R. Kastenbaum (New York: Springer, 1992), 307–351.
5. Kenyon, et al., "Elements of a Narrative Gerontology."
6. Ibid.
7. S. Kaufman, *The Ageless Self* (New York: New American Library, 1986).
8. A.J. Traxler, "Let's Get Gerontologized: Developing a Sensitivity to Aging," in *The Multi-Purpose Senior Center Concept: A Training Manual for Practitioners Working with the Aging* (Springfield: Illinois Department on Aging, 1980), 88–89.
9. T.A. Glass, et al., "Population Based Study of Social and Productive Activities

as Predictors of Survival among Elderly Americans," *British Medical Journal* 319 (August 21, 1999): 478–482.

10. E. Palmore, *Ageism: Negative and Positive* (New York: Springer, 1990).

11. M. Silverstein and X. Chen, "Too Much of a Good Thing? Intergenerational Social Support and the Psychological Well-Being of Older Parents," *Journal of Marriage and the Family* 58 (1996): 970–982.

12. J. Feezel and R. Hawlins, "Myths and Stereotypes: Communication Breakdowns," in *Human Communications and the Aging Process*, ed. C.W. Carmichael, C.H. Botan, and R. Hawkins (Prospect Heights, IL: Waveland Press, 1988), 81–94.

13. M.W. Riley, A. Foner, and J.W. Riley, "The Aging and Society Paradigm," in *Handbook of Theories on Aging*, ed. V.L. Bengston and K.W. Schaie (New York: Springer, 1999), 327–43.

14. L.L. Langness, *The Life History in Anthropological Science* (New York: Holt, Rinehart and Winston, 1965).

15. S.J. Mann, "Telling a Life Story: Issues for Research," in *Management Education and Development*, ed. S.J. Mann (London: Sage, 1992), 271–280.

16. J. Kotre, *Creativity and the Interpretation of Lives* (Baltimore: Johns Hopkins University Press, 1984).

17. K. Kelly, "Building Aging Programs with Online Information Technology," *Generations* 21, no. 3 (Fall 1997): 15–18.

18. Economics and Statistics Administration, U.S. Department of Commerce, "Sixty-Five Plus in the United States," http://www.census.gov/socdemo/www/agebrief.html, May 1995.

19. American Association of Homes and Services for the Aging, *The CCRC Industry 1997 Profile* (Washington, DC: American Association of Homes and Services for the Aging).

20. Kenyon et al., "Elements of a Narrative Gerontology."

21. A. Danto, *Narration and Knowledge* (New York: Columbia University Press, 1985).

22. P.G. Coleman, *Aging and Reminiscence Processes: Social and Clinical Implications* (Chichester, UK: Wiley, 1986).

23. L. Tornstam, "Gero-Transcendence: A Theoretical and Empirical Exploration," in *Aging and the Religious Dimension*, ed. L.E. Thomas and S.A. Eisenhandler (Westport, CT: Greenwood, 1994), 203–225.

24. W.R. Fisher, *Human Communication as Narration: Toward a Philosophy of Reason, Value, and Action* (Columbia: University of South Carolina Press, 1987).

25. Kenyon et al., "Elements of a Narrative Gerontology."

26. W.A. Villaume, M.H. Brown, and R. Darling, "Presbycusis, Communication, and Older Adults," in *Interpersonal Communication in Older Adulthood: Interdisciplinary Theory and Research*, ed. M.L. Hummert, J. Wiemann, and J.F. Nussbaum (Thousand Oaks, CA: Sage 1994).

27. C.S. Bergman, *Aging: Genetic and Environmental Influences* (Newbury Park, CA: Sage, 1997).

28. D.A. Ritchie, "Memory and Oral History," in *Doing Oral History, Twayne's Oral History* Series No. 15 (New York: Twayne, 1995), 11–17.

29. A.R. Herzog and H.R. Markus, "The Self-Concept in Life Span and Aging Research," in *Handbook of Theories on Aging*, ed. V.L. Bengston and K.W. Schaie (New York: Springer, 1999), 227–252.

## Bibliography

American Association of Homes and Services for the Aging. *The CCRC Industry 1997 Profile*. Washington, DC: American Association of Homes and Services for the Aging, 1997.

Bergman, C.S. *Aging: Genetic and Environmental Influences*. Newbury Park, CA: Sage, 1997.

Coleman, P.G. *Aging and Reminiscence Processes: Social and Clinical Implications*. Chichester, UK: Wiley, 1986.

Danto, A. *Narration and Knowledge* (New York: Columbia University Press, 1985).

Economics and Statistics Administration, U.S. Department of Commerce. "Sixty-Five Plus in the United States." http://www.census.gov/socdemo/www/agebrief.html. May 1995.

Entman, R.M., "Framing: Toward Clarification of a Fractured Paradigm." *Journal of Communication* 41 (April 1993): 51–58.

Feezel, J., and R. Hawlins. "Myths and Stereotypes: Communication Breakdowns." In *Human Communications and the Aging Process*, ed. C.W. Carmichael, C.H. Botan, and R. Hawkins, 81–94. Prospect Heights, IL: Waveland Press, 1988.

Fisher, W.R. *Human Communication as Narration: Toward a Philosophy of Reason, Value, and Action*. Columbia: University of South Carolina Press, 1987.

Glass, T.A., et al. "Population Based Study of Social and Productive Activities as Predictors of Survival among Elderly Americans." *British Medical Journal* 319 (August 21, 1999): 478–482.

Herzog, A.R., and H.R. Markus. "The Self-Concept in Life Span and Aging Research." In *Handbook of Theories on Aging*, ed. V.L. Bengston and K.W. Schaie, 227–252. New York: Springer, 1999.

Kaufman, S. *The Ageless Self*. New York: New American Library, 1986.

Kelly, K. "Building Aging Programs with Online Information Technology." *Generations* 21, no. 3 (Fall 1997): 15–18.

Kenyon, G.M., H. Ruth, and W. Mader. "Elements of a Narrative Gerontology." In *Handbook of Theories on Aging*, ed. V.L. Bengston and K.W. Schaie, 40–58. New York: Springer, 1999.

Kotre, J. *Creativity and the Interpretation of Lives*. Baltimore: Johns Hopkins University Press, 1984.

Langness, L.L. *The Life History in Anthropological Science*. New York: Holt, Rinehart and Winston, 1965.

Mann, S.J. "Telling a Life Story: Issues for Research." In *Management Education and Development*, ed. S.J. Mann, 271–280. London: Sage, 1992.

Nunemacher, E.M. In *I, Witness to History* http://larksfieldplace.org/iwitness/nunnemacher/duststorm.htm. July 5, 1999.

Palmore, E. *Ageism: Negative and Positive*. New York: Springer, 1990.

Polster, E. *Every Person's Life Is Worth a Novel*. New York: Norton, 1987.

Ritchie, D.A. "Memory and Oral History." *Doing Oral history (Twayne's Oral History Series No. 15)*, 11–17. New York: Twayne, 1995.

Riley, M.W., A. Foner, and J.W. Riley. "The Aging and Society Paradigm." In *Handbook of Theories on Aging*, ed. V.L. Bengston and K.W. Schaie, 327–343. New York: Springer, 1999.

Silverstein, M., and X. Chen. "Too Much of a Good Thing? Intergenerational Social Support and the Psychological Well-Being of Older Parents." *Journal of Marriage and the Family* 58 (1996): 970–982.

Tornstam, L. "Gero-Transcendence: A Theoretical and Empirical Exploration." In *Aging and the Religious Dimension*, ed. L.E. Thomas and S.A. Eisenhandler, 203–225. Westport, CT: Greenwood, 1994.

Traxler, A.J. "Let's Get Gerontologized: Developing a Sensitivity to Aging." In *The Multi-Purpose Senior Center Concept: A Training Manual for Practitioners Working with the Aging*, 88–89. Springfield: Illinois Department on Aging, 1980.

Villaume, W.A., M.H. Brown, and R. Darling. "Presbycusis, Communication, and Older Adults." In *Interpersonal Communication in Older Adulthood: Interdisciplinary Theory and Research*, ed. M.L. Hummert, J. Wiemann, and J.F. Nussbaum. Thousand Oaks, CA: Sage, 1994.

Wyatt-Brown, A.M. "Literary Gerontology Comes of Age." In *Handbook of the Humanities and Aging*, ed. T.R. Cole, D.D. Van Tassel, and R. Kastenbaum, 307–351. New York: Springer, 1992.

# Index

# About the Contributors

**Deborah Lines Andersen** is an Assistant Professor of Information Science and Policy at the Rockefeller College of Public Affairs and Policy, University at Albany, State University of New York. She teaches statistics, research methods, and information policy to graduate students interested in librarianship, archival administration, and records management and preservation. Her research interests are in the use of electronic information access technologies by special user populations, particularly by academic historians.

**Terryl M. Asla** has devoted his professional career as a gero-informaticist to enhancing the quality of life for older persons through technology and promoting appreciation for the benefits that come with aging. He is the creator of the award-winning *I, Witness to History* program and a regular speaker at national and international conferences. He is presently working on a doctorate at Emporia State University in Information Sciences.

**Douglas J. Cremer** is Associate Professor of History and Chair of the Department of Natural and Social Sciences at Woodbury University in Los Angeles. He has presented papers on the interface between history teaching and technology for H-Net, the AAHC, and regional accreditation agencies in California. He has also written on the history of religion and the problem of modernity in modern Germany in *The Journal of the History of Ideas* and *The Journal of Church and State*. He holds a Ph.D. in intellectual history from the University of California, San Diego.

**A. Keith Dils** received his Ed.D. from West Virginia University and has taught widely with technology as a social studies instructor at the Wellsboro Rock L. Butler Middle School, Wellsboro, Pennsylvania, as an adjunct sociology instructor at Penn State's Pennsylvania College of Technology, and as a teaching assistant at West Virginia University.

**Larry Easley** is an Associate Professor of History and a Technology Associate in the Center for Scholarship in Teaching and Learning at Southeast Missouri State University, where he teaches courses dealing with Africa, American film, and Progressive America His interest and research in multimedia education date back more than twenty years.

**Kathleen Ferenz**, BANDL director and coach, is a visiting educator with the Bay Area School Reform Collaborative. She taught middle school for over ten years and is a lecturer in the Instructional Technologies Department at San Francisco State University. She is also a 1997 American Memory Fellow.

**Steven Hoffman** is an Associate Professor of History and Historic Preservation at Southeast Missouri State University. His research focuses on the role of race and class in the city building process and on the role of technology in history. He has published and presented widely in both areas.

**José E. Igartua** (http://www.er.uqam.ca/nobel/r12270/) teaches Canadian economic and social history, as well as the use of computing tools for historians. His recently published work includes *Arvida au Saguenay* (Montreal: McGill-Queen's University Press, 1996), an account of the creation of an instant company town in Quebec in the 1920s and 1930s, as well as articles on the evolution of representations of national identity in English-speaking Canada since 1945. He heads the Canadian History Electronic Resource Centre Project of the Canadian Historical Association (see http://www.millennium.gc.ca/cgi-bin/mill_srch.cgi?view_record_e&1193).

**Stephen Kneeshaw** is Professor of History at College of the Ozarks in southwest Missouri. He is also involved with the teacher education program, specifically history and social studies education. He completed his B.A. in history and English at the University of Puget Sound and his M.A. and Ph.D. in American history at the University of Colorado, Boulder. Since 1972 he has been on the history faculty at College of the Ozarks, where he was named the first recipient of the college's Distinguished Faculty Award for excellence in teaching, scholarship, and service. He has held fellowships for study and research at the Newbery Library, Harvard, MIT, and the U.S. Military Academy at West Point. He is the founder and editor of *Teaching History: A Journal of Methods* and for several years has presented workshops on "Active Teaching and Learning" at high schools and colleges. His publications cover a wide range of topics from diplomatic history to history education, active learning, and writing to learn.

**R. Bruce Lewis** is an Assistant Professor of Education, Instructional Technology, and School Counseling at the School of Education at Freed-Hardeman

University. He received his Ed.D. in curriculum and instruction, with a concentration in educational technology, from Tennessee State University. His dissertation focused on the use of software to teach social studies.

**Margaret M. Manchester** is an Assistant Professor of History and Director of the American Studies Program at Providence College.

**Cheryl L. Mason** is an Assistant Professor of Social Studies Education in the Curry School of Education at the University of Virginia. She received her Ph.D. in social studies education from North Carolina State University. Currently she is a faculty member in the Curry Center for Technology and Teacher Education and leads the Virginia Center for Digital History's Teaching Initiative. Her interests in social studies education include using technology to develop preservice teachers' reflective thinking and teaching strategies.

**Scott A. Merriman** is a doctoral candidate in modern American history at the University of Kentucky. He has previously taught history at the University of Cincinnati, Northern Kentucky University, and Thomas More College. His books include *The History Highway: A Guide to Internet Resources* and *The History Highway 2000*. He is also an associate editor for *History Reviews On-Line*. He has contributed to the *Historical Encyclopedia of World Slavery*, *American National Biography*, and *Buckeye Hill Country*.

**Rita S. Pearce** holds a Master of Arts in communication from Wichita State University. She is currently a human environmental science doctoral candidate specializing in gerontology at Oklahoma State University. Her two most recent presentations occurred at the 1999 Annual Meeting and Exposition for the American Association of Homes and Services for the Aging (AAHSA) in Chicago: *A Practical Guide to Creating a Resource Center in Your Retirement Community* and *Senior Scene: AAHSA's Residents Program: Seniors and Technology*.

**Daniel Pfeifer** works in the History Department at Wake Forest University as an academic computing specialist. His background includes degrees in both history and computer science.

**Brian Plane** is a Ph.D. candidate at the University of Connecticut and a visiting faculty member at North Carolina State University, where he teaches modern European history and the history of science. Between 1995 and 1997, he held a Fulbright Dissertation Research Fellowship in Berlin, where he conducted archival and secondary research for a manuscript titled "Science and Dissent in East Berlin: The Havemann Controversy, 1961–1982."

**Arne Solli** is a doctoral candidate in history at the University of Bergen, Norway.

**Dennis A. Trinkle** is an Assistant Professor of History and Associate Director of Faculty Development at DePauw University. He serves as the Executive Director of the American Association for History and Computing (http://www.theaahc.org) and is a Fellow of the International Center for Computer-Enhanced Learning, Wake Forest University. He has published widely on technology, teaching, and history. His books include *The History Highway: A Guide to Internet Resources*; *Writing, Teaching, and Researching History in the Electronic Age*; and *The History Highway 2000*.

**Wilson J. Warren** is Assistant Professor of History and Program Coordinator for Social Science Education at Indiana State University in Terre Haute, Indiana. He received his Ph.D. in history from the University of Pittsburgh in 1992, specializing in twentieth-century United States working-class history. His forthcoming book, *Struggling with "Iowa's Pride": Labor Relations, Unionism, and Politics in the Rural Midwest since 1877* will be published by the University of Iowa Press in spring 2000.

**Ann Wynne** is Professor and Chair of History at Orange Coast College, Costa Mesa, California, and Co-chair of the College Internet Education Committee.